Ways of the Word

Ways of the Word

Learning to Preach for Your Time and Place

Sally A. Brown & Luke A. Powery

Fortress Press
Minneapolis

WAYS OF THE WORD

Learning to Preach for Your Time and Place

Cover image: Art Background/Creative Source

Cover design: Laurie Ingram

Library of Congress Cataloging-in-Publication Data

Print ISBN: 978-0-8006-9922-2

eBook ISBN: 978-1-5064-1030-2

The paper used in this publication meets the minimum requirements of American National Standard for Information Sciences — Permanence of Paper for Printed Library Materials, ANSI Z329.48-1984.

Manufactured in the U.S.A.

This book was produced using Pressbooks.com, and PDF rendering was done by PrinceXML.

Contents

Acknowledgments

Just as the human body has many parts, we recognize that we are part of a larger body of support, a great cloud of witnesses, too many to number, but we will try with this brief literary eucharist. We thank our teaching colleagues and the administration at each of our respective schools, Duke University, especially Duke Divinity School (Luke A. Powery), and Princeton Theological Seminary (Sally A. Brown), for their generous support in varied forms. Abundant thanks goes to research assistants Timothy Buskey (Duke Divinity School) and Jesse Tosten (Princeton Theological Seminary) for securing materials, following up references, and reading early chapter drafts.

We are immensely grateful for the sharp eye and wise counsel of our editorial consultant, David Lott, who embraced from the start our "dialogical" approach to co-authorship, and with that vision in mind, improved our work in many ways. We are grateful, as well, to the editorial staff at Fortress Press for final oversight and copyediting of the text.

Each of us is deeply indebted to our families. Thank you Gail, Moriah, and Zachary Powery, and thank you, Peter Dunbar, for forgiving our too-frequent absences, physical or mental, due to our preoccupation with "Ways." Bless you, now and forever.

Both of us sense how much of our broad ecumenical sense of

faithful Christian preaching, worship, and witness we owe to the diverse settings where we've been privileged to worship, study, or engage in ministry—Presbyterian, Reformed, Pentecostal, Baptist, Methodist, Roman Catholic, Episcopal, UCC, free-church independent, and international-ecumenical. These communities and the preachers, mentors, musicians, and ministry partners who became part of our lives there, have shaped our conviction that the redemptive work of God in the world, in Jesus Christ and through the power of the Spirit, is wondrously diverse and beautiful.

Finally, we thank our students. Year after year, you make us better teachers. We owe much that is in this book to the questions you have raised and the risks you have taken.

Sally A. Brown and Luke A. Powery

Introduction

Sally A. Brown and Luke A. Powery

Every book has its backstory. It can be difficult to pinpoint where that backstory begins; but it is safe to say that this one began in an e-mail exchange. Picture two preacher-homileticians hammering on their computer keyboards in offices some 150 yards apart on an East Coast seminary campus: "We could do this—a new textbook" // "right—tapping into our traditions, Baptist-Pentecostal/Reformed— and crossing race and gender too" // "for changing classroom demographic?" // "right!" //"Spirit-driven" // "yes" // "you serious?" // "of course."

Such exchanges formed part of a larger web of animated dialogue about the changing realities in church and theological education, the increasing diversity of our classrooms, and our search for tools to help us train a rising generation of preachers who would be capable of meeting a future whose contours we weren't able to spell out for them exactly, but which would clearly be diverse religiously, culturally, and ethnically, both inside and outside the church. We wanted to help students take varied contexts seriously as they were formed as leaders.

What anchored these conversations were some deep, shared convictions. Both of us believed strongly (and still do) that Christian preachers dare to dance on the grave of despair and sing in the domains of death in the name of Jesus Christ, crucified God-with-us and firstborn of God's new creation. Beyond that, we had both published work expressing our respective, gut-deep convictions that any preacher or Christian community that hopes to bear fitting witness to the yearning of divine love over the world must learn the language of lament—a language we learn from the Spirit herself.

As fate or providence would have it, we further discovered that our sense of what is at stake in preaching had been shaped by a specific experience etched deeply in each of our memories—a scene that had played out differently in detail, but with similar impact. We had each found ourselves, still in our thirties, standing shoulder to shoulder with parents committing the unthinkable act of burying their greatest treasure—their child. For each of us, this was an experience that marked the depth of despair and tear-stained rage to which Christian preaching must answer. Lowering a small coffin into the ground has a way of sharpening your senses: you hear the groans of the Spirit everywhere. Now, silent news footage of listless refugees waiting for help under a blazing sun has a soundtrack: you can hear the moan of the wind that's blowing dust in their eyes. Or you open the newspaper to yet another photo of an urban mother clutching the junior-high photo of her teenage boy who is no more, his life an unfinished sentence that ended with a pistol shot: the keening grief of thousands of bereaved mothers rises off the silent page. To these groans of the Spirit are added the sighs of deforested Central American mountainsides where dense rainforests—the air-purifying "lungs" of the planet—once stood. The Spirit's groans hollow you out some days. Into those hollow places rushes an evermore intense hope in God's just and righteous future yet to come.

We also share a common vision of theological education as increasingly being an arena where diverse, historic Christian traditions will need to draw strength from each other, be mutually tested and stretched, and give birth to new hybrid languages of lament and hope adequate to our time. Theological education will need to animate new, prophetic practices to challenge the forces of runaway classism, racism, and sheer indifference that cause human beings to withdraw into polarized, sometimes literally armed, camps of suspicion and callous self-interest.

Yet, for all our common concerns, we two preacher-homileticians are different. One is black, the other white. We are of different gender and different age. One was nurtured in the free-church tradition of Pentecostalism and ordained Baptist, whose worship practices lay full claim to the body and voice of not only the preacher but every member of the congregation. The other was raised in the mainline, North American Presbyterian branch of the Reformed tradition—a worship tradition that associates a stone-still body with attentiveness to the presence of the Lord (a concept many Presbyterian eight-year-olds have found mind-boggling). Each of us has had the privilege of spending significant time in worshiping traditions more like that of the other. We've been welcomed there. We have experienced the death-defying power of the Spirit in settings that were not our natural liturgical habitat, reminding us that the Spirit is always on the loose, not constrained by any one tradition.

Finally, we are both preachers and teachers of preaching. Our perspectives on the field of homiletics are stereoscopic; and this has improved our vision. We divided up most of the chapters of this book according to our areas of strength and experience instead of trying to write each chapter together. We trust one another's voices, which are different.

A feature of this book is that in each of the singly-authored chapters (chapters 2 through 10), readers will find "sidebars" in which the other writer reflects on a key point under discussion. Our hope is that the implicitly dialogical nature of this book will evoke, in turn, energetic dialogue among its readers, whether in classrooms or preachers' workgroups. Out of such invested and open conversation may come the hybrid shapes, sounds, and theological frameworks for preaching that will equip the present and future church to bear courageous witness to the work of God in a changing world, one charged with tension, yet full of redemptive possibility.

And Now, a Word from the Manufacturers . . .

These days, every new product comes with a label full of fine print. Whether it's a new treatment for hair loss, a three-wheeler for your nephew (assembly required), or the new Weedwacker you are hoping will outperform the other half dozen you've thrown away in disgust, the fine-print information is always important. It tells you what to expect: "This is what this item can do, this is how *not* to use it ('don't try this at home')." It seems only fair for the authors of a preaching textbook to fall in line and put the "fine print" up front.

First, this book cannot teach you to preach, nor is it intended to. What it *is* intended to do is to accompany you on a journey of learning-by-doing. We take the view here that preaching is an event, not a static object. A written sermon is an artifact, marks on a page that point to an event of sound and bodily gesture. Preaching itself is embodied, vocalized, actively received, here-and-now witness to the ongoing work of God in the world. The purpose of this book is to construct different vantage points—theological, contextual, historical, and so on—from which you can critically reflect on just such embodied events of speaking and hearing—your own, and the preaching of others. The aim of this back-and-forth between the act of preaching and critical reflection upon it is to become more attuned to the Spirit, more adept in preaching's component skills, and more self-aware about all that is at stake in proclaiming the redemptive work of God.

First, a word on what we mean by "critical reflection." To be clear, "critical" reflection does not mean that one's aim is to identify everything that's wrong with the way someone preaches, or to beat down all views of preaching except one's own. Critical reflection is part of any practice-based learning process. Reflecting critically on preaching means taking a deliberate step back to try to understand better a particular sermon event—our own, or that of another preacher. Typically, we evaluate preaching events in relation to particular criteria (theological, interpretive, contextual-rhetorical, and so on) that are agreed upon by the learning community involved. Although critical reflection will reveal flaws or raise questions, it can just as easily foreground strengths in a preaching event, and its ultimate aim is to always build up the preacher, whether the feedback is positive or negative. Within the increasingly diverse preaching classrooms or preachers' peer groups for which this book is intended, critical reflection undertaken in company with other preachers can help us consider preaching from completely new perspectives.

A second "fine-print" assumption that we make in these pages is that preaching is best learned in some kind of group environment, whether physical or virtual (Internet-based). Many who pick up this book will be learning to preach with other relatively new preachers. You may be in a physical space with the rest of the class, or yours may be a virtual classroom you enter periodically to meet with the rest of the community. Regardless, we see this book functioning best when put to work in relation to a fundamentally *interactive* process of learning, whether you are just starting out in preaching or have done it for years.

You may be a working preacher who has picked up this book because you hope to create higher-quality sermons and preach them better. To make the learning process even more effective, consider working your way through this book in company with a small group of other preachers who've committed themselves to mutual support, honest critique, and unflagging encouragement in the work of preaching.[1] Nothing is more valuable than the informed feedback of other preachers. Using a shared set of criteria, such a learning community can surface insights that may never come up in the brief remarks, appreciative or critical, that listeners typically offer after a worship service. At the very least, a preacher reading this book on her own can invite at least one other preacher to read it, too, and commit to a couple of meetings (in shared physical or space) for conversation. Listening to sermons together and evaluating them can be an invaluable exercise.

A third "fine-print" assumption of this book is that we envision your classroom as a place far more diverse than classrooms of even ten or fifteen years ago. Some diversities will be obvious—denominational differences, gender difference, different ethnicities and first languages, along with cultural and generational differences. Other dimensions of difference may be less obvious but will have an impact on what goes on in the classroom, such as different theological viewpoints related to the practice of preaching or its content, or

---

1. Research conducted by the Sustaining Pastoral Excellence Peer Learning Project has shown that preachers who work in committed peer-learning groups with fellow pastors, setting shared goals and achieving them, are more satisfied with their own preaching, as are their congregations. Being committed to shared learning in ministry also correlates with more enduring and satisfying ministry careers. See Penny Long Marler et al., *So Much Better: How Thousands of Pastors Help Each Other Thrive* (St. Louis: Chalice, 2013), 6–9.

the varied worship styles that members of the class prefer or believe are most valid. Not least of all, learners differ in what they consider strengths in a sermon—a matter largely influenced by the specific faith-forming contexts where they have spent significant time. Such dimensions of ordinary life as sexual orientation or political views and affiliations can also affect a learning community.

We are convinced that diversities matter. The increasing diversity in today's preaching classrooms is a gift, not a problem, a beautiful blessing, not a burden. Diversities press us to become more self-aware, challenging us to welcome into our experience persons and perspectives distinctly "other" from ourselves. We have made an effort to keep the diversities that are present in any preaching classroom or learning community in the forefront of our thinking as we've written this book. A community of preachers, novice or seasoned, that gets past surface talk will discover differences among them of all kinds. They will differ in their convictions about preaching—what it is, what it is meant to do, and what makes it excellent.

Differences of opinion in relation to preaching, a practice deeply rooted in distinctive traditions, can run deep. Difference typically produces tension. This tension has potential to "break" either of two ways. If "different" is always presumed to align with "wrong" or "lesser," it becomes the source of mutual distrust, increasing self-protectiveness, and disengagement. In a learning community, especially a preaching community, difference can lead to a closed, dismissive attitude toward styles of preaching other than one's own. Yet, if we can maintain open-minded curiosity about the differences that surface in our classrooms and preachers' learning groups, these diversities become opportunities to enlarge our view of the world and the endless variety of the Spirit's ways with the saving word. Practicing openness of heart and mind to the vast variety within

Christ's church makes better preachers, pastors, and citizens out of us in a world that summons us to live and work in close quarters with those we experience as "other." Until we recognize the "other"—the one who is religiously, culturally, socially, and politically different from oneself—as brother/sister and, indeed, *teacher* and companion on the way, we will miss the presence of Christ.[2]

Whatever the circumstances in which you are developing your preaching skills, this book assumes that real learning happens for preachers when (1) they keep preaching, and (2) they discipline themselves to be self-aware about their work, stepping back from time to time and submitting it to their own critical assessments and those of others different from themselves.

Learning to preach is an open-ended process. Neither of us has ever met a good preacher who thought he or she had nothing further to learn. We ourselves continue to learn. Among our teachers are the everyday folks in the pews; we hope that they, too, will be a resource for you. Some days, listeners will embrace you; other days, you'll just feel grateful that they continue to put up with you. Then there are moments, if mutual trust is strong between pulpit and pew, when a listener will be constructively critical, letting you know where a move in the sermon left them feeling marginalized. Precious are those listeners who bring such gifts of honesty and constructive engagement.

But there will also come a time (by grace!) when a listener looks you in the eye and testifies that while you were preaching, they heard not only *your* voice, but the speaking of Another. We are not alone in the pulpit—ever. Preacher and listeners find themselves on holy ground. The Spirit moves in the assembly, restoring vision,

---

2. The homiletical approach of John S. McClure is notable for its insistence that positioning oneself before "the other" in receptivity and humility is essential for preaching constructively amid the conditions of postmodernity. See McClure, *Other-wise Preaching: A Postmodern Ethic for Homiletics* (St. Louis: Chalice, 2001).

restoring hope. But the power of the Spirit cannot be confined to the sanctuary. The Holy Breath moves into the streets, teaching every believer to bear witness there in word and deed that—even *here,* even *now*—God is making all things new.

Structure of the Book

With these convictions guiding us, we have structured this book in the following manner. Rather than diving immediately into the nuts and bolts of sermon development, we begin with thinking about the theological and rhetorical nature of preaching. Chapter 1 posits preaching as a Spirit-animated event. We consider preaching as a rhetorical act guided by theological convictions rooted in the promises of God. Chapter 2 goes deeper into the Spirit-driven theology of preaching underlying our approach to preaching. Along the way, we invite readers to examine the theologies *of* preaching and *in* preaching that they have internalized, and which will be at play as they learn the skills of preaching.

Having clarified our pneumatological (Spirit-driven) theological lens in chapters 1 and 2 we turn in chapter 3 to the importance of a life of prayer for preaching, a topic that grows out of our pneumatological starting point, one we believe sometimes suffers neglect in preaching classrooms. This leads to reflection in chapter 4 on preaching as an act of worship. Chapters 5 through 8 deal with the traditional tasks and skills of preaching, from the study of biblical text and context to sermon design and performance. Chapter 5 helps readers understand their role as interpreters of Word and world, texts and contexts, including the congregation itself. Chapter 6 maps a method for the study of Scripture for preaching (also known as exegesis), beginning with a contemporized version of the ancient practice of *lectio divina*, a prayerful engagement with one's chosen preaching text. Chapter 7 presents different ways to move from exegetical study to sermon design, exploring different sermon forms. Yet sermons are not ideas arranged on a page. As living events of Spirit-inspired embodied communication, sermons must *take* form through being *per*formed by a human body. Chapter 8 takes a closer look at sermon delivery through human voice and body.

Chapter 9 moves beyond the body to discuss the challenges and opportunities of the relationship between preaching and technology, especially in our digital age. Chapter 10 explores ways that preaching forms Christians to live faithfully in the world, revealing our conviction that the Spirit's work in and through preaching is not limited to the interior of a church building.

Spirit-animated preaching engages the life of individuals, communities, and wider society. Such preaching has centripetal and centrifugal power, shaping both speakers and hearers as agents of witness in the wider world. There, the Spirit is on the loose, blowing where She wills. Our hope is that the sound of this Holy, world-transforming Wind will accompany you as you read these pages and make the practices of preaching your own.

1

The Spirit-Animated Event of Preaching

Sally A. Brown and Luke A. Powery

Preaching is risky business. It is risky because, frankly, its divine aims are impossible to achieve, humanly speaking. There is no set of rules any of us can follow, no book we can read (this one included), that guarantees that when you step up to a pulpit and open your mouth, the words that reach listeners will be a word that is God's own. We can speak with consummate rhetorical skill of things theological, but only God's animating Spirit makes our preaching a life-transforming, world-changing message.

As the chapters of this book hope to show, the skill sets that preaching requires can be learned because preaching is both theological *and* rhetorical. Yet we offer this technical toolkit, recognizing that skill alone can't account for what happens in preaching. The human act of preaching participates in a divine act of new creation that we preachers cannot fully comprehend, let alone predict, produce, or control. Ordinary human voices speaking ordinary human words are taken up into God's project of interrupting humanity's mad dash toward self-destruction. Christian preaching is both news of God's redemptive work in Jesus Christ and the means by which it has an impact upon us, transferring us, as one prayer puts it, "out of darkness into light, out of sin into righteousness, out of death into life."[1]

The Church and Its Preaching:
Open-Ended Events in the Power of the Spirit

There are many ways to begin a book about preaching. We choose to begin by reflecting on preaching from both *theological* and *rhetorical* points of view. Theologically, we see preaching as anchored in an *event*—one that was set in motion two thousand years ago and still continues today: the God-instigated, yet utterly human "event" known as the church of Jesus Christ in the world. This starting point captures for us something essential: both the church and its preaching are best understood as *Spirit-animated, dynamic events* rather than static concepts. From their inception to the present, the church and its preaching have been *more verb than noun*.

According to the New Testament, the outpouring of God's Spirit on the first Pentecost festival after Jesus' resurrection brought the church and its most characteristic public practice, the preaching of the good news of Jesus, into being. In the Gospel of John, Jesus commissions his followers as a community of living witness in word and action to the ways of God (14:15-17; 15:16, 26). To that end, says Jesus, God will send the Holy Spirit upon them (14:26, 15:26). In a post-resurrection account unique to John, Jesus tells his disciples

---

1. *Book of Common Prayer*, The Episcopal Church, U.S.A. (New York: Church, 1978).

not to be afraid and breathes upon them, saying, "Receive the Holy Spirit" (20:22).

More familiar to many of us is Luke's account. Luke ends the Gospel that bears his name with Jesus' promise of the Holy Spirit ("I am sending you what my Father promised," 24:49a). Jesus tells his followers to wait in Jerusalem "until you are clothed with power from on high" (24:49b). This fusion of divine and human agency will be crucial for the mission ahead: that "repentance and forgiveness . . . be proclaimed . . . to all nations" in the name of Jesus (24:47).

The title of Luke's second volume, the "Acts" of the Apostles, indicates that to speak of the church is to speak of action—specifically, acts of "co-agency," human and divine, rhetorical and theological. The Acts of the Apostles explicitly connects the agency of the Spirit with the effective witness of the church three times in its first eight verses (1:2, 5, 8). After Jesus' ascension (1:9-10), his followers do as instructed: they stay together in Jerusalem, actively waiting and praying for the promised divine Spirit (Luke 24:49; Acts 1:14).

According to Acts 2, the church is born *not as an institution but as a preaching event.* The Spirit bursts onto the scene in the city of Jerusalem fifty days after Jesus' resurrection, laying claim to the human bodies and tongues of Jesus' followers with the explosive force of a cyclone. Preachers with tongues set on fire by the Spirit pour into the highways and byways of Jerusalem, their tumultuous, multilingual resurrection proclamation filling the city with new-creation sound. The remaining twenty-six chapters of Acts record the beginnings of the unstoppable, Spirit-driven event of the expanding church—an event that continues even now.

The community that witnesses to God's self-revelation through Jesus Christ is first and foremost a Spirit-driven *doing*, both human and divine: a *proclaiming* and a *testifying* that leaves no heart, no place, no power structure within its reach untouched by its saving disruption. Preaching is a non-optional component of the action-event that is Christ's church. In death-defying Word and life-giving deed, God *does* new creation amid the structure of the old order through Spirit-driven communities speaking and acting in Jesus' name. The lowly are raised up and the powerful humbled. Captives to abusive power are set free. Hungers—for hope, for bread, for justice—are satisfied in the wake of what the Spirit is doing to make all things new.

Christian preachers who have stepped to the pulpit in days of spiritual famine as well as feast, out of utter human weariness rather than strength, can testify that the life- and world-saving effects of the word event cannot be accounted for in terms of human wordcraft and performance alone, though there are rhetorical dimensions to it. This saving event of Christian proclamation depends upon the dynamism of the Spirit for both preacher and hearers. The human tongue speaks (rhetoric) and the life-giving promise of God sounds (theology). The church and its preaching remain *more verb than noun*, God's power turned loose in the world to disrupt the ways of death and to bring forth life.

A Stereoscopic Theology of Preaching as Spirit-Driven Event

Different traditions within Christianity provide us with distinctive theological descriptions of the rhetorical activity we call Christian preaching. Here, we draw on insights from each of our traditions, Reformed and Baptist-Pentecostal respectively, to build a more stereoscopic view of preaching than any single theological point of view can provide. Doing so signals our commitment to dialogue among Christian traditions as an essential feature of preparing for church leadership in the twenty-first century.[2] Readers of this book

---

2. The term "free church" refers to Christian traditions that have always existed independently of the institutions of government. These include Baptist and Anabaptist traditions (the latter

will have their own insights to contribute based on their own traditions and experiences, reminding us that preaching is not just one homogeneous thing. Preaching is many things, both theologically and rhetorically, but we, the authors, have our own inclinations, which will become clearer in what follows.

Reformed Theological Insights:
Three Dynamic Forms of the Word of God

The Reformed tradition has understood preaching as one of three basic "forms" of the divine word expressing itself amid the flux of human experience. In Reformed thought, the three forms of the word of God are interrelated and ordered as follows: first, the living (risen) person Jesus Christ; second, the word that comes through our engagement with the written witness to the living word, which is Scripture; and third, the divine word that addresses us in preaching that takes its point of departure in the interpretation of a biblical passage (or "text," as we say).

This threefold theological map of the ways of God's living word in the world has been helpful in many ways, holding together the coherence of the word as expressed in the incarnation, through Scripture, and through preaching. On the other hand, the language of "form" tends to imply a static structure and fails to capture the living eventfulness of God's word in the world. In keeping with our view that, like the church, the word of God occurs more as an *event* that happens to us than a *thing* we can point to (more *verb* than noun), we suggest thinking in terms of a threefold *dynamic* of the word of God that *does* something to us.

including, for example, Moravians and Mennonites, to name just two), as well as Methodist, Christian Missionary Alliance, Church of God, and Pentecostal in addition to independently organized evangelical congregations and communities that identify with the charismatic renewal movement around the world.

The primary dynamic manifestation of the word of God in the world is God's Word incarnate in Jesus Christ. The amazing (and unsettling) claim of Christian faith is that the God we worship is not distant, passive, and unknowable. Called "the Word [that] became flesh and lived among us" by the Gospel of John (1:14), God entered into the ordinariness and tumult of human experience by way of a human being who acted and spoke, rejoiced and suffered, and was vulnerable to death. The first dynamic way of the divine Word in the world bore the name Jesus of Nazareth; he was nothing less than God-with-us ("Emmanuel," Matt. 1:22-23), a divine–human event.

The second dynamic of the word flows into the world through the Christian Scriptures, comprised of the first (or Old/Older) Testament and second (or New/Newer) Testament of the Bible. (Some Christian communions also include other books they consider authoritative for Christian living, the books of the Apocrypha.) Sometimes the Bible itself—a book we can hold in our hands—is referred to as "God's Word." Yet preachers do not simply reiterate the words on a page of Scripture; they interpret it (some say "apply") in ways relevant to the specific listeners they address. God's Word is living and dynamic; it is revealed through Scripture as a result of Spirit-assisted engagement with the text—reading, meditation, and interpretation. (More will be said of this in chapters 5 and 6 of this book.)

The third dynamic of the word of God moving into the world is Christian preaching. A central claim of Reformed churches' theology is that "the preaching of the Word of God is the Word of God."[3] Preaching is a here-and-now message aimed at a specific context of Christian worship and witness. Preaching flows out of an interpretive process in which the preacher has been prayerfully alert both to the diversities of her congregation and the prompting of the Spirit. As

---

3. Second Helvetic Confession 5.2, *The Book of Confessions*, The Presbyterian Church, U.S.A. (Louisville: Geneva Press, 1999).

noted above, preaching is more than repeating the words on a page of the Bible. The preacher inhabits a lively dialogue between the world of the biblical text and the world of contemporary Christian life, trusting that, as a result of this back-and-forth process, the Spirit will guide him or her to speak a fresh and timely word for a particular time and place.[4]

To summarize, God's word enters historical time and space through three concrete actions: incarnation (the living Word, Jesus Christ), biblical interpretation (the "voice" of the word through Scripture), and public, context-specific proclamation (the "event" of divine address to a specific community through preaching). Thinking of God's word in the world as a living, active event can be unsettling. It is tempting to identify the word *only* with a past historical event (the life, death, and rising of Jesus) or with the words of the Bible, which—with enough effort—we imagine we might master. But this is not the nature of God's living word. The living word of the living God in the world—incarnate, flowing from Scripture, and proclaimed—is dynamic. In the power of the Spirit, these three dynamics of the word lay claim to the church as living witness to its risen Lord.

Free-Church/Pentecostal Theological Insight: Preaching as Spirit-Animated Dialogue

A lively understanding of the Spirit-driven nature of Christian life, worship, and public social witness goes a long way toward helping us avoid a static notion of the ways of God's living, eventful word in the world. Here, we draw upon insights arising from free-church traditions, particularly Pentecostal traditions.

The biblical witness declares that even to make the confession,

4. Thomas G. Long, *The Witness of Preaching*, 2nd ed. (Louisville: Westminster John Knox, 2005), 63–66.

"Jesus is Lord" is only possible when it is "Spirit speech," human speech taken up by the animating presence of the Spirit (1 Cor. 12:3).[5] Without the Spirit's co-agency along with the human preacher, no sermon no matter how rhetorically sophisticated would accomplish the redemptive work of judgment and grace that calls forth new life and leads us out of death into the life of God's new creation.

The Spirit is the animating center of the embodied life of the church, including all the forms of speech and gesture by which it worships God and bears public witness to God's ongoing, redemptive work. This is what makes congregations *more verbs than nouns*; they are social structures that host Spirit-animated action, not institutional hierarchies or brick-and-mortar structures. In fact, the governing structures and worship spaces of Christian communities around the globe differ greatly. What they have in common is that they are zones of Spirited-inspired action. In worship, the Spirit inspires lament for all that is wrong in human lives and in the world, as well as praise for the God whose mercy and power addresses these realities and denies death the final word.[6]

Christian traditions that cultivate expectant openness to the ongoing activity of the Holy Spirit in the church disabuse us of any notion that, with the right education or the right tools, we might become "masters" of God's word. The word of God turned loose in the church and in the world is not ours to control or to predict. At the same time, these traditions emphasize that the Spirit is active in the *whole* congregation during the preaching event, not the preacher alone. The active presence of God's Spirit in pew as well as pulpit produces dialogical forms of preaching in which the congregation

---

5. See Luke A. Powery, *Spirit Speech: Lament and Celebration in Preaching* (Nashville: Abingdon, 2009).

6. See Luke A. Powery, *Dem Dry Bones: Preaching, Death, and Hope* (Minneapolis: Fortress Press, 2012).

enters fully into the dynamic of the in-breaking word, participating through movement of the body and vocal response.

The outpouring of the Spirit in preaching is not for the church only, but for the world. The dynamic of the Spirit in worship is centrifugal—moving believers outward from the core experience of prayer, praise, and preaching into a world of deep hungers and deadly conflicts. The Spirit moves us to witness against all that is deathly in the world—the practices of sin, abuses of power that marginalize the weak, and socioeconomic or cultural structures designed to secure the flourishing of a few at the expense of the many. The Spirit enables believers to speak and enact genuine hope grounded in the love and justice of God. God's transformative energy moves in the world through the bodies and voices, intellects and skills, of ordinary human beings who have been given "Spirit"-sight to discern the outlines of new creation amid the powers and structures of the "old age."[7] Preaching is a primary way that the Spirit provides believers with "corrective lenses" through which to see the world in light of God's redemptive work.

To sum up, preaching is a Spirit-driven event that takes place within Spirit-created communities. Preaching is one of the dynamic forms of the living word of God in the world. Through preaching, God speaks a saving word for a particular time and place, a word derived from prayerful and disciplined study of Scripture. Along with every other practice of the worshiping, witnessing church, preaching bears witness to the incarnate Word, Jesus Christ, crucified God-with-us and firstborn of God's new creation.

---

7. James F. Kay, "The Word of the Cross at the Turn of the Ages," *Interpretation* 53:1 (January 1999): 44–56.

Preaching as a Rhetorical Task:
Exploring Your Rhetorical Understanding of Preaching

Preaching depends on the animation of the Spirit; divine action is indispensable for preaching to happen. Yet, at the same time, preaching requires human effort and skill. Preaching is the dance of the divine and human, the theological and the rhetorical. Without God, there would be no preaching; but without a human preacher, there would be no preaching either! As divine–human event, as more verb than noun, preaching *does* something, and the doing is not just God's doing or the Spirit's doing; it is our doing, action, and skill. As such, preaching has rhetorical substance and uses human tools.

How we experience preaching, rhetorically, varies based on our life histories, particularly the preaching we have experienced. We discuss preaching as a *rhetorical* activity from the point of view of homiletics scholars both ancient and contemporary. As we do, we invite you to explore the rhetorical qualities of preaching as you have experienced it and the impact that has on what you expect from preaching—your own, and that of others. Your experience of preaching as a rhetorical event shapes the images you have of preachers and your expectations of the effects preaching has, or should have, on listeners.

Rhetorical Experiences and Images of Preachers

As you sit in a wooden pew or cushioned chair each Sunday listening to a preacher, you may give little thought to the rhetorical shape and impact of the sermon and the images of preachers and preaching being formed within you because of that experience. Of course, your denominational connections and heritage shape the preaching you hear as does the architecture of the preaching space. A megachurch coliseum showing the preacher on a big screen is quite different from the intimate environment of a storefront church in a shopping plaza. The preacher may use no notes and speak from a stool; or he may use an iPad with PowerPoint; or she may stand firmly in a pulpit with her full manuscript. Some preachers walk while they preach to emphasize points and to engage the audience in the event of preaching. Other preachers stand still behind the pulpit. Some use large hand gestures; others do not. Some sing the sermon, while some of you are very happy that your preacher does not! These choices are part of the varied rhetorical forms that preaching takes. The point here is not to say, "This way is better than the other," but to appreciate how the rhetorical approaches we are used to have an impact on our experience of preaching, shaping our images of preachers.

Different rhetorical choices on the part of the preacher produce different rhetorical effects on listeners. On the basis of experience, one of us might expect preaching to be an intimate experience of very personal address, while another may expect preaching to be a dramatic, high-energy *tour de force* designed to energize an auditorium full of worshipers. Whatever rhetorical mode a preacher uses, the Spirit is at work, animating the life of the preacher and congregation toward a holy dialogue, ultimately with God.

Depending on the rhetorical styles of preaching we have experienced, we tend to have different images of the preacher. In the last few years, several scholars have explored various images of preachers; among these would be some you recognize and others you don't. Homiletician Kenyatta Gilbert suggests seven types of preachers.[8] There is the "Evangelical-Moralist" who takes the biblical record seriously and puts a heavy emphasis on the hearer's need for a personal relationship with God. The "Social Activist" preacher stresses social change through ethical action and has a sociopolitical

8. Kenyatta R. Gilbert, *The Journey and Promise of African American Preaching* (Minneapolis: Fortress Press, 2011), 132–39.

lens on the gospel message. The "Entrepreneurial Agent" is a positive thinker and motivator who preaches to inspire the congregation toward new social and financial ventures. The "Clerico-Politician" is a preacher who leads a congregation but is also a skilled politician, whether elected, aspiring, or neither, and has great focus on civic engagement. The "Rancher-Pontiff" is a charismatic figure who is orally skillful and enjoys a mass following; he or she thrives through their brand of preaching (narrative, didactic, etc.) and tend to have loose, if any, denominational ties. The "Mystic-Spiritualist" is a preacher who focuses on spiritual encounter and uses the sermon to lead people to prayer or greater devotion. The "Social Poet-Technophile" is an innovative preacher who uses popular songs, movies, and technology, in conjunction with Scripture, to convey the gospel. These types—and the list is not exhaustive of all possibilities—are just that because they are not literal but *functional* rhetorical identities of preachers. They speak to what these preachers aim to *do*. Perhaps you know these preachers from experience and they have shaped what you think preaching should do. One must also acknowledge that no preacher is only one of these but most likely embodies a couple or even several of these or other tropes at once.

Still other images for preachers may resonate with your experiences: herald, witness, servant, hope-giver, lover, mystery steward, fool, fisher, host and guest, entrusted one, and one "out of your mind."[9] These rhetorical images may help you name what it is

---

9. See Robert Stephen Reid, ed., *Slow of Speech and Unclean Lips: Contemporary Images of Preaching Identity* (Eugene, OR: Cascade, 2010). In addition to these images, there are many contemporary preaching books that describe preaching as many things: "preaching as local theology and folk art," "preaching as spiritual direction," "preaching as testimony," and "preaching as worship," to name a few. See Lenora Tubbs Tisdale, *Preaching as Local Theology and Folk Art* (Minneapolis: Fortress, 1997); Kay Northcutt, *Kindling Desire for God: Preaching as Spiritual Direction* (Minneapolis: Fortress, 2009); Anna Carter Florence, *Preaching as Testimony* (Louisville: Westminster John Knox, 2007); Michael J. Quicke, *Preaching as Worship: An Integrative Approach to Formation in Your Church* (Baker Books, 2011).

you have experienced in weekly worship or picking up a sermon on YouTube.

It is important to reflect on how preaching has functioned for you (both positively and negatively) and the degree to which you value, or identify with, one or another image of the preacher. Our rhetorical experiences and images shape what we consider the rhetorical purposes of preaching to be and what any one of us hopes to accomplish as a preacher.

Rhetorical Purposes of Preaching

As already noted, preaching is both theological and rhetorical. Our understanding that preaching is more verb than noun implies that preaching does something to hearers and speakers not only theologically but rhetorically. Speech acts upon us; this is what we mean by the rhetorical effect, or function, of an event of spoken communication such as preaching.

In what is considered the earliest homiletical textbook, *On Christian Doctrine*, St. Augustine teaches that preaching has three rhetorical aims—to teach, delight, and persuade. Preaching *does* these things. Augustine goes on to detail some of the linguistic and vocal choices a preacher will need to make to produce these rhetorical effects. Contemporary homiletician Jana Childers has edited a book of essays written by homileticians called *Purposes of Preaching*, and in it we find a range of ideas concerning what preaching is and does.[10] The volume makes clear that there is not one way to name what preaching does or how it functions in the lives of hearers. The list below is suggestive, not exhaustive; but it may help you clarify your own thinking about different purposes in preaching and the varied rhetorical strategies that may best serve them. Keep in mind that we

10. See Jana Childers, ed., *Purposes of Preaching* (St. Louis: Chalice, 2004).

are considering what preaching *does*, or *accomplishes*, in and for the listener.

1. *Historical.* This mode of preaching emphasizes telling of the past, whether it be of proclaiming God's mighty acts in history or illuminating human history of the twentieth century or another time period. This kind of preaching aims to ensure that hearers learn about God's acts through history and learn from people or events of the past.

2. *Biblical.* Preaching's rhetorical purpose, in this perspective, is to make plain textual insights from Scripture. It focuses on reiterating the biblical text, making sure people know and understand Scripture in what might be deemed a biblically illiterate age.

3. *Spiritual.* This suggests that the rhetorical task of preaching is to lead listeners to prayer and other spiritual practices such as meditation or the sacrament of communion. Spiritual growth and practice are the aims in this approach.

4. *Sacramental.* The rhetorical thrust of preaching through this lens is to help people meet Jesus or encounter God. Preaching attempts to usher in the Presence amid the congregation.

5. *Soteriological.* This rhetorical purpose of preaching is to aim for the conversion of the hearers, to preach for a decision by the hearers, a decision to serve God. Ultimately, the sermon attempts to be a vehicle for (personal) salvation.

6. *Theological.* Though one can argue that preaching is a theological venture overall, regardless of its aims, this way of characterizing the purpose of preaching aligns closely with what we state elsewhere in this chapter about preaching as divine promise. Helping others come to know and understand God's redemptive purposes for creation is vital in this approach.

7. *Pastoral.* The main rhetorical aim is to care for the people through the sermon, whether it be healing, comfort, encouragement, or providing calm. It is preaching as pastoral care for the needs of the hearers.

8. *Conversational.* The rhetorical purpose is to foster a conversation between preacher and congregation about the life of faith and to keep the conversation going.

9. *Educational.* One can argue that all preaching teaches in some way or the other but for this rhetorical purpose, preaching is primarily didactic in nature, conveying information about the church or the spiritual life or the ways of God. It aims to form disciples.

10. *Ethical.* Preaching with this rhetorical purpose aims to move people toward acts of justice that resist oppressive powers in the world and fosters hospitality within the community and wider society.

11. *Social.* This type of preaching hopes to help listeners have insights about social innovations such as technology; or what it means to live in society as a good citizen; or ways to embody interfaith etiquette.

12. *Rhetorical.* This is a specialized use of the term, "rhetorical," and suggests that preaching aims to persuade listeners toward some action. In Augustine's terms, it does not focus on teaching or delighting but on moving people.

13. *Narratological.* This is preaching that desires to tell effective stories about God, the community, and world. It is story-driven as a means toward human connection.

14. *Comical.* This rhetorical approach capitalizes on using humor to make people laugh. The effects of comedy are complex. Satire can help us see ourselves for who we really are. Sometimes we

need to laugh, perhaps to keep from crying in a world that is dying.

Considering these rhetorical purposes, and the different genres or strategies of communication that support them, may help you name some of your own beliefs about the purposes of preaching and the rhetoric that supports them. Preaching takes rhetorical form through such tools as language and gesture, and these are adjusted to support a sermon's overall purpose. Just as the Bible is made up of various literary forms to proclaim the word of God—for example, psalms/poetry, proverbs, stories, parables, and epistles—preaching, too, adopts genres appropriate to its rhetorical purposes and theological aims.

Some Key Theological Aims of Preaching

A collection of poems published in 1974 by Catholic storyteller and poet John Shea bore the title, *The God Who Fell from Heaven*. The phrase is based on one of Shea's poems. It begins this way:

> If you had stayed/tightfisted in the sky/and watched us thrash/with all the patience of a pipe smoker/I would pray/like a golden bullet/aimed at your heart./But the story says/you cried/and so heavy was the tear/you fell with it to earth/where like a baritone in a bar/it is never time to go home.[11]

Using many rhetorical strategies, Christian preaching is news of the undefeated love of a God who indeed refused to "[stay] tightfisted in the sky." At the heart of Christian faith is the startling claim that God "'took up residence' among us, full of grace and truth," a line we find in John 1:14, referring to Jesus of Nazareth, a healer and teacher. After he was crucified at the hands of Roman authorities on

---

11. John Shea, "A Prayer to the God Who Fell from Heaven," in *The God Who Fell from Heaven* (Niles, IL: Argus Communications, 1974), 90.

charges of sedition and blasphemy, his followers insisted his was no ordinary martyr's death. They staked their lives on the conviction that God had raised Jesus on the third day after his execution, dealing the death-blow to death itself and establishing in Jesus Christ a new beginning for humanity—a new beginning so radical, in fact, that later, the apostle Paul could only stammer, "Behold—*new creation!*" (see 1 Cor. 5:17).

Preachers step to the pulpit to extend God's loving outreach to any who will listen. Preaching includes many kinds of "speech-action" (rhetorical moves and genres), but all serve three theological aims: 1) communicating God's promise, kept and being kept in Jesus Christ, to redeem and renew all things; 2) reframing the way we see ourselves and others, the present and the future, in light of this promise and action of God; and 3) "rehearsing" us for active participation in the work of God in the world. As we discuss each of these theological aims of preaching in turn, keep in mind that many rhetorical genres and styles of communication may serve each of these theological aims.

The Core Affirmation of Christian Preaching: Divine Promise

The core *rhetoric* of Christian preaching is to declare God's promise to make all things new. The pledge of that divine promise is that Jesus, crucified God-with-us, was raised from death as the firstborn of God's new creation. And this Jesus Christ, who is Lord of the human future, is active in our present lives, through the power of the Spirit, to judge and expose all that is deathly in us and in the world and bring forth in human life and human lives the love and justice of God.

Accenting the promise of God to renew all things prevents preachers from lapsing into moralism. By moralism we mean talking as if by sheer moral effort—by being less lazy and faithless, and by

17

acting rightly—human beings could make the world conform to the wholeness we see in Jesus. Another way to put this is that by beginning with declaring God's promises to our congregations, we make certain that *the divine indicative precedes the human imperative.* This pattern is basic in Christian preaching. We do not urge our congregations to accomplish redemption; we announce redemption as God's doing.

Many of us who studied grammar in school were taught the difference between the indicative and imperative moods of a verb. The indicative mood declares an established state of affairs: "Joe is riding his bike"; "Governments exist to protect all their citizens"; "God is working in the world to expose and judge all that destroys human well-being." The imperative mood of a verb, on the other hand, uses words like "must," "ought," and "should." For example: "Joe *should be* riding his bike"; "Governments *ought to* protect all their citizens, not just a privileged few"; "Christians *must* expose and judge all that destroys human well-being."

Too often, well-intentioned preachers major in this kind of must-ought-should language. This has several negative effects. First, it discounts what God has already done in the death and resurrection of Jesus Christ and the outpouring of the Spirit to fundamentally shift the vector of history toward its redeemed and whole future as new creation. Second, it implies that God's hands are tied without our effort. Third, it places the burden for transforming the world on human shoulders, as if either there is not Holy Spirit, or as if the Holy Spirit were waiting on the sidelines for us to do something worth of divine participation. While there is a place for "must," "ought," and "should" in Christian preaching, its place in sermons is less dominant than we might suppose. We will return to this idea when we discuss the third rhetorical task of Christian preaching, rehearsal.

Renaming and Renarrating the World through Cross and Resurrection

Declaring the promise of God to renew all things "reframes" our understanding of reality. There is a divine redemptive dynamic afoot in the world that may not be obvious to us, but which judges what is wrong in the world. Because God has already acted, and continues to act, amid the here-and-now realities of our ordinary lives, new, life-giving ways of living open up for us, both as individuals and as communities. Thus, the stage is set for a second *rhetorical* task of Christian preaching: renaming and renarrating our listeners' everyday world seen through the lenses of cross and resurrection.

Congregations cannot participate in what God is doing to make things right in the world unless they can recognize what is wrong. Looking at the congregation's world "through the lens of the cross" means recognizing and naming those forces and patterns of action in the world that are sinful, unjust, and abusive. Preaching from the perspective of the cross is, first, truth-telling speech about human sin both on individual and social levels. Greed, dishonesty, abuses of power, self-advancement at any cost, and indifference to suffering are life-destroying for us and for others. Further, preaching that sees the world through the lens of the cross unmasks our futile efforts to mend our lives by our own efforts. Preaching issues an urgent invitation to abandon the notion that we can make ourselves whole through achievement, wealth, and wielding power over others.

Second, preaching identifies social and cultural structures that privilege some and marginalize others. With numbing regularity across cultures, the marginalized prove to be persons who are ethnically different and therefore regarded as "other" and as a threat to those who have power and privilege. God's creation of a new human future in Jesus Christ is often referred to as "salvation." The term suggests that God's design is to deliver us, individually and collectively, from the death-producing consequences of our own shortsighted efforts to build our own version of heaven on earth. Throughout history, despite the highest of ideals and the loftiest of rhetoric, human schemes for constructing a peaceful, prosperous world have been willing to settle for peace and prosperity for a privileged minority balanced on the backs of an impoverished minority, progress at the price of pollution and the "soft" violence of a rigged marketplace, and ever-increasing investment in weapons of violence to protect the wealth of the few from the impoverished masses. Thus the rhetoric of Christian preaching includes lament as well as hope—as did the rhetoric of Jesus himself. We are more inclined to remember and treasure the Beatitudes ("Blessed are the meek, blessed are the poor in spirit, blessed are those who mourn . . .") and imagine them directed at us than to ponder the equally prominent "woes" that Jesus pronounces. Christian preaching has always been risky truth-telling. There are moments in every congregation, and in every society, when the preacher's job is to speak in plain terms about the deathly consequences of human efforts to engineer a secure human future. The cross itself testifies to the violence to which empires resort in the effort to impose their own "saving" narratives on the world. The resurrection testifies to God's determination to expose the empty promises of such violence-driven narratives. Thus, to speak of the cross is to speak lament. Re-envisioning and renarrating the world "according to the cross" is to give visibility and voice to human suffering. It is to declare the steadfast presence of God with sufferers. Jesus' death reveals God as crucified God-with-us. God chose, and still chooses, to be aligned with the world's victims.

The other half of the rhetorical task of "renaming and renarrating" is to re-envision the world through the lens of resurrection. This means identifying amid the ordinary landscapes of our listeners' lives signs of new creation breaking through. Here, the preacher points to evidence of redemptive transformation happening not only within individual lives, but in family systems and corporate environments, in congregations and action groups, in neighborhoods, and sometimes on the world stage. Preachers need to stay alert, especially, to transformative change in the social structures that affect our listeners' lives. As preachers, part of our job is to be alert to transformative initiatives in the immediate communities that affect their lives. The dynamic, redemptive movement of the Spirit is not distant and otherworldly, but near at hand. The preacher can connect the signs of hope she or he discerns in the local landscape with wider realities on a national or global scale.

Imaginative Rehearsal for Public Witness

The third *rhetorical* task of Christian preaching is imaginative rehearsal for action in the world. Awakened to the promises of God and helped to see the world rightly—both its captivity to sin and the dynamic of new creation breaking through—both preacher and congregation are ready to "rehearse" for faithful action in the world. Spirit-driven imagination leads to Spirit-empowered action. In this rhetorical task, a preacher imaginatively projects the possibilities that open up as God's new-created future for humanity lays claim to the present. Preacher and congregation together "rehearse" what it might look like to participate in God's redemptive work in the concrete settings of their ordinary lives. Imaginative rehearsal means reimagining the world with "Spirit"-illuminated insight and with hope grounded in divine promise.

Preachers who declare what God *is already doing to renew all things* before talking about what believers need to do will sense a different energy in their preaching. When we know that God has acted for our redemption and has opened a redeemed future for us, we sense we are being *drawn* rather than *pushed* toward lives of truth-telling and generosity, patience and endurance, peaceability and courage. We will probably use phrases like "we must," "we ought," and "we should" more sparingly—not because we do not need to act, but because the declaration of God's future draws new possibilities out of us. Because God's redemption-working Spirit precedes us into the world and works within us, "we *can*," "we *are able*," "we *may*." The Spirit draws us forward into a transformed life, a future of wholeness for which Jesus is both pioneer and pattern.

As a counterstrategy against the deadly effects of humanity's endless self-absorption and our fearful, frantic efforts to hoard wealth and amass power, preaching seems weak at best, "foolish" at worst.[12] If preaching were a purely human effort to make God's love and redemptive future persuasive by means of human rhetorical skill, it would not stand a chance. But preaching is *not* a purely human effort. Preachers know, from the moment they begin wrestling with a biblical text to the moment they step into the pulpit, from the first to the last word of the preaching event, they are not alone. Preaching, beginning to end, is an event in which divine agency and human agency entwine in a dance as mysterious as it is complex. Wonder of wonders, the same Spirit that turned Jesus' early followers into a preaching church continues to lay claim to the bodies and minds, imaginations and voices of preachers. Young and old, men and women, learned or unlettered, preachers aided by the Spirit are bearers of hope. In Jesus, crucified God-with-us and firstborn of a new creation, God has established a new future not only for human beings, but for all creation.

12. 1 Corinthians 1:18-21 describes Christian preaching as "foolishness" in the estimation of the world at large.

In both a rhetorical and theological sense, preaching is more verb than noun. The Spirit moves and acts through a wide range of rhetorical strategies and styles of preaching to 1) convey the promises of God, 2) rename and renarrate our experience as it is reframed by divine promises, and 3) "rehearse" us for active participation in the new future God is initiating.

In the next chapter, we develop more fully the Spirit-driven theology of preaching with which this chapter began.

Further Learning Strategies

1. Have you thought of preaching as an *event* before? Why or why not? What are the strengths and weaknesses of this way of thinking about preaching?
2. What would it mean if preaching was more noun than verb? How would the rhetorical tasks we named above perhaps differ?
3. Are you drawn to any particular images of preachers? Why do you think that is? Which contemporary preachers represent some of these images? Are there other images of preachers that were not named above? Name them and describe.
4. Watch three YouTube videos of sermons. Analyze them to see to what extent indicative and imperative moods of language are being used. What do these sermons do to you? What do you perceive their rhetorical purposes to be?

Further Reading

Campbell, Charles, and Johan Cilliers. *Preaching Fools: The Gospel as a Rhetoric of Folly.* Waco: Baylor University Press, 2012. An exploration of what it means for the Christian preacher to be a fool inseparable from the folly of the cross.

Childers, Jana, ed. *Purposes of Preaching.* St. Louis: Chalice, 2004. A book of essays from leading homileticians expressing their particular views on the purpose of preaching.

Hogan, Lucy Lind, and Robert Reid. *Connecting with the Congregation: Rhetoric and the Art of Preaching*. Nashville: Abingdon, 1999. This volume approaches the field of rhetoric in a constructive manner and uses the principles of rhetoric to help preachers better connect with their congregations.

McClure, John. *The Four Codes of Preaching: Rhetorical Strategies.* Louisville: Westminster John Knox, 2004 (1991). This book asserts the importance of the rhetorical study of preaching via "codes" as a means to understanding congregational cultures better.

Reid, Robert Stephen, ed. *Slow of Speech and Unclean Lips: Contemporary Images of Preaching Identity.* Eugene, OR: Cascade, 2010. This collection of essays present various tropes for preachers.

Resner, Andre. *Preacher and Cross: Person and Message in Theology and Rhetoric.* Grand Rapids: Eerdmans, 1999. This book addresses the character of those who would preach by examining the relationship between the message of Christian proclamation and the preacher.

2

A Spirit-Driven Theology of Preaching

Luke A. Powery

During my first year in seminary, on a particular weekday in Princeton Seminary's Miller Chapel—essentially a Presbyterian meetinghouse built for worship in 1834—the preacher spoke of the Spirit as if she was his best friend and closest confidante. This senior-class student began to preach and as he proclaimed, he interjected the phrase, "Help me, Holy Ghost!" One time. Two times. Three times—and then I lost count of how many times he said, "Help me, Holy Ghost!" Maybe he was praying for himself in the moment because he realized the sermon wasn't going over too well in this ecumenical seminary congregation made up of students, faculty, and staff. Maybe he thought that if he said "Holy Ghost" ten times, it would make his sermon more Spirit-filled and we might actually pay attention to the sermon. But saying "Holy Ghost" or "Holy Spirit" does not guarantee that one is in the Spirit, led by the Spirit, or bearing the fruit of the Spirit. To play off of a spiritual, "Everybody talkin' 'bout the Spirit, ain't got the Spirit."

Sitting in holy shock that morning, we began to silently affirm his prayer and say our own version of it: "Help him, Holy Ghost. Help him and that sermon." Or, perhaps we said our own "Help me, Holy Ghost"—meaning, "Help me endure what is being said." As he continued, it became increasingly clearer that something was sorely wrong, and our shock reached its unforgettable peak when the preacher announced to us, "You won't praise God because you're just mean." It didn't seem to occur to him that maybe meanness was not the reason we didn't praise God but, rather, because the sermon was very messy and smelly. I don't think the Holy Ghost answered his prayer during his sermon on that day. But our prayer was finally answered and we were helped when he finished his sermon and sat down. This does not mean that we fully understood what happened that morning; indeed, some of us who were there are still searching for the black box from that sermon to see what actually went wrong on that morning in Miller Chapel. There's nothing wrong with saying, "Help me, Holy Ghost," but do we really understand to whom and for what we are pleading?

The Holy Spirit is both a concealed and revealed mystery, a wind that hovered over the face of the waters at creation (Genesis 1), a "wind that blows where it wills and you hear the sound of it, but you do not know from where it comes or where it goes" (John 3:8). On the day of Pentecost, "suddenly from heaven there came a sound like the rush of a violent wind, and it filled the entire house . . . divided tongues, as of fire, appeared among them. . . . All of them were filled with the Holy Spirit" (Acts 2:2-4). Wind. Fire. The Hebrew word for "spirit," *ruach*, means "wind" or "breath"; it is feminine. The Greek word for "spirit" is neuter. We grasp for language to talk about the

Spirit of God—he, she, it. Some "thingify" the Spirit and can't make sense of this third person of the Trinity who is sometimes perceived as the stepchild in the divine family. Yet, the Holy Spirit is the Lord, the Giver of Life, the one in whom, according to German Protestant theologian Jürgen Moltmann, "our life wakes up."[1]

In situations like this, it's hard to say whose experience is more painful, the listeners' or the preacher's. Who knows where the problem lay for this unfortunate preacher? Was he simply lazy and unprepared? Maybe he imagined that if he could *sound* like a trusted mentor his sermon would surely be just as effective, even if the content was thin. Or had he truly wrestled long hours with his text and simply ended up lost in a forest of possibilities, unable to identify one "tree" (or truth) to speak about in the pulpit? Or maybe he had brought his own agenda to the text, yet the text would simply have no part of his ill-conceived idea, leading to a "forced" sermon. Whatever the case may have been, Spirit-empowered preaching only flows from Spirit-inspired preparation.

Nearly every preacher, sooner or later, will feel he or she is going to the pulpit with a ragged sermon. Yet, if we have sought the Spirit in prayer, kept the good company of trustworthy biblical scholars through our study, and grappled with the realities of the lived preaching context, we can at the very least identify one affirmation about the nature or activity of God to carry to the pulpit. On this basis, the preacher can think through what difference that affirmation makes for individual believers, congregation, and/or wider world and illustrate each of these with a simple example or story. Plain food can be as nourishing as gourmet fare. Spirit-empowered preaching flows from Spirit-infused preparation.
– SB

The Holy Spirit is also the one in whom our preaching wakes up. Without God's breath, the Holy Spirit, humanity would not exist (Gen. 2:7; Ps. 104:29-30) and neither would preaching. Human beings would not have life; therefore, no human task could be done or word be spoken. The divine–human venture of preaching would be impossible because the human variable would be absent. But the Spirit also allows us to fellowship with the divine; thus, according to James Forbes, "The preaching event itself . . . is a living, breathing, flesh-and-blood expression of the theology of the Holy Spirit."[2]

---

1. See Jürgen Moltmann, *The Source of Life: The Holy Spirit and the Theology of Life* (Minneapolis: Fortress, 2009).
2. James Forbes, *The Holy Spirit and Preaching* (Nashville: Abingdon, 1989), 19.

Chapter 1 identified both the church and its preaching as Spirit-animated events. This chapter develops more fully what could be called a "pneumatological homiletic," a Spirit-driven theological understanding of preaching that takes context, Christ and his presence, the church, and engagement with the world seriously. In the final section, there will be an excavation of your own theological influences that shape your conception of preaching as a means to further self-understanding; this self-knowledge will make you more aware of why you think of preaching the way you do.

A Contextual Word: The Spirit and Translation

Context is inescapable. Even in our mother's wombs we are already somewhere in time and place. Once we are born with breath, voice, flesh and blood, we enter a new context. We are then somewhere else in our inspirited bodies in time and place. Thus, to ignore context would be to ignore human existence on earth and would make for inauthentic preaching. The incarnate truth of the gospel happens on earth as it is in heaven. The gospel truth is connected to particular contextual experiences. As a preacher within a particular cultural context, I realize that I not only come from within particular faith communities but also from within specific cultural communities, not from outside of them. Preachers are located somewhere in time and place from the beginning. Preachers should begin right where they are as homiletical, enfleshed temples of the Spirit, experiencing the world and God. The word of God proclaimed, therefore, should relate to this human experience on earth because God's Word for the human world became human in flesh and bones.

John writes, "The Word became flesh and lived among us ..." (John 1:14). God's Word was human and manifested himself in a particular concrete way, in a particular context with a particular culture. This Word incarnated in an embodied, concrete person known as Jesus Christ, making him a contextual Word. The incarnation was God's embodied communication or Word to the world. To speak to the human world, the Word of God or God's sermon became human, relating to the experience of humanity. Humanity would not understand the word of God were it not in human form. God translated the divine Word into human flesh so that human life might have the opportunity to hear and comprehend the gospel, to know that it is *pro nobis*, "for us."

In addition, God's Word became human through the agency of the Holy Spirit.[3] The Word was contextual because the Spirit made him concretely human, demonstrating how the Spirit works in specific cultural situations in time and place. At the day of Pentecost, for example, the Spirit manifests in unified particularities rooted in cultural contexts; the people speak in their own native tongue yet they are unified in their praise of God. This means the Spirit translates the word of God so that it might be understood in context, right where we are in time and place.

The translation work of the Spirit is evident on the day of Pentecost (Acts 2:1-13). When the disciples were filled with the Holy Spirit and spoke in other languages as the Spirit enabled them to do so, "Jews from every nation under heaven" become bewildered and amazed because "each one heard them speaking in the native language of each." At two other points in this passage, the writer emphasizes that these Jews hear their "own language."[4] The Holy Spirit gives a contextual cultural word to each disciple for each particular culture represented. The Spirit translated the word about

---

3. See Luke 1:26–2:21. Also, John Thompson notes that in the theology of Karl Barth the Holy Spirit is the agent of the incarnation. See John Thompson, *The Holy Spirit in the Theology of Karl Barth* (Pennsylvania: Pickwick, 1991), 41–52.

4. In Acts 2:8, the Jews ask, "And how is it that we hear, each of us, in our own native language?"; and in Acts 2:11, they say "in our own languages we hear them speaking about God's deeds of power."

"God's deeds of power" into the language of the hearers so that they might understand what is being proclaimed. The Spirit causes the people to hear in their "own language," though the basic message about God's power is the same. The Spirit sparked the particularity and contextuality of these word events, revealing how, in the Spirit, context is inescapable.

Therefore, Spirit-filled preaching should then be contextual and culturally sensitive. There is no such thing as a "universal" homiletical theology. Leonora Tubbs Tisdale argues that preachers should aim for contextual preaching that is both faithful and fitting.[5] The emphasis on "fitting" suggests that preaching is a local word and local theology, which starts with an analysis of local cultures and then develops theological understandings that are appropriate for a particular people. Preachers should embrace their own particularity as well, recognizing that the preached word not only goes somewhere but also comes from somewhere. This is the recognition that the Spirit works within culture, though she is not confined to it. Sensitivity to culture brings the hope that preachers would connect with the people to whom he or she preaches. The Spirit does not cause us to escape the earthiness of reality but immerses us more deeply into the world for ministry in time and place. There is a groundedness to the gospel.

In that way, the gospel is preached in the vernacular of the hearers so that the word may speak to the "felt need" of the hearers. This hope can only become a reality through the work of the Spirit right where we are. Moreover, the Spirit works through the preaching event to help everyone involved know that Christ, the Word of God, is *pro nobis.*

---

5. Leonora Tubbs Tisdale, *Preaching as Local Theology and Folk Art*, Fortress Resources for Preaching (Minneapolis: Fortress Press, 1997), 33. Cf. Henry Mitchell, *Black Preaching: The Recovery of a Powerful Art* (Nashville: Abingdon, 1990), 14–15.

A Christological Word: The Spirit and the Word of God

No one will come to know Christ if the Spirit does not make Christ, the Word, known. Coming to know Jesus Christ, the Word of God, can only happen through the work of the Holy Spirit. "Christian" preaching is necessarily a discussion of Jesus the Christ as Word of God. The Word that preachers proclaim through the Holy Spirit in specific contexts and cultures in time and place is none other than Jesus Christ. One must realize the close relationship between the Spirit and Christ in order to recognize its significance for the event of the Word called preaching. Irenaeus says that the Word and the Spirit are the "two hands of God," implying collaborative interaction between these two persons of the Trinity. Christ's incarnation, anointing (Luke 3), mission (Luke 4), and resurrection are all works of the Holy Spirit. Jürgen Moltmann was right when he said, "The Holy Spirit is the divine subject of the history of Jesus."[6] Therefore, there is no Christology without pneumatology. The work of the Spirit in preaching leads to Jesus; thus, if there is little Jesus in sermons, there may be little Spirit as well.

Jesus is even portrayed as the bearer and dispenser of the Holy Spirit (John 1:32-34). According to the Gospels, the Spirit came to believers after the earthly ministry of Jesus, suggesting the Spirit is the Spirit of Christ as the "remembrancer (John 14:26), not innovator."[7] From a Christian theological perspective, the Spirit's work always has to do with the incarnate Word, Jesus Christ, because "When the Spirit of truth comes . . . he will not speak on his own, but will speak whatever he hears. . . . He will glorify me, because he will take what is mine and declare it to you" (John 16:7-14). Therefore, the Word event of preaching is an event of the Holy Spirit.

6. Jürgen Moltmann, *The Church in the Power of the Spirit: A Contribution to Messianic Ecclesiology*, trans. Margaret Kohl (Minneapolis: Fortress Press, 1993 [1975/1977]), 36.

7. George S. Hendry, *The Holy Spirit in Christian Theology* (London: SCM Press, 1965), 89.

This rich connection between the Spirit and Christ, the Word, reflects the biblical tradition overall in which there are numerous references to the relationship of word and Spirit.[8] The Spirit is the presence and power of the Word throughout Scripture. For example, Jesus is able to *preach* good news to the poor *because* the Spirit of the Lord was upon him (Luke 4). In other New Testament writings, the Spirit is linked to bold speech (Acts 4:8, 29-31) and effectiveness in teaching (Acts 6:10). The apostle Paul is very clear that his own preaching can only be effectual with "a demonstration of the Spirit and of power," not through human wisdom (1 Cor. 2:1-4). Any event of words limps to its death without the power of the Spirit moving through and working with the frail human tongue. Paul even says, "No one can say 'Jesus is Lord' except by the Holy Spirit" (1 Cor. 12:1-3). What preachers proclaim in general is "Jesus is Lord"; thus, if the Spirit does not empower preachers, this proclamation (Jesus is Lord!) is not possible and the gospel sermon, whose content is Jesus Christ, would be nonexistent. The Spirit points us to Christ through preaching. Without the illumination of the Spirit, the Word will do nothing. But with the Spirit, the real presence of Christ, the Word of God, will pervade the event of preaching such that the speakers and hearers *experience* the living God through the Word who is Jesus Christ.

A Sacramental Word: The Spirit and Presence

Preaching's aims should not solely be to talk about Christ but to offer Christ in such a manner that the community may meet Christ. Preaching is a divine event because God is encountered in and through it. This "encounter" is experiencing the real presence of God in Christ through the Word proclaimed such that people know about

8. See Gen. 1:2ff.; 2 Sam. 23:2; Isa. 59:21; Ps. 33:6; 147:18; Ezek. 2:2; Matt. 10:19-20; Mark 13:11; Luke 1:41-42; 12:11-12; Acts 2:4; 1 Thess. 1:5.

God but also come to know God. As early as the patristic period, the preached word was considered sacramental because the mystery of divine revelation was believed to continue in this word such that the Word himself spoke.[9]

Following this progression of thought, contemporary homileticians affirm this by asserting Jesus is the preacher in the sacramental moment in which we experience his presence. Homiletician David Buttrick asks, "Is it any wonder that we can speak of a kind of 'transubstantiation' through preaching?"[10] Through the Spirit, Christ is made present through the proclamation of the Word and, really, this is what people desire—the real presence of God. Counterfeits will disappoint when you are hungry and thirsty. You want real bread and real wine, a real body of Christ materially, even though there are varied perspectives on how Christ is present in the sacraments across denominational traditions (see chapter 4).

Through preaching, Christ's presence blesses human bodies by using us as conduits of grace. To speak of sacramental presence means one must turn to the physical world as the visible conveys the invisible. Preaching in the Spirit makes visible God's love in Christ through human words and bodies of preachers. Particularly in African American contexts, the climactic ecstasy of some preachers indicates to the congregation the sacramental presence of divine grace. In this celebratory moment, the preacher *is* the Word but this is not surprising because God uses material means to convey grace. The Word is always incarnate, even through human bodies and voices. The Word takes on the flesh of the preacher to speak the good news of God.

The preacher becomes a sacramental "letter" (2 Cor. 3:3) to the

9. Bernard J. Cooke, *Ministry to Word and Sacraments: History and Theology* (Minneapolis: Fortress Press, 1980), 256.

10. David G. Buttrick, *Preaching Jesus Christ: An Exercise in Homiletic Theology*, Fortress Resources for Preaching (Philadelphia: Fortress Press, 1988), 83.

people as the Spirit works within all participants in the preaching event. The real presence of God permeates the human road of voice and body for both preacher and congregation because ideally what happens in the pulpit is happening in the pew.

An Ecclesial Word: The Spirit and the Church Community

Preaching is an event among the people of God. Preaching cannot be limited to what just happens to the preacher because preaching is an event of the church, the body of Christ, the living and primary context for the proclaimed Word. When God reveals God's self by God's grace through the Spirit in preaching, it is not for one person but for an entire community; thus, preaching in the Spirit involves the whole church. Theologically, preaching presupposes a church community, which is created by the Spirit (Acts 2). Preachers belong to communities; thus, in reality, preaching is not a solo performance. It is a practice of and for a faith community. The call of preaching, just like gifts of the Spirit, is given to an individual for the benefit of the church and world.

The preacher maybe inspired by the Spirit, but his or her goal is to ignite the imaginations and hearts of the hearers. As the Spirit creates, nurtures, and sustains the church through preaching, the Spirit continues to work in the hearts and minds of everyone involved in the preaching event. Thus, preaching is one aspect of the broader work of the Spirit to empower and guide the church to build the kingdom of God on earth. Preacher *and* congregation have a role to play in the sermon event. As the body of Christ, all are essential to preaching, which does not let preachers off the hook nor does it allow listeners to ignore their contributions to the preaching moment. As Fred Craddock writes, "Listeners are active participants in preaching."[11] Without someone to listen, there can be no sermon in the power of the Spirit because the Spirit shapes a message for particular hearers as a guide in the spiritual life and testifies to hearers what is truth in the proclaimed message. This mutual, communal dimension to preaching is a work of the Spirit in the church. Many homileticians have taught practical ways to live into this communal ideal more concretely—for instance, as obviously expressed through the call-and-response dynamic of much of the cultural preaching in African American traditions.[12]

Preaching is "participant proclamation," indicating that the sermon belongs to both the preacher and entire congregation. This is more than a method but, rather, is God working through the community of the Spirit.[13] Preaching is a practice of the church. But this action is not confined to the church in traditional ways. The Spirit is centripetal in developing community but the Spirit is also centrifugal, sending followers into the world to proclaim the gospel. With the Spirit at work in the congregation in both the centripetal and centrifugal directions, preaching happens both inside and outside of the church walls. Homiletical pedagogy may center on what happens between pulpit and pew but it is vital to remember that the church's preaching life does not stop there. It moves into the world in the power of the Spirit.

An Ethical Word: The Spirit and the World

The Spirit's work is holistic through preaching and cannot be limited to personal context or ecclesial settings because God is concerned with the whole of life, and preaching empowered by the Spirit aims

11. Fred B. Craddock, *Preaching* (Nashville: Abingdon, 1985), 25. For more about the role of listeners in preaching, see pp. 84–98.
12. For example, see John S. McClure, *The Roundtable Pulpit: Where Leadership and Preaching Meet* (Nashville: Abingdon, 1995); and Lucy Rose, *Sharing the Word: Preaching in the Roundtable Church* (Louisville: Westminster John Knox, 1997).
13. Evans Crawford, *The Hum: Call and Response in African American Preaching* (Nashville: Abingdon, 1995), 15.

to transform the world, not just the church. The Word, even Jesus Christ, is for the world; thus we can consider the Spirit's work through preaching in the ethical domains of society, affirming the centrifugal impulse of the Spirit.

The Spirit as the Spirit of life gives life even in the social-ethical realm as the source of ethics. Any response to the proclaimed Word can only truly occur by the Spirit, including social acts of justice or what John Wesley called "works of mercy." This is not to say that the Spirit is not at work in the world already, because the Spirit works with or without us. The world is the domain of the Spirit's work; thus, the movement of the Spirit in preaching is not bound to the corporate worship experience, but its influence reaches far beyond the confines of the local church in matters of social ethics because sermons "travel on in the lives of those who listen."[14] Through the Spirit, preaching becomes a socio-ethical act. The experience of the Spirit in preaching does not stop when the sermon is finished because the work of the Spirit through preaching continues in the public realm. Anointed preachers and churches expose death and its structures of oppression; make truth plain, which leads to transformation of life for the oppressor and oppressed; overthrow powers of death in all their forms; and cast out demons of institutions, whether ecclesial, political, or social. In the Spirit, the people of God are living witnesses of the Word made flesh because the Spirit empowers the church to live out its ethical obligations shaped by God's justice.

Through preaching, the Spirit fights for life and seeks to resist any form of power that would aim to destroy humanity. The Spirit resists oppressive powers in the world, and this is a sign of God's love for the world. In light of the resurrection life of Jesus in the power of the

---

14. Arthur Van Seters, *Preaching and Ethics*, Preaching and Its Partners (St. Louis: Chalice, 2004), 132.

Spirit, preachers can proclaim Jesus Christ as the one who can redeem the powers to create a new social order aligned with the gospel. God's social order is one of charity instead of profit, peace instead of war, and mercy instead of power. The world's social order of power is a power of death and is thus self-destructive, whereas God's power brings life as the power of the resurrection. Preaching can unmask the powers in the face of principalities and powers with the "sword of the Spirit, which is the Word of God."[15] The Word is the tool that the Spirit uses to resist. The Word, the sword of the Spirit, is the only weapon wielded by Jesus in his nonviolent action against the powers of death. With the Spirit's help, preaching becomes active resistance as opposed to a passive, irrelevant act in the world. A Spirit-driven theology of preaching propels preachers into the world with a word of hope and life because the Word in the power of the Spirit is an incarnate one. The proclaimed word must be practiced in loving and just ways, for preaching without works is dead, incomplete, and not fully the embodied Word the Spirit intends.

Exploring Your Theological Contours

Many influences on your thinking pertain to a theological understanding of preaching. None of us are without context. We come from somewhere and we cannot escape our skin, heritage, culture, background, family history, education, denominational upbringing, and overall life events. It is impossible to do so nor would we want to do so because, ultimately, we would lose who we are and who we are becoming. In the same way, our theology is always becoming, always fluid and on the move in the wind of the Spirit. Some may prefer a stiff system of thinking but God's work never has been confined within any human system or expectation. God is

15. Charles Campbell, *The Word Before the Powers: An Ethic of Preaching* (Louisville: Westminster John Knox, 2002), 43.

free and our theologies are also free, free to expand and explore, to be changed and challenged over time. This section aims to help you reflect on the shape of your own theology-in-the-making that has an impact on your theology of preaching. The work of homiletician Ronald J. Allen, specifically his book *Thinking Theologically*, is a highly useful resource for this exploration.[16]

Personal-Contextual Influences

What Allen and other homileticians emphasize is the way in which our theological frameworks are shaped by our social location and the contexts that we inhabit. It has long been acknowledged that the sources for theology are tradition, experience, Scripture, and reason. The Wesleyan tradition refers to these sources as the quadrilateral. Experience is an especially key source; thus, preachers are never blank slates because who we are and who we are becoming are shaped by where we have been and what we have experienced. We cannot live our lives as "neat freaks," expecting everything to fit a preset pattern. Rather, if we were to analyze our own histories and experiences we would most likely see a mosaic, composed of pieces of our life journey. Since this mosaic is inescapable, as preachers we should never try to ignore who we are and where we have been.

I can never escape the fact that I was born to parents from the West Indies. My father is a minister, making me a "PK" (i.e., a preacher's kid, though there are other meanings for PK as well—party kid, problem kid, etc.!). My father stems from the Wesleyan Holiness church but has had an ecumenical ministry for many years. I was born in the Bronx, New York, and grew up in Miami, Florida, both cosmopolitan cities consisting of many ethnicities and cultures. I am the fifth and last child in my family. We attended a Holiness-

---

16. See Ronald J. Allen, *Thinking Theologically: The Preacher as Theologian*, Elements of Preaching (Minneapolis: Fortress Press, 2008).

Pentecostal congregation in Miami while I was growing up, but after high school, I explored other denominations, eventually being ordained in the Progressive National Baptist, Inc., a historically African American denomination. I went to a university in Palo Alto, California, attended a Presbyterian seminary in Princeton, New Jersey, served a congregation as an associate pastor in an interdenominational English-speaking church in Zurich, Switzerland, did doctoral work in Toronto, and am now in the South at a university with historic Methodist ties. There is so much more that I can say about my own life history and experience, but my point is that this ecclesial, cultural, geographical, and educational boundary crossing has influenced what I think about God, the church, humanity, and the world in general, and how I act toward others in the world. These contexts I have inhabited or still inhabit make me who I am and who I am becoming theologically. My theology may be embedded and explicit. These variables may not be nice and neat but it is necessary to make them explicit in order to reflect on my own life.

Consider your own "locations"—ethnicity, race, gender, class, age, educational level, political commitments, line of work, values and demographics of your local community, nation in which you reside (colony or imperial power), denominational history, family history, current family situation, community-service involvement, and leisure activities. You embody all of these parts of your self, whether you recognize it or not. Ask yourself, "Who am I? Where have I been? Where do I come from? What do I do? How is it that I am going where I am headed?" Movement toward self-knowledge is an act of self-care and provides deeper understanding of the influences on your theological perspectives. All theology is contextual because it comes from a human being in particular contexts. This may not be acknowledged, as some may take their locations for granted.

Exploring your own personal-contextual variables is an aid to help you not take for granted who you are as a person and preacher, but to become more aware of oneself. In so doing, you may realize why certain things are important to you and other things are not. Excavating your personhood may reveal the why of your passion and interpretive inclinations. Your interpretations and perspectives come from somewhere—your life.

Interpreting the Bible is not as simple as: "The Bible tells me so," therefore this is what I will preach. How you interpret Scripture is linked to your theological assumptions and life presuppositions, all of the variables listed above, and plenty more. Plus, we are not called to preach the text alone, but the gospel. When I was a child in Sunday school, we used to sing a song, "The B.I.B.L.E., yes that's the book for me, I stand alone on the Word of God, the B.I.B.L.E.!" The Bible, the Holy Book, was and is revered still, but these days there are numerous views of Scripture, high views and low views. I have discovered through my own contextual journeys that the Bible is not God; rather, when we approach it, we do so through human lenses that influence what we see and what we do not see. When I was growing up, we could not place anything on top of a Bible because it was deemed holy. Not only have my views changed, but my contexts and locations have altered my opinions and help shape the questions I ask of the Bible today. If we never ask about the marginalized figures in a biblical story, maybe it says something about our theologies. If we never ask about God, that may also imply something about our theological understanding of what we should be doing in a sermon. The point is, when it comes to preaching, there is more than the Bible and definitely more than the King James Version, which some say is God's language. You do not just stand alone on the word of God, Scripture—you also stand in your own particular history and experiences, reason, as well as tradition, all of which give you theological impulses about preaching. As you continue to ponder how you have been shaped through many contexts and uncover your presuppositions, let us now turn to an exploration of denominational historical influences.

Historical-Denominational Influences

Once again, it is important to note that this may not be neat either. Of course, there are those who may be born and bred and eventually dead in one denominational tradition. But there are others who have crisscrossed denominations or parachurch organizations on their search for God. As noted above, I have been influenced by the Wesleyan tradition, Pentecostal church, and Baptist denominations (particularly historic Black Baptist ones). There was a short time during college when I had heavy nondenominational or independent church influences. Some may view this crossing of denominations as having made me something of a "theological mutt." Nonetheless, where life and God lead you, you have to go, mutt or not. What I have learned is that there are lots of mutts out there, though some do not want to claim it!

The phrase "theological mutt" is a good one; it describes many of us! Being shaped by different communities, each with its own preaching traditions and its distinctive expectations about what preaching is and does, leaves us with a broad appreciation for the diverse ways the Spirit uses the human voice and body to convey the Word.

Preaching is a practice deeply marked by its cultural location. Every culture of preaching is rooted in a particular tradition and "sound" of worship, with its own history. Another gift of a mixed theological and liturgical heritage is that you can give yourself over to many kinds of worship. Theological "mutts" recognize that God chooses to communicate God's present Word through radically different preachers, preaching styles, and theological traditions.

I try to stay aware that my "mutt" identity, in terms of worship and preaching has conferred both benefits and baggage. For example, as a woman who experienced a call to preach despite being raised in a tradition that discourages women from preaching, I can find myself harboring a kind of habitual defensiveness about my preaching. This kind of emotional baggage can only get in the way of the Spirit's work.

Being a theological "mutt" also means your theological views have been shaped gradually, over years, possibly by Christian congregations or communities that would regard each other with suspicion! When a student or a preacher is expressing ardent views very different my own, I remember chapters of my life when I thought differently about theology and preaching than I do today. To say we are all "in the Spirit" and "of the Spirit" is not to say that we all think alike—not now, and perhaps not ever. – **SB**

Either way—whether you have been a member of one denomination your entire life or have experimented with a few—it is vital to think about how these denominational perspectives have shaped you. The influence may not be explicit but, rather, more embedded, yet it is still there. One of the first questions fellow classmates may ask a new seminarian is, "What denomination are you?" Somehow, our denominational connections are a part of our identities. They are not the only aspect but a key part of our theological contour. Allen lays out some of the main themes related to preaching within ten historical-denominational families: Orthodox, Roman Catholic, Anglican-Episcopal, Lutheran, Reformed, Wesleyan, Anabaptist, Society of Friends, and Pentecostal.[17] Are you a member in one of these? Or have you been a part of several of these throughout your life? Pay attention to your denominational past and present

17. Ibid., 9–15.

histories because they may tell you why you think what you think. For instance, a Lutheran perspective asserts the idea that Christ is truly present in the sermon and that God speaks when the preacher speaks. Also, a Lutheran sermon may include aspects of law and gospel, a prominent marker in Lutheran theology. A Reformed take on preaching may center on preaching as teaching, in which congregations learn how God is gracious and how that grace is still active in the world, hopefully leading the congregation to respond in faith. In general, Baptists have a high view of the Bible for guidance and, through the Spirit, the sermon is an expression of God's word for the people who are invited to repent and renew their faith and respond in some way. In a Society of Friends meeting, there is emphasis on silence and various members stand and speak out of the silence as the Spirit leads them.

These nuanced understandings of what happens during preaching have a theological impact on those who experience these differing denominational settings. Again, it is not that these ideas are explicit, but they undergird these historic theologies; thus, it becomes critical for those who desire self-awareness to uncover what is behind preaching in these denominations. However, as human beings, we are always more complicated than any one denomination. It might even be that you have grown up in a denomination yet do not hold to all of its teachings and practices. It is also important to acknowledge that no denomination is homogeneous. All Pentecostals are not alike. All Roman Catholics are not the same. Therefore, one has to ask, "What other theological influences might there be on me that put me in tension with my own denomination at times?" This brings me to a discussion about various theological schools of thought that may be at work in your thinking as well.

Theological-Familial Influences

Beyond our denominational influences, there are "theological families" that we may consider in order to determine how we do or do not resonate with them. We may be informed and formed by some theologies without even really knowing it. Some of the major theological families that Allen identifies are: liberal theology, mutual critical correlation theology, process theology, evangelical theology, neo-orthodox theology, postliberal theology, confessional theology, radical orthodoxy theology, otherness theology, liberation theology, and ethnic theology.[18] No one theology can encompass the totality of a person's thought and perspective. We are always more complicated and beautiful than that, yet it can be helpful to reflect on where we locate ourselves within these theological streams.

Because the Bible is such a critical partner in preaching, presenting how some of these theological families approach the Bible may help you to determine which of these approaches resonates with you or if you are already relating to Scripture in a particular manner. There is more to these theologies than interacting with the Bible, and you can read Allen's work for more detailed insights. But I hope this will stoke your flames of curiosity to do further investigation.

Put succinctly: liberal theology believes the Bible is a human interpretation of divine activity. Mutual critical correlation theology sees the Bible as a library of views, some of which are trustworthy while others are not. Process theology sees the Bible as perspectives on ancient worldviews regarding God's power and purposes. Evangelical theology believes the Bible is a factual record of God's activity. Neo-orthodox theology believes that an encounter with the Bible releases God's Word. Postliberals view the Bible as a source

18. Ron Allen explores the major motifs in these theologies and compares them in a table at the end of ibid., 23–86, 89.

of Christian identity and practice. Confessionalists see the Bible as a series of confessions. Radical orthodoxy believes the Bible contains assertions of orthodox Christian theology. Otherness theology presents the Bible as a library of others. Liberation theology views the Bible as a record of God's liberating action. Ethnic theology views the Bible as a key to Christian understanding and expression of cultures.

Our theologies are shaped by many influences, including the Bible; at the same time, our theologies shape how we interpret the Bible. Do you find yourself in any of the above perspectives on the Bible? Maybe you are located in one family or you are a part of a "mixed family." The point is to discover and uncover the layers of your theological self so that you can realize the impact this has on your understanding of preaching. What we present in this introductory book is a Spirit-driven theology, which is not to imply it is the only approach. There are many approaches yet none of them is truly possible without the Spirit. As noted before, Reformed and Baptist-Pentecostal lenses shape the perspective driving this book but we recognize your particularity and the gift that is to the church and world. The aim here is to help you uncover the fullness of your own theological contour. And, since its shape is fluid, thus your thinking now may not be your thinking in the future.

Current Operative Theology

One last item may be helpful to this exploration of your theological inclinations: What are your operative theological views *today?* Where you stand now will most likely shift in the future based on many of the things named above; however, knowing what you believe today can be helpful in realizing your current homiletical theology. Homileticians John McClure and Burton Cooper created a theological profile as a way to help preachers assess their own theological perspectives.[19] This could be useful for self-assessment and locating oneself in relation to certain theological *topoi*. The following questions may also be helpful for naming where you are today theologically:

- What is your operative view of God? Which member of the Trinity do you emphasize most (or least)? Is God primarily immanent or transcendent? A judge or merciful parent? Who is Jesus to you and what role does he play in salvation? Does the Holy Spirit hold a prominent place in your thinking?

- What is your operative view of human beings? Are people primarily viewed as sinners? Children of God created in God's image? What is valued more in human nature—being, doing, or becoming? What is your perspective on evil and humanity's relationship to it?

- What is your operative view of the church and its mission? Is the church a hospital for the sick or a community of saints? Is the mission of the church more activist, civic, evangelistic, or sanctuary in nature? How is the church supposed to relate to the world?

- What authority does the Bible have? How is it God's word, if indeed that is what you believe?

- How does Christianity relate to other religions—exclusivist, inclusivist, or pluralist?

- What is your view of the end/*eschaton*? Is the kingdom of God above, coming, here, present in part?

These questions are not exhaustive but an attempt to prompt further reflection on where you are right now in your theology. It would be

---

19. Burton Z. Cooper and John S. McClure, *Claiming Theology in the Pulpit* (Louisville: Westminster John Knox, 2003), 135–41.

interesting to compare your answers to these questions to where you locate yourself in the theological families and historic denominations. For instance, are there similarities or differences between your operative thought and the traditional perspectives of the denominations in which you reside?

The shaping of your theology is a lifetime affair. Where you are now may not be where you will end up and that is fine when you take the Spirit seriously. Yet it can always be helpful to discern and learn how you arrived to the place where you currently reside theologically. The Spirit is key to all of this, just as the Spirit is crucial for preaching. The Holy Spirit breathes life into preaching, thus the Spirit is the life of preaching. Without the Spirit, effective preaching would be buried in the tomb of death. With the Spirit, however, there is the hope of experiencing resurrection life through the Word. This chapter has attempted to place the Holy Spirit at the core, not the periphery, of our understanding of preaching. Preaching in the power of the Spirit is contextual, Christological, sacramental, ecclesial, and ethical. Preaching is a Spirit-empowered Word in the church for the world. It may form a community but it can also shape a world through the work of the Spirit. It does not all depend on the Spirit because preachers are co-laborers with the Spirit; therefore, what you think matters because what you think preaching is will shape your preparation and practice of preaching. Yet, the Spirit is the lifeline of preaching, thus the first word preachers must proclaim as they enter the pulpit is not to the congregation but to the Spirit—"Come." This is why the next chapter explores prayer as a vital practice for preachers.

Further Learning Strategies

1. Write down the major points of your theological understanding of preaching. What factors led to your current theology of

47

preaching? How does your theological contour converge and/or diverge from what was presented earlier in relation to context, Christ, the church, and world? How does your theological contour shape your preaching?

2. Create a visual map of the personal contextual variables that shape your theology. Include a timeline and even highs and lows, if relevant.

3. Do you lean theologically in more contextual, christological, sacramental, ecclesial, or ethical ways as it relates to your conception of preaching? Why do you think that is? Find a partner with whom to discuss this.

4. Write a poem about how your theology has changed over time and what it is becoming.

Further Reading

Allen, Ronald J. *Thinking Theologically: The Preacher as Theologian.* Elements of Preaching. Minneapolis: Fortress Press, 2008. An exploration of the preacher as theologian, reflecting on the historic theologies of denominations and contemporary theological families that influence preachers. It aims for preachers to become more self-aware of their own theologies and how that influences their preaching.

Bartow, Charles L. *God's Human Speech: A Practical Theology of Proclamation.* Grand Rapids: Eerdmans, 1997. A theological and practical study of how the Bible read and sermon delivered are means of grace, stressing aspects of embodiment.

Brown, Sally A. *Cross Talk: Preaching Redemption Here and Now.* Louisville: Westminster John Knox, 2008. A reclamation of "cross talk" in the pulpit and a proposal of a metaphorical and pastoral model for preaching about the crucifixion.

Buttrick, David G. *Preaching Jesus Christ: An Exercise in Homiletic Theology.* Fortress Resources for Preaching. Philadelphia: Fortress Press, 1988. This book centers on Christology as the heart of homiletic theology and is basically a theology of Jesus for the purpose of preaching.

Campbell, Charles L. *The Word Before the Powers: An Ethic of Preaching.* Louisville: Westminster John Knox, 2002. This work focuses on the way preaching is nonviolent resistance to the powers rooted in the ministry of Jesus and offers some practical ways of embodying this ethic.

Cooper, Burton Z., and John S. McClure. *Claiming Theology in the Pulpit.* Louisville: Westminster John Knox, 2003. Presents how theology informs preachers and facilitates a process by which preachers can create a theological profile in order to be more self-aware.

González, Justo L., and Catherine G. González. *The Liberating Pulpit.* Nashville: Abingdon, 1994. This book aims to present what preaching is from the perspective of the oppressed and liberation theology.

Hilkert, Mary Catherine. *Naming Grace: Preaching and the Sacramental Imagination.* New York: Continuum, 1997. Drawing on Catholic thinkers, this work presents how preaching is a sacramental practice.

Kay, James F. *Preaching and Theology.* Preaching and Its Partners. St. Louis: Chalice, 2007. A detailed historical and theological analysis of the theologies of preaching that have dominated Protestant thought.

LaRue, Cleophus J. *The Heart of Black Preaching.* Louisville:

Westminster John Knox, 1999. Argues that the extraordinary character of black preaching derives from a distinctive biblical hermeneutic that views God as a sovereign mighty deliverer of the oppressed.

Lischer, Richard. *A Theology of Preaching: The Dynamics of the Gospel.* Nashville: Abingdon, 1981. A discussion of how theology informs preaching and preaching informs theology with a clear aim of affirming preaching as a theological enterprise.

Mitchell, Henry H. *Black Preaching: The Recovery of a Powerful Art.* Nashville: Abingdon, 1990. A classic text that presents the major themes, ideas, and approaches within Black preaching in order to illuminate this distinct embodiment of cultural preaching.

Moltmann, Jürgen. *The Church in the Power of the Spirit: A Contribution to Messianic Ecclesiology.* Translated by Margaret Kohl. Minneapolis: Fortress Press, 1993 (1975/1977). A rich in-depth theological study of what it means to be the church in the world.

Powery, Luke A. *Spirit Speech: Lament and Celebration in Preaching.* Nashville: Abingdon, 2009. A homiletical study that emphasizes pneumatology of and in preaching, advocating for a pneumatological approach to homiletics that takes seriously both lament and celebration in preaching.

Tisdale, Leonora Tubbs. *Preaching as Local Theology and Folk Art.* Fortress Resources for Preaching. Minneapolis: Fortress Press, 1997. A study that stresses the importance of exegeting the congregational culture as a way of fostering more fitting sermons. It provides helpful tools to do so.

3

———

Preaching and Prayer

Luke A. Powery

It may not always be obvious to human eyes, but to the One who sees the heart as an altar, it is clear that what is inside preachers is just as important as what comes outside of preachers through words and actions. In the long view of life, it may be possible to discover that an altered life is an altar-ed life, though in the micro-moments of the everyday this may be hard to discern. Even more, when it comes to preaching, we may not be so sure what impact the spiritual life truly has on our preaching and what role prayer plays. Despite the ambiguity, we know that Jesus, during his ministry, took times to get away in order to pray. As he carried the weight of the world on a cross, he continued to pray to God, the Father. In life and death, prayer is important. The same is true for preaching, especially if we believe it is a vocation of agony, not one of pristine glory. When life is rough and tough, even in the lives of parishioners, how do we respond as preachers? When we survey the wounded terrain of the world, including the perpetuation of human violence and senseless natural disasters, how should we respond?

In the aftermath of the 2010 Haiti earthquake, a TV camera showed a Haitian man lying on his side, trapped under a slab of concrete from a collapsed building. And where there's a TV camera, you can bet there will be a news reporter right there ready to get high ratings. Conducting an interview with this man immobilized under this bone-crushing rubble, the CNN reporter asked, "What are you telling yourself?" I had to say to myself, "Well, what do you think he's telling himself? A cement block is on top of his body, squeezing the life out of him! 'I didn't respond to that e-mail'? Or, 'I really would like a Starbucks caramel macchiato right now'?" "What are you telling yourself?!" What if he had said, "I'm asking myself why a news reporter is interviewing me right now!"? Or he could have uttered angry lament from his lips toward the reporter or God. Rather, in response to the misguided question, this man said, "Jesus, Jesus, my life is in your hands." He prayed in public what Jesus prayed on a cross—"Father, into your hands I commend my spirit." Under the weight of a broken concrete slab, in the heap of dust and ashes, this man of faith prayed to Jesus—"Jesus, my life is in your hands." When hell was breaking loose and hope appeared to be on life support, this Christian man showed the spiritual way for every Christian, including preachers, who may bear the weight of life and of a congregation. He demonstrated that prayer is a lifeline even in the face of dying and death.

Spirit-animated preaching leads us to consider the spiritual discipline of prayer because it is the Spirit who enables us to pray, "Abba, Father" (Rom. 8:15). Preaching in the Spirit is fueled by prayer, a free divine gift, unlike those who promote a prosperity, capitalistic approach and charge people for prayer by pleading with them to send $19.99 for a prayer cloth with "holy Jerusalem oil" on it. This chapter will explore prayer's essential relationship to preaching as an attempt to spark self-reflection on your own spiritual life as a preacher, a topic usually muted in the teaching of preaching.

In *God's Trombones*, a collection of seven sermons in poetic verse, published in 1927, James Weldon Johnson includes a prayer as an attempt to capture the prayer life of early black preachers, especially before they preached a sermon. Yet I would also claim that this prayer is included there as an implicit suggestion of the vital connection between preaching and prayer. Prayer is a reminder that we are, as Johnson suggests, "Like empty pitchers to a full fountain / With no merits of our own."[1] To begin with a prayer is to suggest that praying is the beginning of preaching. Though we see prayers offered before and after sermons during worship services across denominations to indicate that preaching is none other than a prayer itself, an *epiclesis*, the following discussion about prayer and preaching encompasses prayer outside of the sermonic moment and, perhaps most importantly, in private. If a preacher only prays in public, then there may be a spiritual problem. But what follows is an exploration of ways of thinking about prayer and how it relates to the preaching life, concluding with some practical suggestions for praying and deepening your own spiritual life.

Have Preaching Classes Lost Prayer?

If you were to judge the importance of prayer in the preaching life based on some preaching course syllabi, you might think that prayer is not necessary for the ministry of preaching. Many course syllabi for introductory preaching classes assume a lot about the preacher,

---

1. James Weldon Johnson, *God's Trombones: Seven Negro Sermons in Verse* (New York: Viking Penguin, 1927), 13.

for instance, that preachers believe what they preach. But the truth is there may be no guarantee about that. Others assume that preachers know the God whom they proclaim, but talking about God does not mean one knows God. As Brad Braxton notes, "It is possible to have a master of divinity without being in relationship with THE Master of Divinity."[2] Moreover, many assume that preachers pray and nurture the spiritual life in an ongoing manner; thus, the topics of prayer and spiritual practices are excluded from many classes on preaching. The absence of prayer's presence is sometimes glaring. Even a recent collection of essays on teaching preaching as a Christian practice does not include an essay on prayer or the spirituality of the preacher among its key topics.[3]

The "external" work of preaching is prized, despite its vanishing glory days of unquestionable authority, compared to the "internal" work of prayer, especially if we take hints from our curricular practices. Prayer is not viewed as a priority, at least compared to biblical exegesis, a theology of the word, or dialogue about sermon form. This is not to say that prayer is not taught in seminaries and divinity schools, particularly with the rise of "spiritual formation" or "'spirituality' classes"; but if it is taught, it is not necessarily in tandem with preaching. Therefore, prayer is placed on the homiletical back burner even though, ironically, it is the spiritual practice that fuels the fire of preaching. The hard work of preaching is actually the internal spiritual work. In fact, the most difficult sermon you may ever preach is the one you preach with your life. The real challenge for preachers is to pray better than we preach and we may never reach that *telos* if we never discuss it in the homiletics classroom.

2. Brad Braxton, "Sanctification and Proclamation: Walking with God," in *A Spiritual Life: Perspectives from Poets, Prophets, and Preachers*, ed. Allan Hugh Cole Jr. (Louisville: Westminster John Knox, 2011), 232.
3. See Thomas G. Long and Leonora Tubbs Tisdale, eds., *Teaching Preaching as a Christian Practice: A New Approach to Homiletical Pedagogy* (Louisville: Westminster John Knox, 2008).

Prayer as Prerequisite for Preaching

Prayer's absence in syllabi does not mean it has been absent from homiletical thought throughout past and present history. From the late nineteenth century until today, there has been a basic implicit agreement among thinkers that a vital spiritual life is critical for vibrant preaching. Prayer is clearly assumed as a prerequisite for preaching practice. It is a means for a preacher to open him- or herself to the divine presence, the same presence one hopes will permeate the preaching moment. If one desires for a sermon to be touched by God, prayer as receptivity of God's presence is essential. Through prayer, a preacher receives the One proclaimed. From a rhetorical perspective, it is even bad rhetoric to ignore prayer because of its influence on preaching. In his lectures to students, Charles Spurgeon taught, "It will be in vain for me to stock my library, or organize societies, or project schemes, if I neglect the culture of myself; for books, and agencies, and systems, are only remotely the instruments of my holy calling; my own spirit, soul, and body, are my nearest machinery for sacred service; my spiritual faculties, and my inner life, are my battle axe and weapons of war."[4] Generally, preachers tend to think of the "outer work" of preaching and all of the tasks needed to create a sermon; however, the nurturing of the inner life is also vital, since preachers "outer what they inner." If a preacher runs away from prayer, he or she should run away from the preaching ministry.

This is so because preaching has to do with God, and prayer enables us to come to know God and implicitly says that we desire God. To pray is an acknowledgment that the proclaimed word that is spoken and heard is not ours but a gift, because the power of

---

4. Charles H. Spurgeon, *Lectures to my Students: A Selection from Addresses Delivered to the Students of the Pastors' College, Metropolitan Tabernacle* (London: Passmore and Alabaster, 1875), 12. Cf. John Broadus, *On the Preparation and Delivery of Sermons* (New York: Harper & Brothers, 1926 [1870]), 7.

the word is given by the Spirit (Acts 2). Any homiletical success, therefore, depends on God; prayer reveals dependence on God as it sighs, "Come, Holy Spirit." This prayer means that the future of the word is in the hands of God and reminds us that, ultimately, preaching should be about God. In prayer, preachers cooperate with the Spirit, and yield to the Spirit as a sign of openness to the future of the word. Through prayer, God will speak, breathing life into homiletical practice. Any strategies imagined and implemented "find their deepest origins not in human calculation but in prayer."[5]

Preacher as Pray-er

A focus on prayer as a prerequisite for preaching does not always translate into conceiving the preacher as a pray-er. This is often overlooked: before you are a preacher, you are called to be a pray-er, a worshiper. Preaching, then, has deep spiritual roots in the triune God and is grounded in prayer and fellowship with God. In recent years there has been a "spiritual turn" in homiletics, with books being published on spirituality and preaching; these volumes can help bring preachers back to their roots for ministry when other homiletical tasks may vie for their attention.

These recent works are a gentle reminder that to preach is to pray and that preaching is in and of itself a spiritual practice. We normally hear about preaching *in* worship, but preaching itself *is also* worship. Before you take a biblical text for a sermon, you should take time to pray, because the power of preaching comes from God. Prayer implies a Power outside of ourselves, but without the presence of prayer one might assume that we create effective preaching moments on our own. The practice of prayer places emphasis on the Spirit and

---

5. Thomas Troeger, *Ten Strategies for Preaching in a Multi-Media Culture* (Nashville: Abingdon, 1996), 8, 120.

reminds us that before we speak to others, we must first speak and listen to God.

When a pastor steps into a pulpit, she or he brings her or his prepared sermonic offering to burn on the coals of an altar—the pulpit. Of course, it may be a good thing that at times our sermons are burned up! When a pastor calls a congregation to worship, everyone is being called to worship, including the pastor. Pastors lead worship and lead public prayer, but are also participants in worship and prayer as pray-ers. Preachers may easily perceive themselves as rhetoricians, biblical scholars, theologians, philosophers, or even cultural analysts; but do we view ourselves as worshipers, as doxologians? As the Westminster Shorter Catechism (1647–48) states, humanity is "to glorify God and to enjoy [God] forever." The heart of the Christian vocation beats with doxology. Thus, the heart of any preacher should burn with this same desire, a yearning to glorify God in word and deed, including the preaching moment.

Prayer guides preachers to become doxologians. A traditional saying from the Eastern Church states that a theologian is one who prays. Maybe we should likewise say a preacher is one who prays; this may shift our syllabi content and affirm that preachers work for the glory of God alone. Being a pray-er signifies this. At times the doxological focus may become blurry because some sense that their chief homiletical labor is to find a funny story or some clever scriptural insight, rather than to labor intensely to please and worship God—that is, to pray. We pray to God because we preach for God and at the core of why we preach is love for God. Prayer is an act of love and preachers are lovers—lovers of God and the Word of God, Jesus Christ, and are therefore called to love others. Who we are before God shapes what we do on behalf of God.

This is why the spiritual formation of the preacher through prayer is critical. How spiritual intimacy with God looks may vary according to traditions and cultures, but having a spiritual relationship with God is essential. If preachers do not know God, how can we expect others to come to know God? If preachers do not love God, how can we expect those in the pews to love God? Prayer nurtures the rhetoric of the heart. Some say prayer changes things, but actually prayer changes us, the preachers; God changes things and works through prayer, even our own sermons.

In the small group sessions where my students preach, I ask a class member who is not preaching that day to pray for all of us, both the ones who will preach and the rest of us who will listen. There is nothing "pretend" about these preaching moments. The classroom becomes holy ground. We await God's own Word, addressed to us.

Praying for the Spirit's presence doesn't mean that we have foreclosed on the possibility of giving feedback after the sermon is preached, including critical feedback. In a preaching class, students and their teachers covenant to give feedback on classroom sermons, pointing out theological and rhetorical strengths, as well as adjustments that could facilitate a clearer and more engaging "hearing" of the Word.

The Spirit honors our classroom prayers. I may have heard a familiar text preached thirty or forty times; yet again and again, students will preach utterly fresh sermons. Sometimes it is the sermon's pastoral word, connecting unerringly with someone in our company who is suffering. Other times, a sermon jumps the gap from classroom to street so compellingly that the atmosphere is electric at sermon's end. We are poised to act. God honors the prayers of those who preach and those who listen. – **SB**

The preacher being a pray-er is really the beginning of sermon preparation and fuels the entire preaching event. Biblical exegesis, congregational analysis, sermon development, and sermon delivery are also acts of prayer as an extension of the preacher's life. Without this understanding, one can think of preaching as being about ourselves and not God; but a preacher who prays as an expression of worship signals implicitly that the power in preaching really has nothing to do with us at all. Of course, there is human agency and a Spirit-animated perspective embraces, not erases, the enfleshed human being. However, prayer is dependence on God and includes the understanding and the hope that God would shape a preacher's *whole* life into one of doxology, not just personally or individually, but in one's social interactions and involvement such that preachers are not just speakers and hearers of the word, but doers of it.

When this happens, onlookers can declare about us what has been said about Jesus: "his life was the 'amen' to the proclamation of his lips."[6] A preacher's goal should be to live better than one preaches because prayer can be viewed as a way of life, shaping one's life into an eloquent sermon à la St. Augustine. Prayer is more than a utilitarian magic trick for a "home run" sermon. It is an integrated part of a preacher's life that implies the essential movement of God within a preacher, whether preaching or not. It provides an interior space where the Spirit may work on us before she works on others in the congregation. It is a willingness to be touched by God. Prayer is more than an act we do just for the purpose of preaching; it is not a means to an end. It is a way of life that forms everything about a preacher.

Sermon as Prayer

With this formational view of prayer, the entire ministry of preaching is prayer: prayers for illumination of Scripture, writing the sermon on a laptop as an altar, embodiment of the sermon in a church, and so forth. But the holistic integration that is required for preachers wanes if the preacher is not a pray-er at heart. In light of this, it may sound like the sermon is not the top priority for preachers (and maybe it is not!). This may trouble the waters, especially in an introduction to preaching textbook, but what is essential to remember is that your life is a sermon and it is the most difficult sermon you will ever have to preach. Matching one's lip service and life service is vital. In this age of the Spirit, the integrative

---

6. James Forbes, *The Holy Spirit and Preaching* (Nashville: Abingdon, 1989), 43.

life, a life of integrity, is important because the Spirit cannot be compartmentalized; thus, we cannot truly separate our public and private lives just as prayer cannot be divided between sectors of life or between sacred and secular realms.

However, it would be silly for a teacher of preaching to center only on the preacher's prayer life and thus negate the importance of what the preacher actually proclaims with his or her lips. What is proclaimed, the gospel, is still significant, and how that is done most effectively is critical. The sermon itself is not unimportant. It is a prayer offering, an extension of the preacher's life of prayer. It is an act of worship for God to others. The effort and care invested into the biblical, hermeneutical, theological, cultural, and rhetorical substance of any sermon is ultimately for the glorification of God, or at least it should be. As an oral/aural offering, though imperfect and fallible, the sermon can still be received by God through grace. Seeing the sermon as prayer may lighten the burden on the preacher because it suggests that the ultimate impact of the word rests with God's will. It may be a cliché but it is nevertheless true: we do our best and God will take care of the rest. We offer what is on our heart and mind through study and ask God to bless the homiletical mess that we form.

A sermon as public prayer also means that it should lead others to pray and return praise to God. Through the Holy Spirit, the sermon may form the hearers of the word to be doers as well, to be a community of prayer, that the church may once again be called "a house of prayer" (Mark 11:17). The sermon as prayer is not only an aim for the preacher but the entire congregation because, through prayer, we meet the living God and through that encounter we are changed.

Passion through Prayer

Through that encounter with God, a passion for God and the gospel are ignited. To discuss prayer invites a conversation about the experience of God. This is not to negate tradition, reason, and Scripture, but the practice of prayer is a theological experience of a Reality embodied in Jesus Christ, completing what we spoke of in the previous chapter as the quadrilateral. Prayer is a practice, something a preacher does, thus it is primary theology in which one engages a holy God and experiences the Spirit (Gal. 4:6-7). Through this experience, one may develop a heart moved by God because prayer may be thought of as a rendezvous of love. It is a love that is the source and summit of preaching, as preachers should preach out of the love of God and because we love God and God loves the world. We learn this love and nurture this love through prayer.

Another name for this love in and through preaching may be called *passion* because this experience of God in and through prayer awakens preachers to be fully alive to God, the world, and the gospel. This love ignites preachers to such an extent that homiletical bodies may become ecstatic bodies literally as an example of human temples of the Spirit (1 Corinthians 6). This is more prominent in some churches than others. But passion, or what might be called "cruciform love," is not just an emotional display of dancing bodies or loud shouts of praise, though the human body is vital to homiletical practice. "Passion" stems from the Greek word *pascho*, which means "to suffer" or "to endure," linking itself to the suffering of Christ and his paschal mystery. Passion in and for preaching is formed through prayer and shapes one into the gospel pattern and passion of Christ, voiced through the sorrows of the crucifixion and joys of the resurrection. Passion is not about "feeling good" but is an immersion into the Good Friday-Easter motif of the life of Christ. Like the experience of love, sometimes passion may hurt, and preaching should articulate this when appropriate. Passion stems from the prayerful experience of Jesus who lived, died, rose, and will come again. It embodies the full spectrum of human expression found in Jesus Christ but this will only come through prayer, unless it is fabricated. Spurgeon echoes this when he teaches,

> There is no rhetoric like that of the heart, and no school for learning it but the foot of the cross. It was better that you never learned a rule of human oratory, but were full of the power of the heavenborn love, than that you should master Quintilian, Cicero, and Aristotle, and remain without the apostolic anointing. Prayer may not make you eloquent after the human mode, but it will make you truly so, for you will speak out of the heart; and is not that the meaning of the word eloquence? It will bring fire from heaven upon your sacrifice, and thus prove it to be accepted of the Lord.[7]

Fire in preaching is fostered through prayer in which one is mentored in love at the foot of the cross of Christ. There, passion will be formed and sustained and one will discover, like the prophet Jeremiah, something within "like a burning fire shut in my bones" (Jer. 20:9). It will be uncontainable because the gospel is that free and generous.

Passionate fire of and for the gospel has to be shared openly as a gift of grace. This internal fire expressed externally is sparked by the Spirit when one makes oneself available to the breath of God. Prayer is important in helping preachers become open to God so that there is something present, like their hearts, with which to ignite, once God blows on it. "Passionless preaching is deadly dull."[8] Passion in and for Christ nurtured through prayer is what makes preaching alive. Thus, no Jesus means no passion, no life, and entombed preaching. Moreover, if there is a hope that others may have their hearts ignited

---

7. Spurgeon, *Lectures*, 44.
8. Lucy Lind Hogan and Robert Reid, *Connecting with the Congregation: Rhetoric and the Art of Preaching* (Nashville: Abingdon, 1999), 71.

on fire, it is even more critical that a preacher prays for his own warm illumination because "you can't give what you ain't got."

Prayer as Listening

"The getting," or more accurately, the receiving, occurs through prayer, but it may not happen when speaking to God. It may occur when we listen to God and when we hear what God has to say; when God speaks, we receive more than we ever imagined—the gift of the word that we are called to share with the world. The absence of the topic of prayer in many courses on preaching could be because preaching is seen only as a vocation of the word, and not also as one of the ear (listening). In the Protestant tradition, words prevail. Maybe for a course on preaching and all of the theo-rhetorical work that needs to be done to accomplish it, talking about prayer seems insignificant or irrelevant, though prayer, too, can be speech. Hopefully, this chapter has made you reconsider the vitality of prayer for Christian preaching.

Nonetheless, receiving the gift of the word through prayer is not only about speaking; it is about listening. Prayer suggests that we may actually have to do some listening and not just talking. As preachers, this may be difficult because some of us like to hear ourselves. However, "Spiritual discipline is first and foremost the fine art of listening."[9] Preachers should aim to listen with the ear of their heart to the heart of God because silence is a portal to God. In this rapid-fire, Internet-driven, texting, tweeting, sound-byte society, it is vital that we center ourselves and slow down.

Pastors are so busy engaging in community activities, leading small groups, and preaching weekly, that rarely do we discuss silence. The listening posture is not something preachers explore much. We

9. Kay L. Northcutt, *Kindling Desire for God: Preaching as Spiritual Direction* (Minneapolis: Fortress Press, 2009), 81.

specialize in speaking, not listening. One does not attend seminary to learn how to listen. This may be an educational faux pas. In the Spirit, it is important to center oneself, even though we may not want to do it because we do not want to watch ourselves pass by; we may not like what we see when we slow down. But in the pause, the waiting moment, while we listen, we may see the vision of God for the church, ministry, and world. The sacrament of pause is essential for the ministry of preaching. In the silence, we may hear the voice of God as our own voice is silenced and hear a sound beyond earthly noises. Preachers should declare, "Speak, Lord, your servant is listening" (1 Sam. 3:10). This acknowledges that holy speech comes out of silence in the presence of the Holy. This presence may come through Scripture, the word of God, as one reads the words to listen for the Word.

Listening suggests the Word we proclaim comes from outside of us, to us, and through us. We receive it through grace as we listen and center ourselves. The first task of a preacher is not to speak but to listen in prayer. As the proverb says—a still tongue makes for a wise head and, we can add, "a wise preacher." We may think that contemplative prayer and ministerial action, including preaching, are opposed to each other rather than existing in a mutually supportive relationship. This is not the case, and the legacy of the Rev. Dr. Martin Luther King Jr., is a fine example of this.

Prayer and Action

Dr. King was a preacher, pastor, and civil rights activist. When people remember Dr. King, one of the first things they may recall is his "I Have a Dream" speech, delivered before the Lincoln Memorial on August 28, 1963, for the March on Washington, D.C., for civil rights. He was a gifted orator rooted in the black Christian church tradition. But he was so much more than an effective communicator.

He had a deep concern for the racially and socioeconomically oppressed who suffered under the unjust hands of modern-day pharaohs.

This concern led him to fight for human rights through nonviolent resistance. He fought for racial justice on behalf of those who were deemed nonhuman to such an extent that policemen could fire-hose them down like dogs in the streets. He fought for economic justice, working on behalf of the poor, and died fighting on behalf of sanitation workers in Memphis, as part of the Poor People's Campaign. He called for peace and an end to the Vietnam War. King was indeed a "drum major for justice."[10] But what many tend to overlook is the spiritual foundation for that particular drumbeat.

King organized, marched, preached, and prayed. It is the latter that is not usually discussed when we talk about his legacy. But Dr. King reveals what other prophets affirm: prayerful listening leads to prophetic proclaiming. King believed that activism prefaced and bathed by prayer could be effective. In other words, personal spirituality grounds social transformation. The roots of social and civic engagement are listening skills learned in prayer. Before speaking into situations of injustice in the world, silence is required, with an open ear to the One who loves the world. The question is not whether God is speaking; the question is whether we are listening like the prophet Samuel (1 Samuel 3).

Hearing God's voice in prayer was critical for King's prophetic witness. In January 1956, during the Montgomery bus boycott, he received a threatening phone call late at night and he went to his kitchen table and prayed. It was there he experienced the inner calm of God amidst the outer storm and was ready to face whatever might

10. Martin Luther King, Jr. "The Drum Major Instinct (1968)," *I Have a Dream: Writings and Speeches that Changed the World*, ed. James M. Washington (New York: HarperCollins, 1992), 191.

come. The outer life of prophetic witness found its strength in the inner sanctuary. God provided the interior resources for King to do his social justice work. He listened prayerfully then proclaimed prophetically. King's life and ministry showed the interrelationship of prayer and protest continuously, according to historian Lewis Baldwin.[11] Prayer was vital to the civil rights movement to such an extent that it began and propelled the movement. King took "days of silence" regularly, indicating that his active prophetic work of protest was rooted in prayer. Prayer was not a waste of time for his ministry. It was a matter of life and death in the civil rights movement.

Prayer is not escape from the world God so fiercely loves, but a commitment to engage that messy, material reality. Jesus often withdraws to pray; yet, he turns from these solitary interludes straight into the vortex of human need and conflict. It is not too much to say that prayer in the Spirit drove Jesus into the danger zones where, ultimately, he was betrayed and sent to his death.

The robust, visceral understanding of prayer developed in this chapter shows up again in chapter 6 in relation to interpreting Scripture for preaching. There, an updated ancient prayer practice called *lectio divina* ("divine reading," a process for "praying" a text) engages the preacher physically, not just mentally. Walking, dancing, running, physical artistic expression, and vocalization, including speech and song, are all embodied ways that preachers can "inhabit" the Word. Prayer practices that involve the body turn prayer into groaning, en-Spirited love for a world of human flesh and bone, at risk in myriad ways around the globe. Prayer does not distance us from our bodies or anyone else's. Prayer takes up our bodies and sends them into close quarters with other ones, especially bodies troubled by disease, bodies gripped by various addictions, and dark-skinned bodies whose very appearance puts them at greater risk of untimely death around the globe. – SB

Civil activity began with a heart as an altar of prayer with the posture of listening. Just as King recognized, God is the source and guide of just action in the world. There are theological roots to sociopolitical activity. The two are not separated. As a public "servant" one does not just serve society but God. Thus, to act justly in the world is to follow God's ongoing activity in the world. But to know what God is

11. See Lewis V. Baldwin, *Never to Leave Us Alone: The Prayer Life of Martin Luther King Jr.* (Minneapolis: Fortress Press, 2010).

doing, one has to listen prayerfully. Subsequently, one may discover that civil disobedience and prophetic proclamation are rooted in theological obedience, prayerful listening to the call of a God of justice who says, "Let justice roll down like waters, and righteousness like an ever-flowing stream" (Amos 5:24).

If one does not pause to pray, one may become so enthralled with the flurry of "good" activity and "getting high" on activity that he or she neglects to pursue the practice of prayerful listening. Prayerful listening is critical, yet this does not mean that one sits in a pew of passivity and does not act. There is a story about a missionary who was walking in Africa when he heard the ominous noise of a lion behind him. "Oh Lord," prayed the missionary, "Grant in Thy goodness that the lion walking behind me is a good Christian lion." And then, in the silence that followed, the missionary heard the lion praying, too: "Oh Lord, I thank Thee for the food which I am about to receive." In that moment the missionary needed to do something, like run—or at least run while praying!

The witness of Dr. King shows the integral relationship of prayer and action. The legacy of King and the civil rights movement is such that it was permeated with prayer. There were "calls to prayer," "prayer meetings," "prayer pilgrimages," "prayer vigils," "prayer rallies," "prayer marches," "prayer circles," "services of prayer and thanksgiving." There were prayers in church seats and on the streets. King did not relegate prayer to being a second-class citizen in the struggle for justice and equality. It was just as vital to the success of the movement as picket lines, sit-ins, freedom rides, and marches. Prayer was a "secret [nonviolent] weapon" of the movement.[12]

The prophetic legacy of Dr. King points to the Power behind his words and work and it points to the practice of prayer. It points to listening as a lifeline. It was not just a critical part of his prophetic

---

12. Ibid., 85.

witness, but in fact, the beginning of it. King took time to listen in order to do God's work of love, mercy and justice in the world. The Martin Luther King Jr. National Memorial in Washington, D.C., is now built in solid stone, but one of the best living memorials to King may actually come in the form of an open ear turned to God.

The weight of ministry, the weight of preaching in our day, calls us to tune our ears to the One who is greater than us. If we fail to do this, we may be crushed by the weight of the world rather than held by the One who has the government on his shoulders (Isaiah 9:6). Preachers will dig their own homiletical grave if they are more interested in "taking a text" before taking the time to pray—"Jesus, our lives are in your hands."

Exploring Ways of Prayer

We have seen the following in this chapter: how prayer is a prerequisite for preaching; the preacher is a pray-er; the sermon is prayer; passion for the gospel comes through prayer; prayer is listening; and prayer is connected to action. As noted above, prayer can be viewed as a way of life and not a limited practice that only includes kneeling at an altar or by the bedside and bowing your head with eyes closed. Hopefully, it is clear that prayer is more than that. It is paying attention to and being present to God. As such a way of life, it necessarily includes different approaches. Just as wide and deep as the nature of God, there are infinite ways to broaden and deepen your spiritual life of prayer in order to inform and form your preaching life. What follows will not be exhaustive but an attempt to foster further exploration of your own spiritual practices that may lead you to be present to God. Because of physical or other limitations, not every practice will work for every person, but most are adaptable to one's abilities.[13] The works of Marjorie Thompson and Mike Graves are helpful conversation partners in this endeavor.[14]

1. *Studying.* It has already been said that the entire process of preaching is prayer. This understanding may help those who feel burdened or overwhelmed by the whole process of preparation. With this in mind, studying may be thought of as a form of prayer. One may struggle intellectually for insight and desire emotional connection that is slow to come and not as soothing as, say, sitting in a sauna. Through the study of Scripture, however, via various hermeneutical approaches, one can be brought into the presence of God. "Aha!" moments come. Connections with the world and your life are made. You realize finally that even your exegesis could lead to ecstasy because all along it has been a prayer for and to God. Studying, in whatever form, can be an encounter with God. Your paying attention to texts can be a door to paying attention to God.

2. *Reading.* If you want to become a better preacher, search for ways to become a deeper person.[15] The practice of reading can deepen our lives. Naturally, this includes reading Scripture, and some will read the Bible daily following a set pattern or program. This reading is done apart from any lectionary texts you might use for your upcoming sermons. Rather, this reading of Scripture is purely done for your soul, not your role as preacher or pastor. Jesus read Scripture as a part of his own religious heritage, knowledge, and devotion. We read Scripture to become acquainted with the Word more, to absorb it, such that we know it in word and deed. As many New Testament writers quoted the Old Testament because of their familiarity

---

13. Some of these practices are incorporated into the *lectio* process that you will find in the chapter on exegesis (interpretation) of the biblical text.
14. Marjorie J. Thompson, *Soul Feast: An Invitation to the Christian Spiritual Life* (Louisville: Westminster John Knox, 1995); and idem, "Habits of a Whole Heart: Practicing Life in Christ," in *A Spiritual Life*, 53–64. See Mike Graves, *The Fully Alive Preacher: Recovering from Homiletical Burnout* (Louisville: Westminster John Knox, 2006).
15. Graves, *Fully Alive Preacher*, 7.

with it, preachers should also develop a similar intertextual ethos in their lives, not just in their sermons. In addition, in some ecclesial traditions, such as the Anglican-Episcopal tradition, some may read the *Book of Common Prayer*, which includes daily Scriptures and prayers. We can read prayers from other Christian brothers and sisters throughout church history, making their sentiments our own. Beyond these typical "spiritual" readings, it is fruitful to think beyond these to other kinds of literature, such as fiction, memoirs, and poetry. As we read various kinds of literature, even Scripture, we may engage our senses and ask, "What do I smell, taste, touch, hear, and see as I read?" Reading as prayer is not to fill one's homiletical quiver with stories or illustrations for sermons. It is to learn from God about life and creation. To read is to stay alive in heart and mind and to stay connected with the world and human experience. All of this will help one's preaching, but the end goal is to pray and encounter God.

3. *Writing.* At its best, writing the sermon is a spiritual exercise. The Lord tells Habakkuk to "Write the vision. And make it plain . . ." (Hab. 2:2). Yet, writing is more than sermon writing. Perhaps it is journaling about life, joys and sorrows, and learnings about self and others. You can write prayers and thoughts about what's happening globally and locally. Those prayers may be intercessions, thanksgivings, or your own psalms or paraphrases of psalms. Throughout the day, ideas may come to you and you may decide to write them down. In some way, writing can capture parts of your life on the page, and it can be useful to return to those pages at future dates because it will allow you, as the church song says, "to look back over your life and think things over . . ." You may discern what God has been saying all along. Writing things down may help you focus your

thoughts and foster deeper reflection as you outer what you inner. Writing can be prayer on the page.

4. *Walking.* Just as we see God encouraging writing, we also hear about the children of Israel wandering in the wilderness, Jesus in the wilderness, and other figures walking with God. The imagery of Christians being wandering pilgrims leads us to consider walking as prayer. In particular, walking in silence may provide the benefit of listening to sounds and voices other than our own, hearing the echoes of the gospel in creation. This is particularly important for preachers who embody a vocation of the Word. This spiritual migration can allow us to take in the sounds of the flowing river, the crashing ocean, the singing birds, or children playing in a neighborhood park. Walking itself gets us in touch both with our physical bodies and with the physical world. Walking can occur by oneself or with a companion such as a dog. Walking is an implicit prayer to God, "Guide my feet while I run this race." The practice of walking reminds us that one day we will finish the race but until then we keep praying with our feet.

5. *Watching.* We might even say we pray with our eyes, paying attention and being present with God. The psalmist proclaims, "Taste and *see* that the Lord is good" (Ps. 34:8). In the Garden of Gethsemane, Jesus urges the disciples, "Stay here and *watch* with me" (Matt. 26:38). Watching is praying in the night (e.g., Watch Night), but it is also a way of reading the book of nature—soaring mountains, towering oaks, daisies dancing in the breeze, birds flying, gorillas and alligators at a zoo. You can watch ocean waves splash and even watch people at an airport or mall. What do you read as you look? What story is being told? What do you hear with your eyes? Try paying attention to what you see by walking where you would normally drive. Also,

when you keep watch, you may notice specific facial features of a person, which you've never noticed before because prayer makes you more alive to the world. Watch the hospice nurse feed your loved one on his bed or a spiderweb in the bottom right corner of your living room or the hail falling like buckets during a thunderstorm or the steam floating up out of your cup of coffee or the shape of the clouds in the sky. When you watch you can be more present to God. You can engage a piece of artwork from another culture and see how God works in other lands. You may also watch, pay attention, and pray through icons as a way to God, a rich practice in the Eastern Orthodox traditions.

6. *Playing.* Keeping watch does not mean that prayer is always serious and dour. Prayer can be playful because playing itself is a distinct way of praying. This perspective, along with others, requires a deep sense of sacramentality. Playing embodies enjoyment of God and God's creation. It portrays a joy of living, which can spill over into the joy of preaching. The idea of play is not popular in preacher parlance, which could be because preaching has to do with divine things, the gospel, and life and death. You may hear preachers talk about playing with words in a sermon, indicating a sense of delight in preaching. This is important, but for this consideration of prayer, it goes beyond the sermon. It has been said that Americans live to work rather than work to live, caught up in the so-called Protestant work ethic—even non-Protestants do this! The prominence of capitalism and its linkage to spirituality makes it difficult at times to embrace play as a key part of the spiritual life of prayer. Play as prayer is an act of resistance against the constant drive of work. Play allows us to participate in the joy and goodness of God. It is a way of praying such that we can *be* human rather than only do

things. It reminds us that we were created not solely to work but to worship and play in the presence of God. When was the last time you played at full throttle? Bowling, cards, dominoes, board games with your family, golf, tennis, racquetball, jump rope, basketball and the game H.O.R.S.E., swimming, laughing and telling jokes, making funny faces with your children, dancing to reggae or waltzing in the rain, restoring the woodwork of an antique table . . . When you play, you remember that you are human, even before you are a preacher. You are a child of God.

7. *Singing.* One of the activities most children love to do is to sing. Singing is a key way of praying in the church, too, and has been so for centuries. An early church adage is "He who sings prays twice." Mary sings the Magnificat in the Gospel of Luke. The story of Christ in Philippians 2 is known as the "Christ hymn." The story of our future is told with hymns in Revelation as well (chs. 4, 5). The writer of Ephesians exhorts the listener to "be filled with the Spirit as you sing psalms and hymns and spiritual songs among yourselves, singing and making melody to the Lord in your hearts . . ." (5:18-19). It is common knowledge that much of the church's theology stems from hymnody. Martin Luther said that music is the handmaiden of theology. You can sing ancient hymns or contemporary praise songs or hum spirituals. Singing is a spiritual practice that helps us tap into an acoustemology such that our preaching is not verbal discourse alone. It is sonic and somatic and can provide surplus of meanings that mere speech cannot do. Though I focus on singing, this does not neglect other forms of music-making. Playing instruments can also be a form of prayer. It is worth noting that singing and any music-making do not just happen alone either, especially in the church. They happen in

community and strengthen communal bonds. Music can draw people together, and it does so through sound.

8. *Eating.* As the body of Christ, we sing but we also eat together and have communion. Obviously, there is the sacrament of communion in which we partake of bread and wine. It is a Eucharist, a thanksgiving, not only because of the presence of Christ at the meal, but because we are the visible body in that moment. All have something to eat and drink in that moment. No one goes hungry or thirsty. We come together even though we are not always together in heart and mind. Eating together points us to the hope for our future and the wedding feast to come. Eating reminds us of God's provision through creation and it reminds us of the fellowship we have with one another. Like the early disciples in Acts, eating allows us to share a meal in common (Acts 2). We can break bread in homes and coffee shops and be glad that we are together in the generous grace of God. We do not only pray before meals or say grace before meals. The meal itself is a grace. The eating is a prayer.

9. *Serving.* In the eating, we share the body and blood of Jesus Christ, and there are people in the community, not just clergy per se, who serve. This spiritual practice of prayer is linked to mission and service in the world. In Isaiah 58, the people are indicted for fasting, an ancient spiritual practice, because they mistreat other people. They not only fast from food, but from acting justly toward others. They are self-serving and oppressive in their spirituality. God is not happy and ends up redefining what fasting really is: "Is not this the fast that I choose: to loose the bonds of injustice, to undo the thongs of the yoke, to let the oppressed go free, and to break every yoke? Is it not to share your bread with the hungry, and bring the homeless poor into your house; when you see the naked, to cover them, and not to

hide yourself from your own kin?" (Isa. 58:6-7). Basically, God redefines fasting as just service, linking an ancient practice of prayer to mission in the world. Serving can be prayer, just as Jesus "came not be served but to serve" (Mark 10:45). This form of prayer follows in his steps and brings us closer to the heart of his enfleshed Word.

These ways of prayer are practices to explore in your own life as a means to deepening your preaching. Many of them are not explicitly connected to preaching tasks, but they are connected to the preacher, who is essential to preaching, for "how shall they hear without a preacher?" (Rom. 10:14). If prayer shapes you, it will shape your preaching. Prayer will inform and form your preaching of the gospel. But most of all, it is a sign that you offer yourself to God as Archbishop Oscar Romero did in the movie *Romero*, by praying, "I can't. You must. I'm yours. Show me the way."

Further Learning Strategies

1. Considering this exploration of prayer, what is prayer to you? How have you practiced it in your life or congregation? Does the notion of prayer as suggested in the discussion about the different ways of prayer diverge from your own practices? What other ways of prayer are there? What is missing above? What do you do that is not listed and how does it feed your soul?

2. Take a silent retreat for at least a day. What do you hear? What are you learning? What is the role of silence in your current spiritual practices? How can you create more space for silence? Why is listening so important for preaching?

3. Be rebellious and read something you have been yearning to read but have not taken the time to do it. Perhaps find a local reading group.

4. In light of Isa. 58:1-12, how is your understanding of prayer altered by engaging this passage? What does it mean for the preaching life? What are hindrances to this life of prayer? Draw your answer to this question and discuss in a small group.
5. What other figures embody the interrelationship between prayer and action like Dr. King? Who are they and how are/were they able to do it? Share answers in a small group.

Further Reading

Cole, Allan Hugh, Jr., ed. *A Spiritual Life: Perspectives from Poets, Prophets, and Preachers.* Louisville: Westminster John Knox, 2011. A collection of interdisciplinary essays about different aspects of the spiritual life, demonstrating the rich mosaic of what it means to be spiritual.

Forbes, James. *The Holy Spirit and Preaching.* Nashville: Abingdon, 1989. This book is the publication of the Yale Lyman Beecher lectures that focused on the topic of the Holy Spirit and preaching.

Foster, Richard, and James Bryan Smith, eds. *Devotional Classics: Selected Readings for Individuals and Groups,* rev. ed. San Francisco: HarperOne, 2005. A wide spectrum of readings from various denominations and theological perspectives across history, including a practical reflective section for individual or group learning.

Graves, Mike. *The Fully Alive Preacher: Recovering from Homiletical Burnout.* Louisville: Westminster John Knox, 2006. This book aims to diagnose why preachers may be burnt out and offers some meaningful reflections and exercises to renew preachers.

Northcutt, Kay L. *Kindling Desire for God: Preaching as Spiritual*

Direction. Minneapolis: Fortress Press, 2009. A distinct contribution to reframing preaching as spiritual direction.

Thompson, Marjorie J. *Soul Feast: An Invitation to the Christian Spiritual Life.* Louisville: Westminster John Knox, 1995. A classic introduction to some of the theories and practices of the Christian spiritual life.

Thurman, Howard. *Meditations of the Heart.* Boston: Beacon, 1999. Spiritual reflections on various topics and themes of the spiritual life.

4

─────

Preaching as an Act of Worship

Sally A. Brown

As any naturalist would tell us, if we want to understand how a living creature normally functions, we need to observe it in its natural habitat. Something similar is true of preaching. There are undoubtedly people whose lives have been transformed by a sermon they picked up on the car radio while driving across Texas or stumbled upon while searching the Internet for a long-lost friend. But a stand-alone sermon, like a single shot from a film, is lifted out of its native setting. In this chapter we consider preaching in relation to its natural context, Christian worship.

The worship characteristic of Christian faith since its beginnings is Spirit-animated divine–human encounter. As the book of Acts records the spread of Christian faith, the outpouring of the Spirit accompanies preaching and precedes baptism.[1] Prayer, hymn singing, and the breaking of bread with thanksgiving (a eucharistic act) all appear in Acts as well.[2]

Worship is the center and pivot of a life that seeks to bear witness to Jesus Christ in the world. Although some North Americans think of worship as a weekly "time out" from real life, that view misses something of the real significance of Christian worship. When worship is functioning as it should, all its components—song and prayer, preaching and praise, baptism and Lord's Supper—tell the redemptive story of Jesus that, for Christians, makes sense of their lives.

Worship reframes our view of the world within the presence and action of God so that, at the end of the worship gathering, we move into the world with corrected vision. We perceive ordinary situations as places where God is redemptively at work. Knowing God has gone ahead of us into every situation, we can take action that testifies to the compassion and justice of God. Thus, the Spirit not only enables our worship, but also moves us from sanctuary to street and continues to animate the people of God for public witness.

Preaching as Worship

Preaching is as much an act of worship as praise or confession, baptism or prayer. Sometimes folks will talk as if the praise songs, hymns, and prayers are the "worship" part—and what follows is a cognitive interruption called the sermon. On the one hand, the notion that preaching "interrupts" worship arises when preaching offers little more than instruction and advice. But Christian preaching that educates the mind but does not move the heart misses the mark,

---

1. The Greek word *pneuma* ("spirit") appears sixty-nine times in the book of Acts.
2. See, for example, Acts 16 (Paul and Silas sing in prison), and Acts 2:46 and 27:35 for the phrase "breaking bread" in connection specifically with prayer. Baptism is mentioned over a dozen times in Acts, and prayer in chapter after chapter.

as the prominent African American homiletician Henry Mitchell insists.[3] On the other hand, some overemphasize preaching as the "main event" in preaching, treating praise and prayer as "warm-up" exercises before the "feature" (preaching). Either under- or overemphasizing preaching tends to throw all of worship out of balance. Proclamation—the communication of the saving news of God's acts—is larger than preaching itself. Many acts of worship in addition to preaching proclaim God's self-giving love for the world, most notably the sacraments of baptism and the Lord's Supper.[4]

In a church where I often preached, one of the "subcultures" in the congregation consisted of mentally challenged adults from a nearby group residence. They came eagerly to church every Sunday and sat in the front rows. During the sermon, their attention often flagged. But when it came time for communion, a hush fell over these worshipers. They received bread and cup in focused reverence, fully absorbed in each action of the Lord's Supper. I am convinced they understood the self-giving love of God and our need for this sacrament more deeply than any of us other worshipers. Yet, for many, preaching proves to be an indispensable act of worship by which the Spirit brings us into transformational encounter with the living God.

This chapter begins with a condensed sketch of the development of Christian worship from the first centuries of Christianity to the present. We focus especially on the role preaching has played in Christian worship in the Western tradition. (The "Western" worship tradition refers to churches, including Protestant ones, that trace their roots to the pre-Reformation Roman Catholic church, rather than the Eastern Orthodox tradition.) Most Protestant Christians cannot

---

3. Henry H. Mitchell, *Celebration and Experience in Preaching* (Nashville: Abingdon, 1990), 22–23, 26–29.
4. In this chapter we refer to these worship actions as "sacraments," recognizing that in other Christian worship traditions they are termed "ordinances."

imagine a Christian worship service without a sermon. Yet, at a critical point in Christianity's past, preaching had all but disappeared from the weekly worship of average Christians.

Toward the end of the chapter, against the backdrop of this historical overview, we'll take up the subject of worship change and the factors that prompt it. Change is inevitable in Christian worship, since Christian faith has rooted itself (and continues to root itself) in an array of cultures, as well as settings where multiple cultures meet and mix. We'll also note ways that pastors and other church leaders can ensure that a congregation's deliberations about worship change will be well informed, fair and open, and alert to the purposes or functions of different worship practices. Paying attention to these things makes it more likely that discussions about worship will lead to results that make sense theologically and culturally for a particular congregation.

The Role of Preaching in the History of Christian Worship

I. Preaching: A Jewish Practice Adapted to Christian Faith

As we noted in chapter 1 of this book, *Christian* preaching came into being on the first Pentecost festival following the resurrection of Jesus. On that day, the Holy Spirit came in power upon Jesus' followers as they were praying in Jerusalem, as Jesus had told them to do (Acts 1:4-5). Filled with the Spirit, they poured into the streets proclaiming God's redemptive acts in Jesus, crucified and risen as Lord. But preaching as a practice of worship did not originate with the Christian church.

Preaching was already a long-established practice in Jewish worship. Nehemiah 8:1-8 tells us that when the Jewish exiles returned to rebuild Jerusalem, they all assembled to hear the public reading of the long-forgotten Book of the Law (what we know as the Pentateuch, the first five books of the Bible). Leaders of the community well-versed in these books, known to Jews as Torah, stood before the people, giving interpretation, "so that the people understood the reading" (v. 8). By Jesus' time, when the synagogue was the weekly gathering place for Jewish worship, the reading of Scripture, which by Jesus' day also included the books of Wisdom and the prophetic books, was customarily followed by interpretation—in other words, preaching. Prayer completed Sabbath-day worship.

We find Jesus in synagogue worship often in the Synoptic Gospels (Matthew, Mark, and Luke). According to the Gospel of Luke, the synagogue in Capernaum is where Jesus announced his ministry as he interpreted the day's reading from the prophet Isaiah (Luke 4:16-30). We also know that Jesus preached in towns and rural areas in Galilee, Judea, and beyond, announcing that the reign of God had drawn near.[5] He taught his disciples to carry this message, too.

Luke's second book, the book of Acts, provides a sampling of early Christian preaching, including what are likely abbreviated versions of particular sermons of Peter, Stephen, and Paul. The earliest Christian sermons reinterpret the Torah, the psalms, and Old Testament prophetic texts in light of the ministry, death, and resurrection of Jesus. In keeping with Jewish custom, the apostles first took their message to the Jewish synagogues, beginning in Jerusalem, Judea, and Samaria, and later spreading to synagogues of the Jewish Diaspora (scattered Jewish populations across the empire).[6]

When Jewish opposition to Christian claims intensified, the apostles were no longer welcome in synagogues. We find them preaching instead before religious councils (Acts 7:1-53), in the homes of prominent non-Jewish citizens (Acts 10:30-48), in the

5. See Matt. 4:17; Mark 1:14-15.
6. See, for example, Acts 9:20; 13:5, 14; 14:1; 17:1-2, 10, 17; 19:8; and elsewhere.

halls of government (Acts 5:27f.; 25:23—26:32), and elsewhere (Acts 17:22-33). This suggests that, particularly in times of persecution, preaching may occur outside the framework of public worship.

II. The Classic Pattern Emerges:
The Service of the Word and the Service of the Table

Evidence shows that by the third century, Christian worship had assumed a distinctive shape. Held on the first day of the week rather than the Jewish Sabbath, Christian worship combined the word-centered worship of the synagogue with the distinctive table fellowship Jesus established on the eve of his death. From the synagogue, Christians adopted a summons to worship, prayers, Scripture reading, and preaching. From the upper-room tradition came the unique manner of sharing bread and wine in Jesus' name described in the three Synoptic Gospels.

This "di-polar" (double-centered) pattern for Christian worship is suggested in Luke's story of two disciples walking from Jerusalem to the town of Emmaus late on the day of Jesus' resurrection (Luke 24:13-38). As they walk, they discuss not only the shockingly violent end to Jesus' ministry three days earlier, but odd rumors that, early that very morning, some had seen him alive. At this point a "stranger" falls in step with them. He asks what they are discussing; and when they explain, the stranger *preaches* to them. He interprets "Moses and all the prophets" to show that the suffering, death, and rising of God's Anointed One (Messiah) is indicated in their Scriptures.

Strikingly, although their hearts "burn" within them as they listen, it turns out that *preaching alone is not enough* for these disciples to recognize that the stranger is their risen Lord. It was only later at the table, when Jesus "*took* bread, *blessed* and *broke* it, and *gave* it to them," that "their eyes were opened, and they recognized him" (Luke 24:30-31).[7]

By the sixth century, the word-and-table pattern for Christian worship is attested in ancient manuscripts from many locations with only minor variations, with baptism (often at Easter) another prominent practice. Neither preaching nor the table stood alone in the churches' early centuries; neither dominated worship. Yet, this balance between the service of the word and the service of the table has been jeopardized at some points in Christian history.

III. The Classic Balance of Word and Table Tested

After the legalization of Christianity under the Emperor Constantine (fourth century), Rome became a major center of ecclesiastical influence. Later, Constantinople (located in present-day Turkey) became central for churches of the East. Increasing friction between authorities in Rome and those in Constantinople over ecclesiastical and theological matters led in 1054–55 to a series of events known as the Great Schism. Thereafter, Christianity developed along two independent lines, one constituting the history of the Western churches, the other the Eastern (Orthodox) churches, a difference that continues to the present day. Today, Roman Catholic, Reformed, and other Protestant churches around the globe trace their lineage to the Western church, while Orthodox churches comprise the Eastern branch of Christian faith.[8]

Orthodox churches can point to a nearly unbroken worship heritage that retains the word-and-table balance. But in the Western church, the balance between word and table began to shift. One

---

7. To this day, the fourfold action characteristic of every Christian celebration of the Lord's Supper is take, bless, break, give.
8. Typically grouped with the Eastern churches are distinctive traditions such as India's Martoma church, which traces its heritage to Syria as well.

factor in this shift was theological debate about whether or not the literal body and blood of Christ was being "sacrificed" by the priest in the communion rite. The authorized interpretation that emerged stated that the bread and wine, although their appearance is unchanged, *become* Jesus' actual body and blood, which is called "transubstantiation." The priest literally presides over a recapitulation of Jesus' sacrificial death.

This official doctrine contributed to a growing sense of mystery and awe surrounding the rites of communion. In addition, ritual action leading up to the sacrificial rite became more elaborate. As a precaution, lest the sacred blood of the Lord be spilled, the cup was no longer offered to ordinary worshipers. Eventually, even the bread (the "host") was reserved for the priests only. Further contributing to the sense of dark mystery surrounding the altar was the fact that the language of the Mass was Latin, a language no one spoke. Many priests could read it, but without understanding.

At the eve of the Reformation, across Europe, the priestly rites at the altar had come to dominate worship. The apex of worship was the moment when a chime would sound, and the celebrant would lift the bread high for all to see, intoning, *"hoc est corpus"*—"This is my body." This moment signified the transformation of the bread into the body of Christ. Medieval piety revolved around this priestly action and the consecrated "host." The host and other holy objects, such as relics of the saints (a lock of hair, or a piece of bone) were venerated and seen as means for warding off the dangers of disease, death, and damnation.

At this point in Christian history, preaching was rare, partly because the Bible, too, was in Latin and many priests could therefore not interpret it. For many worshipers, the vivid portrayals of scenes from the life of Jesus and the saints that decorated the interior of churches formed their understanding of the stories of the Bible.

Periodically, itinerant monastic orders emerged (notably the Franciscans in the late twelfth century and the Dominicans in the early thirteenth) that promoted a revival of preaching.[9] Their efforts did much to keep the practice of preaching alive and form popular understanding of Christianity, but did not precipitate change in worship. Only later, through the efforts of church reformers of the sixteenth century, did preaching regain its place as a regular practice in Christian worship.

The Protestant Reformation and the Return of Preaching to Worship

When the reformist Catholic priest, Martin Luther (1483–1546) legendarily nailed his 95 Theses to the door of All Saints' Church in Wittenberg, Germany, in 1517, his immediate concern was clerical abuses, particularly the sale of "indulgences" to secure forgiveness of sin. While Luther had no intention to break from Rome, his action sparked what we now call the Reformation. In northern Europe, the movement was advanced by the more radical Swiss reformer, Ulrich Zwingli (1484–1531) and in Strasbourg by Martin Bucer (1491–1551), whose mediating views fell between those of Zwingli and Luther. These reformers shared concern not only about clerical abuses, but about the absence of Scripture reading and preaching in worship. In Germany, Luther campaigned to restore these practices to weekly worship. He also translated the Bible into vernacular German to make it accessible to priests and literate laypeople alike, composed numerous hymns, and wrote several catechisms to help teach the essentials of faith in Christian households.

Luther also argued that the bread and wine did not *become* Jesus'

---

9. For a fascinating study of Franciscan preaching, see Timothy J. Johnson, ed., *Franciscans and Preaching: Every Miracle from the Foundation of the World Came About through Words* (New York: Brill, 2012).

body and blood, but that, as the priest spoke the authorized words (words of institution) of the Lord's Supper, Jesus' broken body and shed blood became "co-present" with the bread and wine (or what Lutherans refer to as the "sacramental union"). In this respect, Luther meant to correct misunderstandings of the service of the table, but not to diminish its significance in any way.

Zwingli took a different view; pointing to Luke 22:19 ("do this in remembrance of me"), he argued that the sacrament of the Lord's Supper is a memorial meal. He objected strenuously to any notion that the body of Jesus is "re-sacrificed" at the table. Jesus' once-for-all, fully effective sacrifice of himself for our redemption can never be repeated; the bread and cup are memory aids by which we might understand our need of redemption and respond to God in gratitude. Zwingli's view continues to influence many branches of the Protestant tradition today.

John Calvin (1509–1564), who belonged to the next generation of ecclesiastical reformers, followed Bucer in charting a middle way between Luther and Zwingli. Like them, Calvin insisted that sermons must be part of Christian worship. Calvin agreed that Jesus' sacrifice is not repeated at the table, nor do the presiding priest's words "make" Christ's body present. Yet, argued Calvin, as we partake of bread and cup, we are truly being fed *spiritually* by Christ at the Lord's Supper—and the risen Christ is truly present. The Holy Spirit "lifts" us to be united with the Christ, seated at God's right hand; and thus we feed on Christ in a way that is essential for us.

So essential is this means of grace, said Calvin, that we ought to come to the table every week. But the city council of Geneva, the city where Calvin lived and preached, disagreed. Many Reformation leaders took the view (citing 1 Cor. 11:27-28) that each worshiper should undergo examination by the elders of the congregation before every Lord's Supper—a procedure that could prove extremely unwieldy week after week as Reformed congregations grew. This purely practical consideration added weight to the resistance to weekly communion. Ultimately, in most Reformed churches, the Lord's Supper occurred about four times a year, and sometimes less often.

If preaching had suffered diminishment in the medieval Catholic church, the ultimate effect of the reformers' efforts was to throw worship out of balance in the other direction. Protestant services of worship became largely preaching events. The effects of this overbalance toward the pulpit instead of the table can still be detected in the worship patterns of many Protestant churches, especially in North America.

V. Balance Restored: Twentieth-Century Roman Catholic and Protestant Worship Renewal

During the Second Vatican Council ("Vatican II," 1962–1965), a convention of Catholic bishops and scholars undertook a thorough examination and reform of Christian worship. The local vernacular replaced Latin worldwide as the normative language for worship. A regular cycle of Scripture readings (the lectionary) prescribed weekly readings from both Old and New Testaments, the Psalms, and the Gospels. Thus, Scripture reading and preaching took a much more prominent place in the weekly Mass. Protestant worship scholars followed suit. By the late twentieth century, several major Protestant denominations had renewed their worship—at least at the "official" level. New service books recommended a balanced service revolving around both preaching and sacraments. Yet, long-standing habits are difficult to change, especially when it comes to religious practices. Congregations embraced the new services reluctantly. Preaching continues to play a dominant role in Protestant worship. While a high proportion of congregations have shifted to celebrating communion monthly, or even weekly, others do so only four times a year. Some offer communion just once a year—a far cry from the stress placed upon the Supper from the earliest decades of Christianity, and for centuries thereafter.

The conversation about the balance of word and table is an important one especially for those denominations that emphasize aligning worship practices with long confessional and historical precedent. However, I can't help but wonder whether this topic occurs as much to those congregations that have been shaped out of revivalist traditions. There may be discussions about the frequency of communion and the method for serving communion, but in these settings it may be more important to explore the role of the heart in worship just as Jesus quotes the prophet Isaiah and reminds his listeners that it's possible to honor God with lips and still have hearts far from God (Mark 7). In light of these ecclesial spaces where hearts may be "strangely warmed" like John Wesley, it is prudent to talk about how human hearts can be altars and how the impulses of one's heart shape what is seen even in worship. For a God who looks on the heart (1 Samuel 16), it is always necessary to ask, "What is the heart of worship in spirit and in truth?" (John 4) – **LP**

The late twentieth century's energetic reexamination of the history and theology of worship reminded Protestant Christians of many things long forgotten. Not least of all was that every part of worship can proclaim the gospel. The Spirit works throughout worship, not just in preaching or through the communion rite. Hymns function as proclamation, prayer, lament, and celebration. Prayers signify our confidence in a God who listens, comforts, strengthens, heals, and guides. Personal testimony points to the ongoing activity of God in ordinary lives. Both the Lord's Supper and baptism are enacted, participatory proclamations of the saving news of redemption through Jesus Christ.

The practice of testimony is prominent in free-church traditions. It allows for the gospel experienced by individuals to be voiced within the faith community. Considering preaching as testimony opens up the possibilities of who might be thought of as "preachers." This becomes important particularly in those denominations or congregations where women or other marginalized individuals are told they cannot be ordained. Historically, when women were not deemed "preachers" officially, women evangelists would still "preach" in their own right, even if from the floor of the sanctuary and not the pulpit and even if what they said was called a "testimony" and not a sermon. They had a word from the Lord on their lips that stirred the people to holy living. Ordination did not guarantee "the anointing," thus these testifiers were fully enabled to proclaim a Spirit-filled word for the people of God. Testimony is a terrific egalitarian speech act within the church and should never be underestimated. It may be the word the community needs to hear in any given moment. In fact, it might be more effective than the so-called sermon. – **LP**

Worship that balances word (Scripture readings and preaching) and table (communion) has positive effects, even on preaching. First, it is less likely that the effectiveness of worship is going to be measured solely in terms of the quality of the sermon. Second, congregations whose worship is balanced are less likely to suffer traumatic swings in membership when a gifted preacher departs for a new post. Human nature being what it is, congregations are likely to idolize a good preacher and vilify a weak one, blaming all the congregation's ills on him or her. Third, as noted earlier, for some the ritual action of the Lord's Supper forms faith more surely than word-centered parts of worship. Fourth, the close relationship of word and sacrament as proclamations of the gospel can be strengthened through preaching that conscientiously moves *toward* the table, as is the case in some Lutheran and Episcopal communities of worship. Finally, when the action of the Lord's Supper is not regularly part of worship, singing may be the only part of worship that requires active participation, making worship less relatable for children and for some adults.

At its best, accessible, engaging worship strikes a balance among all the senses, appealing to eye and ear, touch and taste and smell. Cultures vary in the degree to which they utilize these avenues of communication, and in an increasingly multicultural context, worship that opens all of these avenues as pathways of divine–human communication will be more inclusive of all ages and all cultures present.

Balanced worship is durable and hospitable worship. Its pattern has stood the test of time. While not every part of worship is equally accessible or energizing to every worshiper, Christian worship that combines song and silence, lament and praise, spoken word and active, tactile ritual action allows worshipers to encounter and be taught by the Spirit in many ways.

Worship Change: More Constructive than Contentious?

Worship is shaped and reshaped by the cultures in which it is embedded. This means that as the cultural environment around worship shifts, some members of a congregation may press for change in the cultural "feel" of worship in their church. Conflicts over the style of music and language in worship have been a major source of tension in congregations in recent decades.

This dynamic is likely to continue in our globalized world. The pace and depth of cultural change is accelerated by the influence of the Internet, which instantly delivers whatever is "trending" in music, ideas, fashion, and religion. Thanks to Web-browsing and social networks, congregation members inevitably feel the impact of trends in Christian preaching and worship music, often associated with charismatic preachers and performers. Congregational leaders need to welcome the questions about local worship practices such exposure prompts, helping a congregation weigh the value of a deeply held worship tradition amid pressures to embrace whatever is "new and next."

The pace of worship change under cultural pressure is moderated somewhat if a congregation is part of a centralized ecclesiastical structure that determines the structure and language of worship. Worship's pattern, along with texts for spoken or sung prayers and litanies, is stabilized in a service book, such as the Episcopal *Book of Common Prayer*. But even in these settings, musical style can become a matter of debate. This is not surprising; music is perhaps the fastest-changing stream of popular culture. Music is not only a memorable carrier of ideas. It reaches deep into the emotions and the body's sense of rhythm, and is one of the most distinctive markers of a generation's and culture's self-understanding.

Discussions about potential changes in worship are bound to arise. Such discussions can take one of two routes: they can lead to rancorous and potentially destructive conflict, or they can result in fresh understanding and constructive change. When questions about worship style and pattern arise, leaders need to pay attention to four key processes that turn difference into constructive change. Wise leaders will: (1) create an open, accessible process in which different stakeholders (different, for example, in terms of past worship experience, musical culture, and/or generation) can share their worship experience without judgment; (2) see that this sharing process integrates well with whatever structures for decision making exist in the congregation; (3) create multiple opportunities for members (including youth!) to learn about the history of Christian worship and the theological function of different parts of worship; and (4) create deliberative settings—settings that move toward concrete change—in which all of the other three elements are brought together.

Keeping worship *accessible* to all present may not be the same thing as making worship *comfortable* in every detail for everyone present. A few years ago I visited a church that had earned a national reputation for its multicultural worship. At coffee hour after worship, I stepped over to a woman who seemed to carry the years and comfort level of a "veteran" in this community. Stirring my coffee, I asked her, "So how do you all work this out, so that everyone's comfortable with all the diversity of music, choral styles, testimonies, prayer—all of it?"

"Comfortable!" she crowed. *"Comfortable?!* Why, no one's *comfortable,* really. I'm pretty sure there's something in worship every week that makes at least a couple of people uncomfortable. But one thing we agree about: God's called us to a unity in the Spirit here that goes beyond comfort. So we try to honor every culture present in our pews but focus mainly on what the Spirit is asking us to become for our neighborhood and city."

Pastors and church leaders can evaluate worship by conducting interviews with one or two dozen representative attendees. The most useful questions will be open-ended ones that can't be answered simply "yes" or "no," but give worshipers the chance to express how and where they experience God's presence in worship. When that does not happen, what is getting in the way? People will be honest if they do not fear that those "in charge" will discount or dismiss their feelings.

Theological Functions of Worship:
Divine Promise, Reframing, and Rehearsal

In chapter 1, we discussed three functions of Christian preaching under the headings of the declaration of divine promise, reframing experience, and rehearsal for faithfulness in the everyday world. Through its different actions, worship functions theologically in these same dimensions.

First, some elements of a worship service announce what God has done, is doing, and has promised ultimately to do to renew humanity and all creation. In the words of Martin Luther King Jr., "the arc of the moral universe is long, but it bends toward justice."[10] The pledge and anticipation of the just restoration and reconciliation God is bringing about is the risen Jesus Christ, called in Scripture the "firstborn" of God's new creation (Col. 1:15).

The rhetoric of promise abounds in Christian worship. Hymns and praise songs, Scripture readings, and litanies of thanksgiving celebrate what God has done, is doing, and will do in the world for our redemption. The sacraments—baptism and the Lord's Supper—are enactments of the promises of God to us in Jesus Christ. Baptism, whether of infants or adults, declares our destiny by identifying our life stories with the story of Jesus' death and resurrection. The Lord's Supper is *eucharist*, "thanksgiving." It points backward to what God has accomplished in Jesus Christ, gathers us into Christ's immediate presence in the here-and-now, and anticipates that future in which God "will make for all peoples a feast of rich food, a feast of well-aged wines . . . and will swallow up death forever" (Isa. 25:6-7). Joyful music, especially congregational song, has been a basic form of response to the promises of God.

Second, different parts of worship reframe and re-narrate present human experience in light of God's love and justice. This reframing functions in two ways. On the one hand, evaluating human experience through the lens of God's new creation revealed in Jesus exposes sin and evil. This leads us to confess behaviors, individual and corporate, that promote self-interest at the expense of others. Admitting the truth of our situation calls for a language that weeps and sometimes rages at the life-destroying systems we help to create (even if unwittingly). Lament, the rhetorical form of about a third of the psalms and many other biblical texts, teaches us a language of sorrow, anger, frustration, and confession that we need in worship. When we speak and sing lament, the Spirit groans with us, appalled

10. Quoted by John Craig, "Wesleyan Baccalaureate Is Delivered by Dr. King," *Hartford Courant*, June 8, 1964.

at how greed, abusive uses of power, lies, and indifference destroy human lives.

Thankfully, on the other hand, worship also reframes our lives positively. Because God has acted to deliver us from sin and its deadly consequences for us and for others, we experience forgiveness and the power to live differently. Assurances of pardon, songs, and testimonies bear witness that we were lost, but are found; we were blind, but now we see.[11] Feasting together at Christ's table, we get a foretaste of the just, inclusive will of God for human beings.

Worship, like preaching, has a third theological function. Worship "rehearses" us for Spirit-animated action in the world. In the preaching event, preacher and listeners imaginatively rehearse for creative, sometimes risky action in the world that testifies to God's mercy and justice. Giving is also a crucial rehearsal for faithful life, especially in societies where buying power and self-worth are too often connected. Monetary gifts signify giving our very selves over to the purposes of God in daily life. Even church announcements, far from being an unfortunate "interruption" of worship, ready us for creative witness to the love of God. They throw open opportunities to feed and shelter the homeless, offer pro bono legal help, teach children, deliver meals to the isolated, and visit the incarcerated.

Worship turns our hearts to God so that we may turn our wills and bodies toward the world. There, the Spirit of God has preceded us, stirring the tides of compassion and justice. Worship sends us out to participate in the redemptive love of God for the whole world.

Further Learning Strategies

1. On the basis of reading this chapter, what insights have you gained, or what questions do you have, about the balance among

---

11. These phrases allude to the hymn text "Amazing Grace," composed by Isaac Watts.

different parts of worship in the setting where you usually worship?

2. Visit two Christian worship services in traditions distinctly different from your own. What surprised you? What intrigued you? Which of the elements of worship discussed in this chapter seemed to receive the most emphasis? What emphases did you appreciate most?

3. List as many different "subcultures" as you can that are represented in a congregation you know well (generational, ethnic, style-preference, theological, etc.). Which among these subcultures seem to have greater influence over the current style of worship in the congregation? Which have less influence? What do you think accounts for this?

4. This chapter argues that preaching is just one part of a whole tapestry of worship practices that declare God's promises, reframe our experience in the world, and rehearse us for faithful living. Sketch a series of sermon topics that could help a congregation gain a greater appreciation for every part of worship.

Further Reading

Costen, Melva Wilson. *African American Christian Worship.* 2nd ed. Nashville: Abingdon, 2007.

Dix, Dom Gregory. *The Shape of the Liturgy.* New ed. New York: Bloomsbury/T&T Clark, 2015 (1982).

González, Justo L. *¡Alabadle! Hispanic Christian Worship.* Nashville: Abingdon, 1996. An introduction to varieties of Hispanic Christian worship, emphasizing cultural, denominational, and generational factors shaping worship today.

Greenhaw, David, and Ronald J. Allen, eds. *Preaching in the Context of*

Worship. Preaching and Its Partners. St. Louis: Chalice, 2000. Essays on preaching and worship that relate preaching to the Christian year, Holy Communion, worship renewal, music, and other topics.

Kelderman, Duane, et al. *Authentic Worship in a Changing Culture.* Grand Rapids: CRC Publications, 1997. A study guide originally designed for churches in the Christian Reformed tradition to help a congregation think about its worship in historical and theological perspective and plan change wisely.

Long, Thomas G. *Beyond the Worship Wars: Building Vital and Faithful Worship.* Bethesda, MD: Alban Institute, 1999 (now: Lanham, MD: Rowman and Littlefield). Provides historical context and frameworks for theological assessment as congregations deal with worship change.

Martin, Ralph P. *Worship in the Early Church.* 3rd ed. Grand Rapids: Eerdmans, 1974.

Troeger, Thomas H. *Preaching and Worship.* Preaching and Its Partners. St. Louis: Chalice, 2003.

White, James F. *A Brief History of Christian Worship.* 3rd ed. Nashville: Abingdon, 2001. A basic overview of the development of Christian worship from New Testament communities to the twentieth century.

5

The Preacher as Interpreter of Word and World

Sally A. Brown

Human beings are nonstop interpreters. From the moment we awake, we interpret our experience through all our senses. The rumble of a truck in the dark of early dawn prompts us to wonder if we remembered to put out the trash. We sniff the cream carton and decide to take our morning coffee black. Gathering clouds prompt us to grab an umbrella on the way out the door. On the morning commute, a sudden flash of dozens of red brake lights ahead alerts us to stalled traffic. In the hallway on the way to the office, a coworker's smile lifts our spirits.

We are all interpreters, but preachers have special interpretive work to do. Preachers stand at a crossroad of interpretation, an intersection where the witness of Scripture and Christian tradition, current events, and the everyday challenges that ordinary human beings face interact with each other. Our congregations count on us to bring specialized skills to our task of interpretation, especially interpretation of Scripture. We use Bible dictionaries and commentaries, consult church history, and in some cases, Greek and Hebrew language tools to explore Scripture from many perspectives. This process, called *exegesis*, which literally means "to draw out," is a core practice in biblical interpretation, and will be our focus in chapter 6.[1]

But we are not commissioned by our congregations to be students of Scripture in a general sense; rather, we are to stand up and preach news of the redemptive work God has done, is doing, and continues to do in the world—especially *their* world. They count on us not simply for news of God in general, but news that matters to *them*.[2] In order to do this, we need to know who they are. We need to know their histories, their current joys and sorrows, and the issues they deal with on any ordinary day. Some wrestle with intensely personal, even private, dilemmas. Others have public responsibilities in city government, the school system, or nonprofit organizations. Many struggle to balance the complex, sometimes conflicting, expectations of them in simultaneous roles as spouses, parents, breadwinners, and children of aging parents. Some come to worship full of faith. Others show up full of doubt.

This chapter focuses on two topics that can help us get a handle on our interpretive responsibilities as preachers. First, we'll briefly

1. Terms differ in various contexts; but homileticians typically use the word *text* instead of speaking of the biblical "passage" to refer to a coherent set of verses that will be interpreted in a sermon (also known as a pericope). In other contexts, the sermon "text" refers to a single phrase or idea from the text that will be emphasized in the sermon.

2. Here, I am in close agreement with Thomas G. Long. See especially his essay, "No New Is Bad News: God in the Present Tense," in *Preaching from Memory to Hope* (Louisville: Westminster John Knox, 2009), 27–53, esp. 34, 38, and 44.

explore some insights of twentieth-century scholars about the interpretive nature of all human experience. This helps us recognize the specialized interpretive work we do against the backdrop of the mostly unconscious interpretive work that we, like everyone else, do all the time.

Second, this chapter focuses on a task too often overlooked in preaching: the "exegesis" of congregations themselves. We preachers don't go to the Christian Scriptures seeking a message strictly for our own benefit, but for the benefit of many others. Our listeners come to worship longing to hear a life-giving message that addresses them where they live. We need to understand these people who are counting on us. We need to use every tool we can so we know them at a level that is more than superficial.

Christian congregations are unique in that, theologically speaking, they are Spirit-animated communities. Thus, while preachers make use of the sort of tools that help ethnographers understand cultures, preachers refine or supplement those tools in order to attend, in particular, to a Christian congregation's theological worldview and self-understanding. Symbols, narratives, interview material, and practices can reveal ways that different members of a congregation understand themselves in relation to God, one another, and the wider world.

To Be Human Is to Interpret

As indicated at the beginning of this chapter, we human beings interpret all sorts of things all the time, although most of us barely notice we're doing it. Reading is an example. We make sense of a complicated array of words on a page without a thought for the complex mental moves we are making. For instance, many words in English (and nearly every language) can have multiple meanings. Consider three words you encountered a moment ago: "complex," "mental," and "moves." Each of these words can have different meanings depending on their context. On the one hand, "complex" can mean "complicated," as it does here. On the other hand, we sometimes refer to a certain type of multiuse commercial building as a "business complex." The word *mental* usually refers to cognitive brain function; but in some regions, it's a somewhat crude slang word meaning that someone's acting crazy ("He's gone mental!"). "Moves" can function as a noun meaning "strategies" (as here) or as a simple verb ("Look—that thing on the rug moves!"). The interpretive moves you made to choose the right meaning for those three words were so quick you never gave them a thought. We do similar interpretive processing constantly. We don't *decide* to interpret; it is our nature as human beings to do so.

Philosophers, theologians, and literary critics have long reflected on the process of interpretation. In general, theory about interpretation is called *hermeneutics*. There are different types, however. Philosophical hermeneutics deals with the general human activity of coming to understand something. Hermeneutics in this sense is mainly *descriptive* (saying what is the case, not what "ought to be" the case). Literary hermeneutics, or the more specialized field of biblical hermeneutics, can be descriptive (reflecting on what it is like to come to an understanding of a text) or *prescriptive*—arguing for a particular method that leads to reliable results.

German philosopher Hans-Georg Gadamer affirmed, along with his teacher and colleague Martin Heidegger, that interpretation (coming-to-understand) is not optional for human beings; it is our mode of being.[3] Interpretive processing is our way of navigating all

---

3. Hans-Georg Gadamer, *Truth and Method*, 2nd rev. ed., trans. Joel Weinsheimer and Donald G. Marshall (New York: Continuum, 1993), 259. Gadamer's work closely follows themes in the work of Martin Heidegger. Both see human existence as inherently and irreducibly "hermeneutical." Human beings are, so to speak, born into a world of interpretation. Both

experience. We can't *not* interpret. Whereas hermeneutical theory up to the mid-twentieth century had mostly dealt with specialized methods for handling different kinds of text, Gadamer set out to describe the interpretive process itself—what goes on when we come to an understanding of anything at all—a situation or a person, an artwork or a written text.

When it comes to interpretation it is always important to acknowledge that it requires more than the Bible. The sources for theological reflection/interpretation are tradition, Scripture, reason, and experience; Methodists call this the Wesleyan quadrilateral. It is an honest way of pointing to what influences any interpreter of word and world. Sometimes it is too easy for some churches to just rely upon "the Bible says" as if that solves every problem rather than acknowledging the various influences on interpretation. Just because one interprets the Bible literally doesn't mean it has been interpreted faithfully. This is not to say that traditions with a high view of Scripture are misguided; rather, there needs to be a more fulsome embrace and awareness of the sources that feed into any interpretation. For example, two people can look at a red robin but one may focus on the color of its feathers and someone else may center on their bill. It's the same robin but what the interpreters see is different based on their locations in the world. There's always more to interpretation than the Bible itself.
– LP

I. The Interpretive Encounter as a Meeting of Horizons

The interpretive encounter between any phenomenon and a human interpreter is complex, Gadamer argued; it is the meeting not simply of individuals, but of distinctly different "worlds." Two different people meeting for the first time bring their often very different "worlds" of experience to the encounter. Similarly, although in a less obvious way, texts, too, are embedded in a "world" different from the "world" that you or I, the readers, bring to the encounter called reading. Gadamer introduced the term *horizon* to speak of the "world" of experience and presuppositions that two persons, or a text and its reader, bring to their encounter.[4]

suggest that we cannot separate ourselves from our matrix of interpretation, as if to gain a stance of perfect objectivity.

The degree of difference between two strangers meeting on an airplane or between a text and its reader varies, of course. An announcement in your church newsletter about next week's youth group retreat represents a horizon of experience closer to your own; the social and religious world it assumes is relatively familiar. Not so if, say, on a tour in Turkey you stop to inspect the inscription on an ancient tomb. You would need considerable help to understand the remote historical and cultural horizon that inscription represents.

II. Interpretation as Dialogue and Play

When strangers meet, their conversation is a back-and-forth between their two "horizons" of experience. Gradually, connections are made. Understanding begins to develop. Similarly, proposed Gadamer, closing the gap between the horizon of a text and one's own horizon as a reader is like a dialogue.[5] As if we were getting to know another person, we ask questions—consciously or unconsciously. Text interpretation is, metaphorically speaking, a dialogue of question and answer. The interpreter raises questions and then patiently explores the text, listening for an answer. Our conversation with a text is often more implicit than explicit. Think back to our earlier example of making sense of words with more than one possible meaning. Through a back-and-forth process of checking the phrase "complex mental moves" against the larger context in which it occurs, we arrive at meanings for the three words that make sense. (Sometimes, of course—in poetry, for example—ambiguity about meaning is deliberate; we're *meant* to keep more than one possible meaning open in our minds.)

The interpretation of Scripture is simply a special and more conscientious expression of this same dialogical process. We arrive

4. Ibid., 245, 302.
5. Ibid., 366–69.

at deeper understanding through a back-and-forth process of questioning and "listening," figuratively speaking. In the case of preachers, of course, many of the questions that will be asked will be, in a sense, "proxy" questions. Preachers enter into dialogue with a text on behalf of the congregation.

Gadamer suggests a further, quite fascinating, metaphor for interpretation: interpreting a text, a work of art, or a film, he proposes, is like playing a game.[6] Just as you allow a game to involve you on its own terms (since "playing" the game means acting by its rules), you allow a text you want to understand to lead you into its world. For example, if you want to join a pick-up game of basketball, you don't trot out onto the court carrying a double-pointed leather ball. Wrong ball, wrong game. You "submit," in a sense, to the terms of the game. You agree to play a particular position, and you play according to the rules of *that* game, instead of some other game.

Philosopher of language Paul Ricoeur speaks of this process, too, but in somewhat different terms. A text, says Ricoeur, "proposes" or "projects" a world. It invites us into a certain way of understanding the world and ourselves. As Ricoeur puts it, "The text speaks of a possible world and of a possible way of orientating oneself within it."[7] Biblical parables are good examples of this function of texts. "There was a man who had two sons," Jesus begins—and we know we are inside a biblical parable.[8] We are meant to give ourselves over to the story Jesus tells, look around inside it, and see if we recognize ourselves there. If we keep our eyes open, we might even recognize traces of God.

To pursue the analogy a step further, preachers enter into dialogue

---

6. Ibid., 102–4.
7. Paul Ricoeur, *Interpretation Theory: Discourse and the Surplus of Meaning* (Ft. Worth: Texas Christian University Press, 1976), 88.
8. This is from what is widely known as the "parable of the prodigal son," although it might more accurately be called the parable of *two* lost sons (Luke 15:11-32).

with a text on which they mean to preach. But first, they "give" themselves to the biblical text and the world of customs, characters, actions, and perhaps even portraits of God that it proposes. They entertain this "possible world" (to use Ricoeur's phrase) and the "possible ways" of understanding ourselves that it offers. Later, they will enter into a back-and-forth dialogue between the world of prospective sermon listeners and the text's world to see what new light each sheds on the other. This back-and-forth of discovery is what leads to the event of insight that produces the sermon.

Preachers as Interpreters of Word and World

As we have indicated, there are not simply *two* horizons involved when a preacher turns to a biblical text on behalf of a congregation. While we might at first assume that the horizons of preacher and text are the only ones involved, we soon see that is too simple a map of the process. A third horizon, which we'll deal with in the next chapter, is that of past interpretations of the text. Preachers consult with other interpreters of the biblical passage at hand, past and present, to discover how they have understood it from their perspective in history and human experience.

Yet, as we've been indicating, there is a fourth horizon—and a fairly complex one: the horizon of the *congregation's* history, experiences, and beliefs about God and the Bible, and even working assumptions they make about the biblical text at hand. Needless to say, this horizon is more plural than singular, since congregations are never singular and monolithic in their points of view about much of anything.

Congregations trust us, their preachers, to wrestle with biblical texts on their behalf. If preachers are going to live up to this trust, we need to know the people in the pews well enough so we can take sermon listeners' hungers and hopes, fears and doubts along with us into the study. What is life like for the childless couple who sits in the fourth pew back on the left? What about the newcomers from Nepal, still struggling with English: what are their beliefs about God? Their hopes for their children? What are their hidden sorrows? What about the two elderly women who come every week and always sit together, third row from the back, near the loudspeaker? What might be their nagging doubts about Christian faith? What brings them joy? Am I preaching to a congregation at peace, or are there conflicts, either open ones or the kind that simmer just beneath the surface of polite coffee-hour conversation?

We need to answer these questions if we're going to live up to our responsibility to these folks. Much is at stake. A preacher seeks nothing less than a Spirit-driven, life-giving word that will give his or her listeners a vision of the world as a place where Christ is alive and God, through the Spirit, is redemptively at work. We need to exegete not only biblical text, but "exegete" the congregation for whom we pray, study, and preach.

Interpreting Your Congregation and Its Cultural Context(s)

Developing a working understanding of your congregation takes time. It won't happen in the first month of your ministry in a particular place; it may only begin to take shape by the end of your first year. Congregational exegesis is an ongoing project. It is more a habit of attentiveness than a single research task. It requires scrutinizing congregational life from different angles and at different levels.

The remainder of this chapter is devoted to sketching out ways to develop a working understanding of the folks for whom you preach. We suggest organizing this exploration in terms of three different views of congregational life: (1) the Close-Up View (a fine-grained portrait of the congregation); (2) the Wide-Angle View (the way multiple cultural contexts, or cultural "formations," shape the congregation's life); and (3) the Hidden View (discerning the way power dynamics work in congregational life).

Since staying in touch with the realities of a congregation is an ongoing task, you will probably be shifting among these views; but they provide a structure for organizing the information you gather. You may decide you need to record some of what you learn, but if so, proceed with caution: such information needs to be kept in a password-protected electronic file. Some of what you learn will be strictly confidential. If it *must* be recorded, it needs to be protected from anyone, including church staff, accidently stumbling over it. Not to do so is unprofessional and potentially damaging—both to pastor and congregation.

With that caution in place, we invite you into a journey of discovery that is likely to be both fascinating and humbling.

Congregational Exegesis for Preaching

I. The Close-Up View:
Understanding a Congregation through Its Symbols and Stories

In 1997, homiletician Leonora Tisdale handed preachers an immense gift with the publication of her first book, *Preaching as Local Theology and Folk Art.*[9] Tisdale uses the instrument of semiotic theory to help preachers better understand their congregations. Semiotics is the study of how cultures use signs, including words, pictures, symbols, gestures, and the geography of space, to express their understanding of themselves in relation to their world. Tisdale also encourages

---

9. Leonora Tubbs Tisdale, *Preaching as Local Theology and Folk Art*, Fortress Resources for Preaching (Minneapolis: Fortress Press, 1997). This section draws generously on Tisdale's guidance, especially pp. 56–90.

accessing a second ethnographic (culture-interpreting) tool, narrative.

Tisdale proposes that by paying attention to these types of signs and the way they function in congregational life, we will have a better understanding of a congregation's view of God and the world, themselves, and those who are "other" from themselves—culturally, ethnically, theologically, and so on.

Symbols and Spaces

Congregations' views of the world and themselves come to expression in many ways. Paying attention to *symbols* around the church building and on printed materials or website displays can reveal much about a congregation's self-understanding and how it sees itself. For instance, the symbols and catchphrases on publicity pieces reveal how a congregation would like to be seen in the public eye. Is there a church logo? What symbols and catchwords does it incorporate? Asking congregation members about the design of the logo can be revealing. If the logos and posters of other community organizations are also on display, this could indicate something of the congregation's sense of responsibility to partner with existing forms of local social outreach.

Architecture, too, reveals something of the character of a congregation. Worship spaces have a story to tell. A worship space may be highly traditional (arched windows with stained glass, and fixed pews in the sanctuary) but show evidence of efforts to adapt it for different types of worship than that for which it was originally designed. A projection screen may cover a carved wooden panel, and wiring may snake along the windowsills. The presence of both a traditional sanctuary as well as another space adapted to accommodate a praise band and video screens may indicate a backstory of either conflict or compromise in terms of worship style. If a traditional sanctuary has recently been renovated, yet its style preserved, that says volumes about the congregation's sense of connection to its past, as well as the way it envisions itself within current debates about worship style. New buildings also say much about the congregation's understanding of its worship and mission. A building in which the architectural markers of Christian worship space (cross, font, table, ambo [reading lectern], and pulpit) are designed to be completely portable and even removable signals a congregation's sense that its space should be easily adapted to multiple uses for the sake of its own members and useful, as well, to its surrounding community. A space without any distinctly recognizable pulpit, yet fitted with a sophisticated projection and amplification system capable of handling multichannel, high-volume sound has translated its worship sensibility and sense of mission into architectural commitments. The condition of a church's space tells a story as well. On the one hand, well-maintained spaces may be a story of sustained prosperity. On the other hand, cracking plaster and crumbling ceilings may point to a grander, more prosperous past. It is worthwhile exploring what current members know of the church's past, and how they feel about it.

Has there been deliberate effort to make the church newcomer-friendly? Check for signs that explicitly welcome newcomers and point them to key spots—the sanctuary, church offices, and nursery. Are the entrances easy to recognize and the interior easy to navigate, or is the church space like a labyrinth so that only "insiders" would know how to get from place to place? Do the church's structures issue a "Come-on-in-you're-welcome-here" invitation, or a "Keep-out-members-only-please" message?

Social Geography

Observing how worshipers use and move about in the church's worship space and other gathering spots can be revealing. How do people distribute themselves in the spaces of worship? (There may be more than one.) Do they tend to sit in the same places, with the same people? Is there a spot in the sanctuary where teenagers generally congregate—or aren't they present in worship? Are children in worship? If they are, do they and their families seem to feel comfortable there, or are adults overly anxious about children's behavior? How do others in the congregation respond to the children?

Pay special attention to worshipers who represent minorities. Do they move easily and comfortably among other members? If a congregation is multicultural, do the various cultures simply co-exist, or do they interact around common tasks or common interests?

Check to see what accessibility adaptations have been made to accommodate wheelchairs and walkers. Do you see evidence of efforts to offer close, oversized parking spaces for persons with mobility issues? If there are hearing-assist accommodations, are they easy to find, easy to use, and functional? Are large-print or Braille versions of worship materials available for those with vision issues?

Take a good look at the appearance of worship from the point of view of the pew. What symbols are points of focus? Is there a direct line of sight with worship leaders in most parts of the room? Whose faces do worshipers see? Do they see both women and men leading from the front about equally, or is one gender disproportionately represented in leadership? What about older adults and youth members?

Many factors influence worshipers' level of participation in worship—but this, too, is worthy of observation. Some worshipers feel uncomfortable singing, or are simply self-conscious if their voices rise above others in prayers and litanies. But if a majority of the congregation seems more like passive observers than active participants in worship, it is worth following up to see what might lie behind this phenomenon.

Notice, as well, how the rest of the building is used. If there is a coffee hour, who attends? Are visitors identified and welcomed? Who provides hospitality? Are the same volunteers tapped week after week, or is hospitality shared among different church fellowship groups, committees, and boards on a rotating basis?

Interviews and Stories

Among the most valuable materials a preacher can access to understand his or her congregation are the *stories* that church members—and sometimes, ex-church members—are willing to share. Tisdale provides excellent *interview* questions for drawing out people's present and past experiences, as well as concerns, hopes, and dreams for themselves or the congregation.[10] Asking people questions like, "What do you see as the strengths of this congregation?" can shine light on what congregation members are proud of and hope others will recognize about their church. On the other hand, a question like, "Have there been situations or incidents for you here that were painful or difficult?" can surface important stories, too. Interviewees need to know for certain that what they share is going to be kept in confidence.[11]

Inviting longtime members of a church to tell *stories of their past* can reveal important information, because they know history that

---

10. Ibid., 65–69.
11. An exception is any report that suggests sexual abuse of any kind; and in this case only designated authorities should receive information. Pastors need to know their state's law about who is obligated to report even suspicion of abuse to authorities.

others don't. At the same time, pastors should also take into account what young parents and youth members of a congregation have to say. They often experience the church differently from old-timers. Likewise, it is useful to talk with *newcomers*. What are their first impressions? After a few weeks or months, ask them in what ways they feel embraced, and whether, in some ways, they still feel like outsiders. Another group to consider interviewing is persons who have left the church. While it can be harder to make contact with them, their stories are important clues to areas of weakness or rigidity in congregational life.

Archival materials—such things as the minutes of church boards and congregational meetings, as well as old service leaflets—can help a preacher understand where a congregation has come from, and what it has valued along the way. These materials reveal much about the congregation's internal fellowship life in the past. Announcements in church bulletins say something about the congregation's history of outreach, or lack of outreach, to its surrounding community.

Nearly every congregation has *stories of trouble* whose reverberations can affect them for decades. The story of a pastor who is seen as having "used" the church for his or her own professional advancement, but did not seem to care for the congregation, reveals a past of hurt and suspicion. Stories of real or even suspected misconduct, financial or sexual, reflect particularly serious and lasting wounds in a congregation, as do stories of broken pastoral confidentiality (parishioners' personal lives being talked about with others in the congregation).

On the other hand, most congregations also have beloved heroes and heroines—both pastors and lay leaders. Listen to these stories with a discerning ear. On the one hand, celebrating key leaders of the past can be a straightforward expression of gratitude and pride in a congregation. On the other hand, nostalgia for leaders of the past can indicate a disconnect from the congregation's current leadership, ethos, and mission.

Stories tell us not only about past events, but indicate how different church members see themselves. Some see themselves close to the church's center, others nearer the margins. Some see themselves as empowered in the church, but disempowered beyond it. For others, the reverse is true. Some speak of God in intimate and personal terms. For others, God is more mysterious and distant. The differences need to be recognized and honored.[12]

II. The Wide View:
Cultural Dynamics That Affect a Congregation's Life

Most Christian congregations do not exist in a bubble of cultural and religious uniformity or isolation. Congregations are living social realities that represent the intersection of multiple cultural "formations." A cultural formation is a group defined by a set of shared self-understandings, shared goals, and shared views of the world and connected by patterns of interaction. In some worshiping congregations, the membership strongly overlaps with a single, distinctive cultural formation. There are numerous Korean American congregations in the United States, for example, that are culturally and ethnically distinctive. More typically, congregations are made up of people whose identities are shaped by diverse cultural formations.

In their book, *Preaching to Every Pew: Cross-Cultural Strategies*, scholars James R. Niemann and Thomas G. Rogers enlarge a preacher's understanding of the way strong, key cultural formations affect congregations' lives.[13] Niemann and Rogers identify four major

---

12. "Appreciative inquiry" is another interviewing practice that can help uncover this sort of information in a congregational setting, particularly when strategic change is in view. Many books on appreciative inquiry are available, including some focused particularly on congregational application, including Mark Lau Branson, *Memories, Hopes, and Conversations: Appreciative Inquiry and Congregational Change* (Herndon, VA: Alban Institute, 2004).

cultural "frames" that can act as lenses to help us focus on some of the strongest vectors of diversity that crisscross a congregation: ethnicity, class, displacement, and belief. (Members of my introductory preaching classes are convinced that *gender-role assumptions* need to be included as a fifth cultural frame.)

Discussing their first cultural frame, Niemann and Rogers argue that the term *ethnicity* offers a more useful and more accurate way to speak of distinct cultural heritages than the term *race*. Ethnicity refers to a shared self-understanding that derives from a commonly held history, community commitments, and intuitively recognized ways of doing things at the basic level of family life: food, marriage customs, child-rearing, and the like. Race or racism, on the other hand, refers to social dynamics of sometimes brutal social marginalization that *relate* to, but are not the *same as* ethnicity.[14] While talk of race or the presence of racist dynamics may correlate with ethnic differences, race as such is not the most apt way to frame discussion of cultural distinctiveness. Ethnicity can be a primary, identity-forming frame for a congregation—one with which newcomers from outside that ethnic heritage must reckon in their effort to find their place in the community. Whether new ethnic minorities are seen as a threat or a gift to the congregation makes a tremendous difference in the success or failure of achieving stable multiculturalism in a church.

Class differences constitute a far more significant grid of division within a congregation than many pastors recognize or would like to admit. The Christian vision of God's new creation calls for a worshiping community of equality and unity. Yet, when we try

13. James R. Niemann and Thomas G. Rogers, *Preaching to Every Pew: Cross-Cultural Strategies* (Minneapolis: Fortress Press, 2001). The authors devote space to "preaching expectations" and "preaching strategies" in relation to four cultural frames: ethnicity, class, displacement, and beliefs.
14. Ibid., 23–27.

to understand congregational dynamics, we can neither deny nor overlook that a combination of factors, including heritage, socialization patterns, vocation, education, neighborhood, and earning power, assign individuals and families to distinct classes that do not socialize comfortably together.

Displacement refers to a sense that some members of a congregation encounter, that wherever they are currently does not "feel like home." The experiences that produce this sense are many, and the impact of displacement on congregations is increasing. Immigration from another country and/or continent is a significant form of displacement, but there are many others, such as loss of mobility through aging, widowhood, marital separation, or divorce. College students far from home and military personnel returned from combat experience displacement. Even persons in recovery from addiction to alcohol or drugs report profound feelings of displacement as they have lost a social context in which they felt significant and understood.

Displacement is not only a cultural frame for reading congregations; it may actually be the reality or experience of the preacher. Where the preacher is "located" internally and externally and who the preacher is shapes how he or she reads. If the preacher is in a "strange land," he or she may wonder, 'How, or what, can I preach (sing) in this strange land?' When the preacher is not "home," this will impact whether there is a hermeneutics of trust or a hermeneutics of suspicion. The strangeness of a people or setting can cause preachers to be cautious, even suspicious, depending on their past experiences. Displacement can be disturbing and disruptive, but perhaps over time with greater familiarity, trust will develop and a more generous reading can occur. Again, what is seen when reading the congregation also says something about the reader-preacher.
– LP

Finally, the frame of *diverse belief* is a dynamic in every congregation. Yet differences do not necessarily have to be divisive. Some congregations prove to be remarkably hospitable to a wide range of core beliefs, both religious and political, while other congregations are brittle and combustible around such differing convictions. Perhaps differences in congregants' view of gender roles, a cultural frame that young professional adults find significant, can be understood within the category of belief. Yet, beliefs about gender roles interact significantly with the other four cultural frames that Niemann and Rogers discuss and may deserve to be considered a distinct cultural frame for congregational exegesis—or even a significant influence in the congregation's power dynamic, a topic to which we turn next.

III. The Hidden View: Power Dynamics in a Congregation

What people believe about appropriate gender roles in church and society points to a factor in congregational life that is pervasive, but receives relatively little explicit attention: power dynamics.[15] Homiletician Adam W. Hearlson argues that it is essential to pay attention to power dynamics in our exegesis of congregations.[16]

Preachers need to note who exerts control over decision-making processes and who is marginalized. This is just as, if not more, important in informal decision-making processes as in formal ones. Tracking the flow of power in a congregation is crucial to wise pastoral leadership, although it takes patience and experience.

To take a fairly simple example, let's say that a pastor's research turns up the same family names over and over, across years of time, in a church's archival materials, in dedicatory plaques on the church

---

15. Power dynamics are but one of several "hidden" factors in congregational life, according to Israel Galindo; however, since the event of preaching interacts with a congregation's existing power structures, both directly and indirectly, it is especially important for preachers to attend to them. See Galindo, *The Hidden Lives of Congregations: Discerning Church Dynamics* (Herndon, VA: Alban Institute, 2004).

16. Adam W. Hearlson, "Preaching as Sabotage: Power, Practice and Proclamation," unpub. PhD diss., Princeton Theological Seminary, 2013. Hearlson offers tools for querying power dynamics in a congregation, as well as homiletical models for addressing this dimension of congregational life.

walls, and in the stories members tell. This evidence could point in one of two directions. On one hand, this could be (and often is) an indication of particularly significant and generous personal legacies in the congregation. On the other hand, this pattern in a small church can be a sign that either the congregation has been overly dependent on a handful of overworked volunteers, or a handful of families has exercised a kind of hegemonic control over congregational life.

Hegemonic systems of power discourage, or even actively suppress, agency on the part of organization members who don't belong to whatever counts as the "ruling class." Newcomers might be attracted to church initially. But soon they discover that, no matter how gifted or willing to be involved they may be, their initiatives are suppressed or sabotaged. Discouraged and disempowered, they drift away. Hegemony by definition acts to protect its marginal control over a social space, whatever the cost to the organization.

Uses and abuses of power are recurring themes in Scripture. There are plenty of preaching opportunities to deal with these realities, but such preaching requires a blend of courage and tact. Congregations need to hear sermons that expose the ways we have of sabotaging one another or shutting one another out of decision making. One can preach about power without "naming names." An apt portrait of a power-abusing biblical character can be sketched in such a way that he or she looks like one of us. A biblical story can function as a mirror for congregational leadership to recognize its own anxieties and imbalances.

It goes without saying that preachers need to counterbalance critique with sermons that present positive uses of power. Power that is distributed and shared empowers, and an empowered congregation is more likely to be creative and effective, both in its worship and its public witness.

At the same time, if we preachers are serious about critically examining power dynamics in congregational life, we have to include ourselves. We need to attend to our own uses *and potential abuses* of the power of our pastoral and preaching roles.

* * *

In the next chapter, we'll discuss the process of interpreting biblical texts for preaching; but before moving on to that task, we can summarize this chapter's main points.

First, human beings are nonstop interpreters. Whether we're driving down the highway, debating national immigration policy with a friend, or studying a biblical text on the way to the pulpit, we interpret. Interpreting a biblical text for preaching is simply a more deliberate and conscious instance of interpretation.

Second, preachers need to do all they can to understand the people on whose behalf they interpret Scripture and preach. We do not presume to be "masters" of theology or divinity, despite the title of some of the degrees we may earn.[17] We are servants of God for the sake of others' faith. We do our best to understand our listeners as individuals and as congregations.

Recognizing that we are always and inevitably interpreters can be both exhilarating and disturbing. The fact that we can never get *outside* the realm of interpretation as human beings suggests that we can never understand anything perfectly—neither the people we serve nor the biblical texts that form the basis of our sermons. In some theological circles, the claim is made that God so illuminates preachers' minds that they *do* in fact have access to "perfect" understanding of the meaning of biblical texts, the nature of God and redemption, and so on.

---

17. Two of the degrees offered at many graduate schools of theology—seminaries and university divinity schools—are called "Master of Theology" and "Master of Divinity."

The stance taken here is somewhat different—and, we believe, faithful. What if God does not choose to *circumvent* (bypass) our interpretive nature, but *uses* it to lead us to understanding that is sufficient to ground our faith and hope and that of our congregations? We believe Scripture itself suggests this is the case. For centuries, the church has relied on the theological writings of the apostle Paul, yet consider what he says: "Now we see in a mirror, dimly, but then we shall see face to face. Now I know only in part; then I will know fully, even as I have been fully known" (1 Cor. 13:12). Despite the partiality of his understanding, God commissioned Paul to preach—and commissions us on the same terms. We can trust the One who knows us fully; and that is enough.

Further Learning Strategies

1. On your phone or in a notebook, keep a diary for twelve hours of the interpretive events you engage in through the day—navigating a highway, a conversation with someone you don't know well, looking something up on the Internet, deciding whether a phone message requires a response, and so on. Reflecting on these, where did you see past experience or your assumptions about what can usually be expected play a role in making sense of a new experience?

2. Over a one-month period, intentionally observe a congregation you know well, keeping notes under the headings suggested in this chapter (Close-up View, Wide-Angle View, Hidden View). *Protecting confidentialities,* which of your presuppositions about the nature of the congregation were reinforced by your observations? Which were challenged?

3. Of the four cultural "frames" that Niemann and Rogers offer as lenses for illuminating a congregation's cultural dynamics,

which of them do you think affects most profoundly the congregation you studied in exercise #2 above? How do you see this playing out?

4. Turn to a biblical text with which you are somewhat familiar (for example, the call of Moses in Exodus 3, or the parable of the compassionate Samaritan in Luke 10). Engage in an exploratory dialogue with the text, raising questions first from the point of view of a member of the congregation's governing board, then from the point of view of a ten-year-old whose school has witnessed several incidents of bullying. What different aspects of the biblical story come to light when explored from the perspective of these different life situations?

Further Reading

Branson, Mark Lau. *Memories, Hopes, and Conversations: Appreciative Inquiry and Congregational Change.* Herndon, VA: Alban Institute, 2004. Among many available titles on practicing appreciative inquiry in congregations, this book gives special attention to churches where ethnic differences are present.

Galindo, Israel. *The Hidden Lives of Congregations: Discerning Congregational Dynamics.* Herndon, VA: Alban Institute, 2004. Galindo provides tools for leaders to analyze the dynamics of congregational lifespan, size, spirituality, and identity, so that congregations may fulfill their vision.

Niemann, James R., and Thomas G. Rogers. *Preaching to Every Pew: Cross-Cultural Strategies.* Minneapolis: Fortress Press, 2001. The authors discuss four "frames" of cultural formation that overlap with, and profoundly affect, congregational life.

Palmer, Richard E. *Hermeneutics: Interpretation Theory in Schleiermacher, Dilthey, Heidegger, and Gadamer.* Evanston, IL:

Northwestern University Press, 1969. A basic introduction to major European figures in the development of hermeneutical theory.

Thiselton, Anthony C. *Hermeneutics: An Introduction.* Grand Rapids: Eerdmans, 2009. A broad, historical introduction to hermeneutics with special attention to the impact of social theory and philosophical hermeneutics on approaches to biblical interpretation.

Tisdale, Leonora Tubbs. *Preaching as Local Theology and Folk Art.* Fortress Resources for Preaching. Minneapolis: Fortress Press, 1997. A basic introduction to congregational "exegesis" and the way it can shape sermons that more directly address a congregation's specific understandings, challenges, and opportunities.

6

Interpreting Scripture for Preaching

Sally A. Brown

Scripture has been the indispensable, authorizing source of Christian sermons since Christianity's beginnings. The sermons of Peter, Stephen, and Paul in Acts all draw on Old Testament texts. The book of Hebrews, thought by some to be a collection of early Christian sermons, draws on material across the Old Testament, especially the Psalms. This chapter provides you with a disciplined, prayerful, and scholarly process for engaging Scripture. Exegetical work (close grammatical, historical, and theological study of a text) is supported in this method by meditative Scripture reading using the centuries-old process called *lectio divina* ("divine reading").

The living word of God for our time and place reaches us, we believe, through informed, disciplined study of Scripture. There are easier paths to the pulpit, and some choose them. Come up with a catchy topic, throw in a couple of video clips, pick up a handful of Scripture quotes, and you can get into the pulpit and back out again with minimal stress. You may manage to be engaging, even amusing, for twenty or thirty minutes, but congregations expect more—and they should.

First, preachers who take such a path do not practice exegesis, in which one's thought is guided and stretched by Scripture. Rather, they practice *eisegesis* (sometimes called "prooftexting"), which means wrenching a phrase or two of Scripture out of context to "authorize" one's predetermined sermon idea. Second, fresh news of God's redemptive work in our time and place comes when preachers *wrestle* with Scripture on behalf of their congregations. The biblical witness to God's redemptive acts in the past, as well as its vision of the future God is bringing about, comes to us through ancient languages and cultures. Historical and cultural distance separates us from the Old Testament world of ritual sacrifice, the lives of tenant farmers in ancient Palestine, and the unsettling apocalyptic imagery of Revelation. Only ongoing study, coupled with congregational empathy and Spirit-enlightened imagination, produces a living testimony to God's redemptive work in our time and place.

Fortunately, preachers have company on the path that leads from study and pulpit. Many others have explored this biblical territory before us. Their trail notes are recorded in Bible dictionaries and commentaries, journal articles, and sermons from the past. Further, as we have argued from the outset of this book, the life of the church in the world, as well as its preaching, are Spirit-animated events. The Spirit, at work in the world around us, brings a living and present word to our listeners through our deep engagement with Scripture. Meditation and study in preparation for preaching is by no means a "substitute" for the inspiration of the Spirit; these are Spirit-infused practices from beginning to end.

In this chapter we offer you a process that unfolds in three stages: (1) *prayerful meditation on the preaching text* through the ancient practice of *lectio divina*, adapted for preachers; (2) *a four-phase exegetical method* that draws on the wisdom of scholarship, past and present, and includes the congregation as a vital conversation partner; and (3) a series of steps to *narrow down the core affirmation* that will anchor your sermon. Many will be familiar with the second stage from their Old and New Testament studies. But why the first and third stages?

The first stage is an invitation to allow the text to engage us personally, setting aside for now concerns about what we will ultimately preach. Preachers report that the first thing to suffer once they take up professional ministry is their own devotional engagement with Scripture. This does not need to be the case. We can make meditative reading part of our ongoing practice of scriptural study. We are more likely to address others effectively when we've been addressed ourselves.

The third stage of interpretation, identifying the sermon's core affirmation, is a discipline that pays immeasurable dividends. Nearly all teachers of preaching are persuaded that coherent, engaging sermons are anchored in a single, declarative sentence, one that shifts our understanding of God, ourselves, and the world in which we live.[1] In this book we refer to this as the core affirmation of the sermon. It is not a question ("Are we *really* ready to follow Jesus?"), nor is it a list of propositions coupled with application statements. These may occur in some sermons, but the sermon's core affirmation

---

1. Samuel D. Proctor, a leading figure in African American homiletics, writes of the core sentence of a sermon, "What should the word [of God] be for them on this day, in this place? [It] comes as a one-sentence statement that embraces a salient truth for that audience at that time. It will have a resonance, a ring, a vibration that assures the preacher that it has the warrant to be preached." Proctor, *The Certain Sound of the Trumpet: Crafting a Sermon of Authority* (Valley Forge, PA: Judson, 1994), 25–26. Proctor is but one of dozens of homileticians who insist on a one-sentence, anchoring statement for every sermon.

is a sentence that combines two things: (1) a clear announcement of something God has done, is doing, or will do; and (2) a here-and-now consequence of God's action for our world. Combined, these statements help listeners see their world differently, envisioning ways to engage it with creative faithfulness. Crafting a core affirmation as the basis for every sermon is liberating, not limiting. It will not stifle imagination, either for you or your hearers; it will energize you.

Think of the process we offer you here as a navigational chart, not a roadmap. While a roadmap assumes a static geography, a navigational chart takes into account dynamic elements like tides, currents, and winds. Like sailors, preachers inhabit a dynamic human environment. They find their way through biblical texts, gauging the effect of cultural currents and the rise and ebb of current events. They sense the winds of God's Spirit disturbing the old order of things and ushering in signs of God's new creation in the risen Christ.

Choosing the Preaching Text

The first interpretive step a preacher takes is to choose the Scripture text that will ground the sermon. To get a sense of the many ways this can be done, let's step into the fellowship hall of Resurrection Baptist Church where about a dozen pastors of all ages, ethnicities, and denominations are just sitting down for their monthly preachers' discussion group. The moderator for the week, a slight, energetic woman with an Asian accent, breaks into the buzz of greetings and conversation to get things started.

"Fellow preachers, last month we decided to talk this time about how we choose our preaching texts. Who'd like to begin?"

A woman in a clerical collar smiles broadly. "I don't have to choose a text; it chooses me. Nearly all Episcopalians use the Revised Common Lectionary. Trouble is, in my parish they expect you to touch on all the texts—Old Testament, Gospel, Psalm, and second

New Testament reading—and all in twelve minutes and seventeen seconds or less. But I like preaching narrative material, so I'd have to say the Gospel gets most of my attention, with the Old Testament a distant second. Those Old Testament stories can be long and strange!"

Around the room, some Lutheran, Presbyterian, Methodist, Reformed, and Disciples pastors chime in that they, too, like to follow the lectionary. But most typically choose just one of the suggested texts, and some stress that they don't follow it all the time.

"You don't always follow it?" asks a newcomer, fresh out of seminary. "How do you decide?"

A thirty-something pastor in black jeans and t-shirt speaks up: "I've got a lot of seekers in my congregation. They don't know the Bible, really. So if I see that the lectionary is going to stay in a single book for a while, I follow it. Sometimes it's one of the big Genesis narratives, or the story of the exodus out of Egypt, or one of the Gospels. But sometimes I choose a book that the lectionary only touches on; then I leave the lectionary aside for a while. Last year I preached through Galatians and Philippians, but each week had a theme. I based each sermon on one major theological question people are asking these days."

A preacher from a lively Hispanic church downtown looks puzzled. "Why a lectionary at all? Doesn't it just repeat over and over and get boring?"

The Episcopal priest speaks up again. "Not really. Over three years, the lectionary gets you all over the Bible. And the realities of your listeners' world are always changing, and that shapes how you see the text. But I'll admit there are big sections of the Old Testament that the lectionary bypasses."

A couple of pastors who head large independent churches have been quiet so far. One of them, an amused smile playing across his face, finally speaks up: "Well, thank God I don't have to worry about any of that. Here's what I do: I think and pray with my congregation in mind. I boil it down to one question I sense coming up from the pews. Then I find a biblical text I think answers it. Eventually I guess we touch on most books of the Bible." A couple of others murmur agreement. Someone points out that this approach keeps things relevant.

At this, a woman across the circle shakes her head vigorously, hooped earrings catching the light. "Congregational questions, biblical answers? I'm not so sure. Does Scripture really answer contemporary questions that directly? Sure, I think about the needs of my congregation, but what I'm looking for isn't an 'answer' but a text I feel helps us *think* our way toward answers that biblical writers themselves couldn't have foreseen and weren't meant to."

A quiet gentleman with a lilting Indian accent picks up the conversation next. "My practice over many, many years, in India and now here, has been simply to preach *lectio continua*."

"*Lecta*—what?" says the black-jeans preacher. "Translate, brother."

"That means I preach very slowly straight through a book. It is an old practice. The great reformer and theologian John Calvin did it year after year. Last year it took me seven months to preach all the way through Revelation. But sometimes, I must interrupt my *lectio continua* approach to address a current event—public unrest, or a natural disaster here or in India that affects my people. At those times I often choose a psalm of lament. It is a time not to explain, but to offer a language for dismay and sadness."

Clearly, there are many ways to choose a preaching text. All have strengths and weaknesses. Using the Revised Common Lectionary spans the canon, and there is a rich array of worship planning material online and in print that coordinates with it. Another week-to-week resource is the African American Lectionary. Its well-maintained website coordinates Scripture texts, exegetical materials, and sermon links related to commemorative dates and cultural celebrations with special attention to African American history and traditions.[2]

> The lectionary can be useful in that it helps preachers to spread across various texts of Scripture in a three-year cycle. As a communal process in its development, it follows a long tradition within the church of faithful people coming together to decide matters of import for the church. At the same, we should recognize that the lectionary itself is not Scripture. It is not the Bible, the Holy Book. That being said, the lectionary at times can miss the "whole picture." Its pericopes can leave out valuable information from the larger literary context and, by doing so, cut out key parts of stories, thus preachers and congregations may not get the sense of the whole. This is why preachers should be sure to read the whole narrative in order to gain a wider perspective. Moreover, what is excluded many times from a lectionary passage can be more insightful to a preacher than what is included. The non-lectionary portion of a story may be the key to aiding preachers to proclaim the gospel. – **LP**

The practice of choosing a theme or a current event and then seeking a text that speaks to it makes sense on occasion, as several of the pastors we met indicated. It is important, though, to access a broad range of texts that shed light on issues or situations instead of hunting for a line in Scripture that backs up the preacher's preset ideas. A weakness of using "preacher's choice" routinely is that preachers can end up preaching a "canon-within-the-canon." The term *canon*, of course, refers to the sixty-six books that, by about the fifth century, were deemed Christian Scripture. If we keep returning to only a few favorite books or themes, we can, in effect, hand our congregation something considerably less than the full biblical witness. We need to let the Scriptures stretch our interests, instead of letting our interests narrow the Scriptures.

Your method of text selection is itself an act of discerning interpretation. With your text chosen, you are ready to begin the work of meditative engagement and disciplined study.

2. See http://www.theafricanamericanlectionary.org.

Stage One: *Lectio Divina* for Preaching (Six Steps)

The *lectio divina* process presented here is an adaptation of the ancient discipline known by this name. We suggest six steps. Four of these—steps 2 through 5—are widely shared in different *lectio* patterns (*lectio, meditatio, oratio, contemplatio*). Steps 1 and 6 (*silencio* and *compassio*) are designed specifically for preachers.[3] We begin *lectio divina* with *silencio*, a process for transitioning away from other pastoral concerns and focusing the mind through centering prayer and silence. We end with *compassio*, moving out of the process of contemplative listening and into the more analytical aspects of exegesis.

Choose a quiet place for *lectio divina*. You will need a Bible and a blank sheet of paper or a personal journal, handwritten or electronic. Some choose to light a single candle as a visual reminder of the presence of the Holy Spirit.

This is such an important idea—inspiration of the Holy Spirit doesn't just begin when the preacher steps into a pulpit. Inspiration should prayerfully be accompanying the preacher along the entire process of preparation through delivery. If one thinks the Spirit only works in the pulpit, this divides up the Spirit's presence when it cannot be done. The fire and wind of God should be burning and blowing before a preacher reaches the pulpit. The whole sermon preparation process should be Spirit-infused and preachers should have this expectation of the Presence. Thus, a prayerful approach is necessary that one might receive a word even while he or she prepares to give a word; before we address a congregation, hopefully we are addressed. Reception mode requires a listening heart. Speech ceases and silence begins to open a door to God amid turbulent sounds. This vocation of speech is also a vocation of silence and as one listens one may be drawn to make unexpected associations with things in daily life, even when the sermon itself may be the farthest thing in one's mind—in the shower, at the store, in the middle of the night while you are asleep. A listening posture is a receiving stance and you never know when the still, small voice of God will be heard. – **LP**

---

3. For these steps, I am indebted to Clay Oglesbee, "From Praying to Proclaiming: the *Lectio Divina* in Sermon Formation," *Preaching* (November–December 1989): 16–19.

1. *Silencio*: Entering through the doorway of silence. Silence electronic devices. Alert family members or church staff that you can't be interrupted for a half hour. With long, slow breaths, *breathe out* tightness in muscles, preoccupying worries and plans, unsettledness in relationships, and thoughts of other obligations, no matter how pressing. Some use visualization to divest themselves of concerns for this meditative time. Visualize a nagging resentment as a sharp stick. See yourself relinquishing it to Christ's outstretched hand. That intractable conflict in the congregation, visualized as a tangled ball of muddy string, gets handed over, too. *Breathe in* the grounding presence and power of the Holy Spirit.

2. *Lectio*: Slow, thoughtful reading aloud. This is the step from which the whole process takes its name. Read the text aloud, slowly, as if hearing it for the first time. Pause, letting the sound of the text resonate in your ears, the texture of the text tug at your tongue, the cadence of the text move your body. Then repeat. Listen for the timbre of the voice. Repeat some phrases, places the stress first on one word, then another. Notice words and phrases that capture your attention. Feel the disturbance the text stirs or the comfort it delivers. Read slowly, with deep pauses, a third time. You may wish to record in a journal phrases that stood out or stirred you in some way.

3. *Meditatio*: Dwelling with key images and phrases. Notice a word, phrase, or image that lingers in your mind and dwell with it. Don't analyze it. There will be time for that in the exegetical phase of your work. For now, let it be. Let your imagination "play" with the human encounters, images, and actions in the text that capture your attention. Jot down a word or phrase in your journal to remind you of your impressions and visual images. Let yourself experience what the text is *doing*, and not

only what it is *saying*.[4] Texts question and teach, convict and console, reflect on the past or point to the future. Does the text draw your attention to a focal point? Does it paint a picture, hold up a mirror, or tease you into the play of a metaphor?

4. *Oratio*: Prayerful presence before God. *Oratio*, at heart, is prayerful presence before God, with an open and receptive spirit. You may wish to use a centering prayer such as the "Jesus prayer," the repetition of the name of Jesus, or a simple phrase like, "Come, Holy Spirit."

5. *Contemplatio*: Attentiveness. In *contemplatio* the busy mind goes quiet. Begin with simple, focused attentiveness to God. Do not rush to leave this phase of *lectio*. It may help you simply to repeat, "Be still, and know that I am God." After a time, you may feel moved to respond to the text in some way. Free-write (writing without pause, punctuation, or editing). Sketch, paint, or work clay. Turn the text into song. Let your body move, expressing the conflict, question, or comfort of the text. Some find it helpful to "walk" with the text in the mall, the train station, or the city park. Others find that the rhythm of running while meditating releases creative thought.

6. *Compassio*: Moving outward, toward your congregation and the wider world. Here, you will begin to capture in writing and by other means (sketching, movement, song) anything that came to mind during the early steps. If you find yourself getting anxious about whether any of this "looks" like a sermon, revert to steps 4 and 5, *oratio* and *contemplatio*. It is too early to scramble toward something "preachable." Now is the time to stay open to the interplay between the world the text proposes and the here-and-now experiences of your listeners. You may wish to picture

4. Thomas G. Long, *The Witness of Preaching*, 2nd ed. (Louisville: Westminster John Knox, 2005), 87–88, 106.

particular listeners in the text's story (if it is a narrative): Where would they stand? How might they react? If it is a psalm, whose prayer would it be? If it is teaching, how would a seasoned Christian respond? A new believer?

You may wish to "free-write" trains of thought or question-and-answer dialogues between the text and your congregation. Don't edit for spelling, punctuation, or even theological correctness at this point. Imagine different listeners' reaction to something in the text that, for them, would be either very good news or very hard to hear.

Many preachers find it useful to step away from preaching preparation for a day or two after their *lectio divina* encounter with the text. Unexpected associations and insights may occur to you in the middle of the soccer game or as you witness a scene in a hospital room. Read. Watch the news. Not everything you do, nor everything you read, should be "for" the sermon or "about" the text. Pay attention to the dynamics of ordinary relationships; this is one of a preacher's best resources. Allow novels, poetry, and films to open up fresh angles on human experience.

An Exegetical Path for Preachers

Exegetical study gets us into focused conversation with potentially dozens of historical and contemporary fellow explorers of the text. Keep in mind as you work that the goal of this study is not to beat the text to a pulp with our exegetical mallets, as if by doing so we could isolate the one and only "right" meaning of the text. Texts typically yield more than one valid insight. You are not trying to master the text, but to let it speak.

Many of the steps in this exegetical process will require you to make use of biblical commentaries. While one-volume commentaries on the Old Testament, New Testament, or whole Bible can be useful, they should not be a preacher's sole resource. They are simply too sketchy in their comments on particular texts. We encourage you to acquire some commentaries of the kind in which the entire discussion is devoted to a single book of the Bible, including those designated as "preaching commentaries." Experienced preachers can recommend helpful ones.

You will want to consult critical commentaries. Recall that critical in this context is a technical term for resources that examine in detail the vocabulary, grammar, structure, genre, likely origin, and purposes of a text. They offer valuable information about the historical and literary context in which a book was written and provide insights into the meaning of the original languages behind the different English translations of the text. They may comment on the way the text has been understood and used in the past. If you are not in a position to acquire commentaries and are not within driving distance of a theological library, there are online sites that give you access to some good commentary material. You can find early Christian commentaries available completely online as well as many journal articles.

Also consider lectionary-based resources, both in print and online, that provide commentary on each of the lectionary readings for each Sunday of the year through the three-year cycle of the Revised Common Lectionary. It is worthwhile to access these even if you do not follow the lectionary, as all of them are searchable by Scripture index. Some include theological and pastoral commentary on the text, in addition to homiletical guidance. Several are included in the resource list at the end of this chapter.

As you work through your text phrase by phrase, section by section, set aside (for now) the conclusions scholars draw about the text's ultimate meaning. Trust your own investigative work, including your personal questions and those you bring on behalf of the congregation. Toward the end of the process, you can return to commentaries and articles you found helpful and compare your own conclusions with theirs.

I. Getting to know the text as a unit and in its literary context

This step in your exegetical work acquaints you with (1) the language of the text; (2) what type of text it is (i.e., genre—story, poem, wisdom saying, prophetic oracle?); and (3) how it might be related to other material in the Bible—the chapter and book where it occurs, as well as other texts on similar topics. Your main tools will be English-language Bible dictionaries and/or original-language lexicons (if you are trained in Hebrew or Greek), Bible handbooks, commentaries, and possibly journal articles.

A. What are the building blocks of the text?

Using Bible handbooks and commentary materials, investigate the following features of the text:

1. Structure: Does the text break down naturally into distinct units (as in the Beatitudes, Matt. 5:1-12), or into a couple of distinct topics or episodes? If it is a story or a parable, who are the main characters and what is the main action? Is there a closing in which the teller of the parable (Jesus or another speaker) makes a statement that focuses the parable's meaning? Is there a parallel or chiastic (symmetrical) structure?
2. Vocabulary: Investigate any words whose meaning you're unsure about. Look up any locations referred to in the text and read what you can about them.
3. Significant grammatical features: Are there questions asked?

Comparisons made? Striking images or metaphors? Commands? Conditional phrases ("if")?

4. Genre: What kind of literature is this? Is it narrative, poetry, doctrinal teaching, or a prophetic oracle? What is its function? In other words, does this text exult, teach, tell a story, or speak of the future? If it is a psalm or is psalm-like, is it a song of praise, a prayer of thanks or lament, a recital of history, or some combination of these?

B. How does the text relate to the various layers of its literary context?

1. What comes immediately before and after? What difference does this make in how we understand the text?

2. To what larger unit in the book does this text belong, and how does that shape its function and meaning?

3. How does this text relate to the themes and/or aims of the book as a whole?

4. If it is a Gospel text, are there Gospel parallels? If so, what are the similarities and differences? How are these differences related to the differences among the Gospels as distinct literary works?

5. How is this text related to other texts within the canonical Scripture, or beyond?

II. Investigating the world that lies behind the text

A. What light does historical and cultural background information shed on this text?

1. What customs and social realities does the text assume? What cultural, religious, economic, and/or moral norms does the text seem to assume?

2. Are there events to which it seems to refer? What was going on

in the religious communities out of which this text arose, or to which it was addressed?

3. What assumptions about the nature of God or of human existence does the text indicate?

B. Origin(s) of the text and history of its reception

1. What might its likely provenance (place/time of origin) be?
2. What can you learn about its use in communities of faith since that time?

III. The text speaks into the world of my listeners

A. Recognizing the cultural and historical distance that separates the world in which my listeners live every day, and the world this text assumes:

1. What vocabulary and other features of this text will my listeners need to understand?
2. What tensions are there between the assumptions of the world of the text and my listeners' everyday world?
3. What surprises and insights in this text could we miss if we didn't know something about the text's assumed cultural context?
4. What different characters or speakers (explicit or implicit) are found in this text? What roles are implied by the text (if it is not explicitly a story)? Are there cohorts within my listening congregation that might identify with some of these roles?

B. Question the text from the point of view of different prospective sermon listeners.

In this section, ask questions of the text from multiple cultural and social perspectives represented within the congregation, or represented in the larger world where congregation members live and work. Say, for example, that you are working with the parable of the persistent widow who wearies a judge by continually demanding justice (Luke 18:1-18). Imagine how different listeners might react to this text. What about the owner of an apartment building who has gotten complaints from tenants about poor maintenance? Tenants who are the victims of a negligent property owner? A defense lawyer? A single mother whose ex-spouse refuses to pay child support? A child who has been pestering his dad lately to buy him a videogame console? What about someone who has been praying for a long time for the healing of a friend whose cancer keeps worsening? What about persons of color in the congregation who, on the basis of their and their friends' personal experience, have good reason to doubt that justice is equal for all persons in North American society?

1. What in your text would sound like good news to some in your congregation? Are there some for whom it would not seem like good news? Why?
2. What in your text would sound like bad news to some in your congregation? Are there some for whom this would not be bad news? Why?
3. Who in your congregation would feel empowered by this text? Disempowered?

C. Finally, raise questions you have about the text. Don't worry about answering all of them. Simply allow yourself to question the text so you can identify your areas of positive or negative feeling about it. Of what does it remind you, either in other parts of the Bible, or in your experience? What troubles you about it? What is exciting about it? What novels, short stories, television series, or films does it bring to mind? If you had to set it to music, what would that music sound like? If you had to choreograph it, what kind of dance would it be? Think about it in relation to this past week's news headlines, and those affected by those events. Who might find hope in this text? Who might it convict? Who might it encourage? If it is a psalm, who might pray it?

IV. Identify key theological affirmations stated or implied by the text

A. Affirmations about divine action in the text

As we have affirmed from the outset of this book, Christian preaching turns on the affirmations it makes about the redemptive ways of God in the world (which, of course, can include acts of judgment against the wrongs that destroy human lives, as well as actions of mercy and pardon). Therefore, it is crucial for the preacher to seek and name this news as she or he studies a biblical text. Sometimes, divine presence or action may be more implicit than explicit. For example, Psalm 88 is the most unrelenting and unresolved lament in the book of Psalms. Yet an affirmation about God is implied in its opening lines: the sufferer addresses this angry cry of emotional and physical pain to God. Raging at God entails the affirmation that God listens. The preacher needs to attend carefully to the dynamics of a text, both its dialogue and its action, to discern what it affirms about God's action in the remembered past, the experience of the present, or a promised future time. With this in mind, answer these questions, as able:

1. What does this text state, imply, or assume that God has done, is doing, or will do to act in redemptive love toward the world? In other words, what redemptive actions/activities of God does this text affirm, either explicitly or implicitly, directly or indirectly?

139

(Keep in mind here that judgment can also be redemptive in that it distinguishes fruitful patterns of life from unfruitful and destructive ones.)

2. What does the text state, imply, or assume about the nature or action of God the Father/Creator?

3. What does the text state, imply, or assume about Jesus? As crucified Savior? As risen Lord of God's new creation?

4. What does the text state, imply, or assume about the activity of the Holy Spirit?

B. If we take seriously the theological claims identified above, how do these shift our perspective on the world? What may be going on that we do not always clearly see? How is our everyday experience reframed?

1. If God is acting in the ways affirmed in #1 above, what is possible for us? In other words, how does God's action change how we see our situation as a community of worship and witness? What are we invited or encouraged to do?

2. What affirmations does this text appear to make about our relationship to the social, cultural, or religious "other"—persons we tend to regard as "foreign" and, in some way, "less" than ourselves?

3. What messages of judgment do I hear in this text? How might they be relevant to listeners today? What self-examination is called for, individually or corporately?

4. What messages of hope do I hear in this text? If we take this hope seriously, what might we dare to do?

C. What does this text state or imply about the nature or mission of the church?

In some Christian communities in this century and the last, there has been great emphasis on the individual in preaching. Yet, in many cases where the English text says "you," checking into the original language reveals that the addressee is the plural "you," not the individual.

Too often, biblical texts that address the plural "you" are misinterpreted and thus reduced to matters of personal morality. When sin becomes strictly a matter of personal confession, and grace and sanctification are limited to the mechanics of soul-salvation, the social and political implications of faith are obscured. In both testaments, sin and righteousness are matters of social practice and social policy. Both testaments emphasize corporate responsibility for the care of the neighbor and stranger, particularly the most vulnerable among us (for example, children, refugees, and the aged).

The church is not a haphazard aggregate of saved individuals, but a new social reality turned loose in the world. The church gathers to worship in Jesus' name in order to bear public witness, through the *social* dynamics of its life, to the love and justice of God. Sermons that address the congregation as an expression of this new social reality are crucial for mature faith.

D. How do my answers to the questions in sections A through C above reinforce, stretch, or challenge my theological understanding? In what ways are these answers likely to reinforce, stretch, or challenge the theological understanding of my listeners? (Keep in mind that all listeners are not the same; your answers might have varied effects on different people.)[5]

---

5. Leonora Tubbs Tisdale suggests that sermons themselves may aim to affirm, stretch, reorder, or challenge a congregation's theological understandings. See *Preaching as Local Theology*, Fortress Resources for Preaching (Minneapolis: Fortress Press, 1997).

Choosing Your Sermon's Core Affirmation

Once you have moved through the four stages of your exegetical and interpretive work with the text itself, you are ready to move to the last stage of interpretation: discerning the core affirmation that will be the energizing center of the sermon you will eventually preach. To get there, you will need to start by discovering the possibilities and then narrow down to one.

Every text yields not just *one* core affirmation, but several valid possibilities. Experience shows us that no two preachers preaching from the same text will deliver the same sermon. As Ephesians says of the diversity of spiritual gifts (1 Cor. 4:4-11), it is "the same Spirit" that inspires different messages from the same text, each fitting to its context.

Valid, possible core affirmations will have three key features. First, as noted earlier, they will not be a question or a lists of ideas, but a declarative sentence. Second, they will affirm some divine action that is either demonstrated, implied, or assumed in the text—something God (Father-Creator, incarnate Son, or Spirit) *has* done, *is* doing, or *promises to do*. Third, they will include some statement of the difference that this divine action makes in the world of human experience. These features produce a structure something like this: "*Because God* has acted [is acting/promises to act] in the following way—[therefore]—*we are able* to do the following . . ." (The sentence finishes with a brief description of some faithful action now made possible for us in the world "opened up" by God's action.)

Imagine, for example, that your preaching text is Luke 13:10-17. Jesus heals a woman who, for eighteen years, has been bent over "by a spirit of infirmity." But there is trouble: Jesus has healed her on a Sabbath, and in the synagogue, no less. The lay leader in charge of keeping worship decent and orderly is incensed. Apparently unwilling to confront Jesus directly, he lectures the crowd on the inappropriateness of coming for healing on Sabbath days. But Jesus counters with an insightful reply that leaves the poor fellow stewing and the whole congregation on its feet, stomping and cheering (so to speak). After studying this text, you come up with these valid affirmations, each meeting the criteria outlined a moment ago:

A. Jesus opens our eyes to those whose suffering has become invisible to us, urging us to make their healing a priority.

B. Just as Jesus truly sees a woman that others have learned to ignore, addressing her spiritual, physical, and social suffering, we can recognize and address the suffering of those we have habitually overlooked.

C. When our preoccupation with policy and procedure causes us to lose sight of compassion, Jesus seeks to liberate us for worship as an experience of healing and joy, not duty. (This affirmation explores the possibility that Jesus means to liberate not only the woman, but the synagogue ruler, too—if he is willing.)

D. Jesus invites us to live with our dancing shoes on—with eyes wide open to the joy that comes with the unexpected outbreak of transforming grace.

E. Jesus seeks out those of us who are spiritually, socially, and physically bent over by forces beyond our control, liberating us for worship and witness.

F. In a synagogue where he encounters, calls, touches, and heals a bent-over woman, Jesus enacts the prophetic vision of Mary's Magnificat, where the lowly are raised up and the mighty brought low. (This last affirmation would depend on drawing together Mary's song in Luke 1 with this scene in Luke 13. This approach theologically frames Luke's observation in v. 17 that "all of [Jesus'] opponents were put to shame.")

Each of these affirmations represents a valid perspective on this text, although some may strike us as stronger and more compelling than others. For the right occasion, any one of them could become the core of a sermon based on Luke 13:10-17. Note that they are not general statements that could be based on any number of texts (phrases like "Jesus heals us" or "God wants us to worship rightly"). General statements may *seem* more useful, but actually, to the extent that they disconnect us from the specifics of a text and its story, they are weak. Good affirmation statements are anchored in the specific action and language of a text.

Consider a somewhat different example, one where the grammar of the text itself seems to resist the preacher's efforts to start with divine action. Let's imagine that we'll be preaching on Proverbs 3: "Trust in the Lord with all your heart, and do not rely on your own insight. In all your ways acknowledge [God] and [God] will make straight your paths" (vv. 5, 6, language inclusive). If we strictly follow the grammatical progression of these verses, we might end up drafting this affirmation: "If we trust God instead of relying on ourselves, God will lead us."

This sentence seems to stand the gospel-shaped grammar we've been talking about on its head. It makes divine action conditional on human action, rather than the other way around. It seems justified—except that the overwhelming testimony of Wisdom literature in general, and Proverbs in particular, is that *God is worthy of trust.* This is a good example of a case where divine action in the text is *more assumed than explicit.* An affirmation that reflects Wisdom theology, yet takes the particular text seriously, could be, "Because God is worthy of trust, we can trust godly wisdom to lead us toward wise decisions."

Exegetical work often turns up multiple, valid affirmations, as the above shows. If this is the case, why not preach several of them in a single sermon? We should not—for several reasons. First, each of these statements offers plenty of territory for preaching. They are too complex to be handled adequately as "points." Second, asking listeners to work through them quickly requires sudden shifts of perspective. We start out standing next to Jesus, then we're the woman, now we're the synagogue ruler, his blood pressure rising as the guest preacher plays havoc with synagogue worship. The result is homiletical whiplash. Third, the affirmations we don't choose this time will be right another time. They are not wasted effort.

Once you've sketched out several valid candidates for your core affirmation, your last interpretive step is to decide which will anchor your sermon—for *these* listeners, in *this* place, at *this* time. Before moving to that last step, you may want to set your work aside for a day or two—or, if time is short, at least a few hours. Let your unconscious sift your material.

Settling on Your Sermon's Core Affirmation

Imagine that your meditation and exegetical work on Luke 13 has generated the list of valid affirmations above. Which of them will become the energizing center for designing and preaching your sermon depends on several factors.

First, does the season of the church year suggest that one option is more compelling than others? Choice F above alludes to Mary's Magnificat. One could imagine an Advent sermon series in which other Gospel stories are paired with more standard Advent texts as visions of both waiting and hope.

Second, is there something about the congregation's current situation that needs to be addressed? What if your congregation is located in a midsized city that has seen its longtime, major employer pick up and move out of town? Sitting in the pews of your church are many people out of work, their mortgage payments in arrears, anxious about their future. They identify with the woman of Luke 13, bent over by forces beyond her control. They will need to experience the compassion of Jesus. Option E may best address their reality.

Options A or B might be well suited to focusing attention on social issues such as child sexual abuse. With as many as a fifth of all children under eighteen estimated to be victims of such abuse, we can assume widespread, unrecognized suffering.[6] On the other hand, it could be that you plan to preach from this text at a leadership retreat for your church's governing board. Either option C or D may fit that occasion.

Finally, which of these core affirmations energizes *you*? Which activates your imagination? Which reframes the world for you as the theater of divine redemptive action and new possibility—so much so that you can't wait to get to the pulpit to describe what you see and hear and hope for? This may be the core affirmation—and the sermon—you need to preach.

In the next chapter we take up sermon design. Our goal will be to create an experience of discovery for the listeners of the same realities our core affirmation announces. We will aim to do that in such a way that their experience of everyday life is reframed, poising them to move into the world with bold faith in the God whose gracious action precedes them.

Further Learning Strategies

1. Interview two or three preachers you trust about their text-selection process and the factors that influence their decisions.
2. Invite three or four fellow students, preachers, or congregation

---

6. See statistics provided by the National Center for Victims of Crime at https://www.victimsofcrime.org/media/reporting-on-child-sexual-abuse/child-sexual-abuse-statistics.

members to engage in a group process of *lectio divina* on a text you will be preaching in the future. At the close, instead of *compassio*, take time for everyone to share what came to them during the process. Resist pushing ahead to text analysis. Emphasize the *effect* of the text on each person present, entertaining the questions and images that occurred to them.

3. "Workshop" a sermon-in-progress with three to four others. You can all work on one text or different ones. Bring along the fruits of your exegetical study. Share resources. One at a time, lay out some valid affirmations from your text and, through group discussion, test their relevance for your preaching context. (This works especially well in busy seasons like Advent or Holy Week when preachers are often working with the same, or similar, texts.)

Further Reading

Bartlett, David L., and Barbara Brown Taylor, eds. *Feasting on the Word: Preaching the Revised Common Lectionary*. 12 vols. (Year A, Vol. 1–Year C, Vol. 4). Louisville: Westminster John Knox, 2010. This lectionary-based commentary series includes essays for each text written from exegetical, theological, pastoral, and homiletical perspectives.

Davis, Ellen F. *Wondrous Depth: Preaching the Old Testament*. Louisville: Westminster John Knox, 2004.

Florence, Anna Carter. "Put Away Your Sword!" In *What's the Matter with Preaching Today?*, edited by Mike Graves, 93–108. Louisville: Westminster John Knox, 2004. Carter Florence encourages preachers to engage texts with freedom and imagination, not strictly by means of analytical tools.

Gross, Nancy Lammers. *If You Cannot Preach Like Paul*. Grand

Rapids: Eerdmans, 2002. Guidance for a lively, dialogical approach to understanding and preaching Pauline material.

LaRue, Cleophus J. *Power in the Pulpit: How America's Most Effective Black Preachers Prepare Their Sermons.* Louisville: Westminster John Knox, 2002. Sermons of prominent African American preachers, both men and women, as well as their personal insights into the process that leads them from study to pulpit.

Wilson, Paul Scott, ed. *Abingdon Theological Companion to the Lectionary.* 3 vols. Nashville: Abingdon, 2012 (Year C), 2013 (Year A), 2014 (Year B).

The African American Lectionary (http://www.africanamerican lectionary.org). A preacher's website that highlights notable dates in the calendars of many African American churches and their communities.

The following websites provide useful information to preachers who either follow the New Revised Common Lectionary (RCL) or have chosen to preach on a text that is included there:

Sundays and Seasons: Preaching (http://www.sundaysandseasons.com). A subscription-based website focused especially on worship planning in churches that use the RCL; the lectionary commentary brings together biblical scholars and congregational preachers (a print version is also available with new editions each year).

Textweek (http://www.textweek.com). This website connects preachers to multiple resources, although some journal articles require that the user hold a license for a journal-access database such as ATLA.

Working Preacher (http://www.workingpreaching.org). A preaching website maintained by the Center for Biblical Preaching housed at Luther Seminary, St. Paul, Minnesota; the site provides commentary on the lectionary texts for each Sunday as well as links to further preaching and worship resources.

7

—

Designing the Sermon's Form

Sally A. Brown

A while back, a pastoral search committee asked me to come help them think about preaching. Confronted with dozens of pastors' dossiers and hundreds of sermons, they asked, "How do you know what to look and listen for?" When we met, I started by asking each one at the table to answer one question: "Let's say that on your way out of church, you've turned to your neighbor and remarked, 'Now, *that* was a good sermon!' Why would you be saying that? What makes a sermon 'good'?" Among the nine or ten folks around the table there were at least seventeen opinions. But on this much, they agreed: A good sermon *takes you to a destination worth getting to*—an insight, a shift of perspective, some strengthened resolve—and *it leads you there by a path you can follow.*[1]

While this is hardly an adequate account of all that goes into a good sermon, theologically and otherwise, it highlights the significance of a sermon's form, or design. No matter how compelling a sermon's core affirmation, listeners will not grasp it or be grasped by it unless the sermon provides a path they can follow. The fact that the Spirit enlivens both speaking and hearing in the preaching event does not excuse us from designing our sermons to be as accessible as possible.

In the first part of this chapter we will consider two basic sermon formats, *deductive* and *inductive*. Sermons organized according to *deductive* logic state the sermon's core affirmation near the beginning and then unpack it, working out its component parts and implications. Strong deductive sermons tap into not only ideas but also emotions, leading listeners to world-reframing.[2] *Inductive* sermons, on the other hand, do not put the sermon's core affirmation up front and build *out* from it; instead, through a series of moves they build *toward* the core affirmation, which ultimately occurs about two-thirds to three-quarters of the way through the preaching event.[3] Inductive preaching coaches listeners to *discover* the core affirmation, instead of proposing it and then demonstrating it. Each of these sermon designs can be handled in different ways and each has its strengths.

In the chapter's second half, we step into a hypothetical congregational setting, watching as its preacher considers different deductive and inductive sermon designs for a sermon on the feeding of the five thousand (Matt. 14:13-21), both aimed at encouraging the

---

1. Homiletician Henry H. Mitchell suggests the metaphor of the "followable path" in *Celebration and Experience in Preaching* (Nashville: Abingdon, 1990), 60.
2. Mitchell commends the widespread practice, common in African American church settings and elsewhere, of ending sermons with a climactic "celebration" of the sermon's news. Ibid., 60–64.
3. I refer to "preaching event" here to emphasize that preaching is a speaking and listening event that unfolds through time. It is absorbed at the ear and evokes internal, imaginative visualization. While listeners have no printed text to scan in order to connect what the preacher is saying, a well-designed sermon unfolds, as Joseph Webb suggests, as a series of sequenced ideas and visual scenes in the mind's eye.

congregation's response to a sector of a city devastated by sudden job losses. We close this chapter with a review of six basic composition skills that can strengthen our sermons.

Sermon Designs: Deductive and Inductive Forms

The parts of a well-crafted sermon flow one into the next so seamlessly that, for the most part, listeners don't notice it happening. A sermon's structure is meant to facilitate listening, not command attention. Although some worshipers like to take notes on a sermon, they shouldn't have to. If the sermon is done well, it will be possible to recall key features or scenes of that sermon without having written anything down.

Every preacher needs to be comfortable with a few basic sermon-design options. This allows him or her to choose the sermon form that best fits the genre or structure of the Scripture text, the listening habits of prospective listeners, and the hoped-for outcomes of the sermon. Preachers who can move smoothly among different sermon formats, week to week, are more likely over time to capture listeners across the range of the listening spectrum.

There are many sermon form options, which can be helpful because there are a variety of listeners in any congregation. No two persons are alike or think the same, act the same, or hear the same things. Knowing different sermon forms can help preachers develop different ways of presenting the gospel so that they can have a hearing from different people. This also acknowledges multiple intelligences and different ways of knowing à la educational theory. Various ways of knowing require various ways of putting a sermon together. Homiletical versatility is a virtue, especially when you are preaching to the same people every week. It is too easy to get stuck in a rut and use the same form each time. But this doesn't mean that one should necessarily pre-choose a form that will be placed on top of a Scripture passage. Through engagement with Scripture and prayer, how to put a sermon together for any given week will emerge (hopefully not at the midnight hour!). There are numerous options and it is wise to give them a try at some point because not every sermon form will resonate with every person. Form variations are an attempt to have a wider hearing on the long journey of preaching. – LP

Some listeners simply prefer deductively designed sermons. Ask them why, and they'll say, "I'm a logical, linear thinker" or "I like knowing right away what the sermon's about without having to guess." Some listeners, in fact, are frustrated by sermons that do *not* start with the sermon's core sentence and then spell out what it means. Ask these folks to listen to an inductive sermon, and they are annoyed; they feel they're being teased. "Just say what you have to say, please, say why it matters, say it again, and sit down." is their plea. Inductive preaching strikes them as somehow devious.

Other listeners, raised on television shows and Web-based games that depend on following clues, prefer inductive sermon designs. Start your sermon by laying out its major claim right away, and you've lost them. A sermon that makes them passive targets for information may leave them disengaged, and clever visuals may not be able to win them over. They prefer sermons that, like movies, unfold scene by scene, letting them assemble the sermon's clues, both conceptual and experiential, and work out the sermon's major claim.

It's a simple fact that not every listener will be equally engaged or helped by every sermon. This is something preachers need to accept, not fret over. Versatility on the preacher's part improves the chances that every listener will be deeply engaged some of the time.

Deductive Sermon Forms

In sermons with a deductive format, the sermon's core affirmation occurs early. Then the preacher develops some component parts and implications of this affirmation. A deductive sermon usually begins with an introduction—either an observation about the biblical text's claims or an observation about some problem in human experience—that makes us *want* to hear the core affirmation and curious to know more.

Imagine that your preaching context is a rural congregation in an area that has experienced severe drought for months. Crops have failed, farmers are deep in debt for equipment, seed, and fertilizer in which they have invested but now can't pay for. Worse, your small town feels ignored by local and state agencies that should be helping them. On every farm in the region, money is tight, discouragement is giving way to entrenched depression, and faith is giving way to doubt.

Imagine a deductively designed sermon on the text we studied in the previous chapter, about Jesus' healing of a woman bent over for eighteen years (Luke 13:10-17). You arrive at this for your sermon's core affirmation: "Just as Jesus focuses his attention on a bent-over woman whose suffering has become all but invisible to her community, God sees and cares about us when we are bent over by forces beyond our control and unable to envision a hopeful future."

A brief sermon introduction might sketch in a realistic way what it's like to wake up and face another day of scarcity: crossing the kids' favorite cereal off the grocery list because it's too expensive; dreading opening the mailbox to face more past-due bills; hoping against hope that a pair of school shoes that fit your daughter will turn up at the local thrift store. Then the preacher states the core affirmation ("Just as Jesus focuses his attention on a bent-over woman whose suffering has become all but invisible to her community, God sees and cares about us when we are bent over . . ."). The sermon might go on to explore what it is like to feel "bent over by forces beyond our control" financially, emotionally, and spiritually, and then explore ways those in the community can pull together, being open with their needs, discouragement, and doubts so that the stronger can help the weaker in these areas. Those who have can share. Those who can, listen. And when it is hard to sing the hymns of faith, hard to repeat the Apostles'

Creed and mean it, and hard to pray, others in a community can sing, believe, and pray on our behalf until we can find our voices again.

Another situation might call for a sermon directed more at caregivers. The preacher might start by reporting how he met a man at the local diner the other day who confided he'd been released from prison after a long incarceration but almost wished he hadn't been. When the preacher asked why, he said, "I haven't been here on the 'outside' [prisoners' term for the world beyond prison] in eighteen years. It's changed. I don't know anybody, I don't know how to navigate public assistance, and everything confuses me. It's painful."

This could lead to a sermon that invites listeners to open eyes and ears to discern types of human suffering that, like that of the bent-over woman whose community may have assumed her condition was simply a just punishment for secret sins, have become all but invisible to us. Starting with a core affirmation that states this, the sermon could explore the implications for sensitivity within our immediate families, our congregation, and our community.

Inductive Sermon Forms

As popular as deductive sermon plans have been and continue to be, many preachers are embracing more inductive sermons designs. An inductive sermon unfolds as a series of moves that "build" its core affirmation, disclosing it well into the sermon. Discoveries about the biblical text and slices of human experience culled from the news, films, church history, or literature converge to construct the core affirmation, step by step.

The Luke 13 sermon for the drought-plagued congregation just discussed can be designed inductively rather than deductively. The preacher might start by exploring at some length the financial, emotional, and spiritual burdens that weigh on church families and then turn to the biblical text. She might simply retell the story of

Jesus' encounter with the bent woman. The core affirmation then occurs, well into the sermon, gathering up the insights that have accumulated along the way: "Just as Jesus focuses his attention on a bent-over woman whose suffering has become all but invisible to her community, God sees and cares about us when we are bent over . . ." We can face our days when we know we're upheld by a God and a community of faith that neither forgets nor abandons us.

Some readers may worry that inductive sermons lack a clear "application" section. We would contend that there is *indeed* application, but it happens differently. Inductive sermons draw their listeners into active curiosity, inquiry, and imagination. The preacher can point to practical consequences of a sermon's core affirmation, but in an open-ended way ("What will this look like? I can't be sure of the answer for you, but it might be that . . ."). When the sermon has activated listeners' imaginations, we can trust them to recognize ways its claim reframes their world and allows them to act differently within it. Homiletician Fred Craddock often suggested that sermons should so activate listeners' imaginations that they leave worship with one foot poised midair, so to speak, ready to be set down in Monday.[4]

Choosing the Best Design for Your Sermon

Determining whether a deductive or inductive plan will serve best for any sermon depends on several factors, among them the text itself and the preaching context. Four questions can help narrow the options:

1. *What are the listening habits of my congregation? Is this an occasion to go with what's most natural to the majority, or is this an occasion to take a path that stretches them?* Considering a congregation's listening

---

4. One of the many occasions when Craddock made this observation was at the "Training in the Art of Preaching" week-long preachers' event held at Kirkridge Retreat Center, Bangor, PA, June 1989.

"habits" is especially important when a preacher is new to his or her congregation. A congregation long accustomed to sermons that stake a claim and then logically unpack it (deductive flow) may be confused the first time they hear you preach a sermon that works inductively. Younger congregants, on the other hand, may experience deductive sermons as authoritarian and heavy-handed. Multitasking fifteen-year-olds listen differently from eighty-year-olds for whom listening to the family radio (which was a boxy piece of furniture in the living room) counts as their first memory of electronic communication. They absorb information differently.

2. *Does the genre of the biblical text suggest a particular shape for the sermon?* If the text itself is a story, it may make sense simply to trust the story's naturally inductive logic. Stories don't introduce a concept, then break it down and apply it. They present us with a situation—sometimes very briefly—and invite us to watch the action. Reducing a biblical story to a series of moral "points" may seriously limit the story's capacity to shed light on listeners' lives. Instead of reducing the story's meaning to a proposition and breaking it down into smaller ideas, why not follow the action itself, interfacing the action in the story with a contemporary situation?

Psalms of lament have a natural movement, as well—from anguished outcry to God to confidence and hope. Psalm 13 is a good example of such a psalm, and its phrases can structure the sermon: "How long, O Lord?" . . . "Give light to my eyes" . . . "I trusted" . . . "I will sing."

A proverb like Prov. 22:6, "Train children in the right way, and when old, they will not stray," could be treated deductively or inductively. Treated deductively, proverbs are truth-claims to be unpacked. Preached inductively, they are the wisdom we discover through life's experience in the presence of God. Imagine that you've met a man whose upbringing by a devout single mother prepared him to cling to faith through several hardships: frontline combat when he was barely eighteen; the failure of his first business at thirty-five; and the loss of a child in later years. A deductively shaped sermon could start with the proverb and let this man's story and others demonstrate it. An inductive plan would explore his and other stories, leading us to embrace the proverb's truth as a result.[5]

3. *Does the structure of my core affirmation itself suggest a good sermon design?* The sermon's core affirmation may be a sermon path in miniature. Imagine that the preacher's core affirmation is: "Jesus' habit of dining with society's outsiders has implications for our own practices of hospitality." This core affirmation suggests a sermon that starts by exploring Jesus' habit of dining with social outcasts. After contrasting this with ways we typically socialize, the preacher could test what hospitality might look like in our homes, at church, and beyond, reframed by Jesus' practices. Keep in mind how important it is to reframe ordinary situations and practices of life, helping listeners to imagine new, more faithful ways of conducting their Monday-to-Saturday lives.

4. *What do I hope my sermon will do? Do I want to provide some basic teaching to newcomers to faith? Or is my aim to equip listeners to work out their own, faithful response to some pressing situation?* Deductive, "teaching"-type sermons work well, at least from time to time, where worshipers are largely new to Christian faith and want help with the layout of Scripture and basic Christian beliefs. (More will be said about preaching to new believers in chapter 9.) Inductive preaching is more effective, on the other hand, when the sermon touches on

---

5. For insight on preaching from Proverbs, see Alyce M. McKenzie, *Preaching Proverbs: Wisdom for the Pulpit* (Louisville: Westminster John Knox, 1996); and Thomas G. Long, *Preaching and the Literary Forms of the Bible* (Philadelphia: Fortress Press, 1989), 53–65.

an issue, within the church or in the public arena on which opinions differ sharply. Here, the preacher isn't so much interested in stabilizing a single perspective as helping Christians think through an issue from multiple perspectives.

Choosing and Sequencing Sermon Material

Sermons that move us to active thought and changed behavior engage us not only at the level of information and ideas, but at the level of experience. They activate intellect, feeling, and imagination. When sermons move us, they engage us not only cognitively, but emotionally; and our emotions are engaged as we identify with vivid scenes of human experience. Much of the Bible portrays scenes in human experience, and good sermons reflect this experiential quality.

How do human beings react to trouble and temptation, competition and conflict, unexpected failure or unexpected joy? Portraying these realities in believable ways means drawing on the human dynamics we discern in popular television shows, movies, literature, sports events, and local news.

Thinking and Preaching Scenes

Homiletician Joseph Webb is correct when he says that a good sermon unfolds more like a series of scenes (as in a drama or film) than a list of points.[6] Points suggest that a sermon is simply information, broken down into digestible portions. While a sermon may *include* information, information alone is not enough.

As the credits rolls at the end of a well-crafted film or when you turn the final page of a gripping novel, you haven't been so much informed by facts as transformed by experience. For a time, you've entered into the frame of reference—the world—created by

6. Joseph M. Webb, *Preaching for the Contemporary Service* (Nashville: Abingdon, 2006).

160

the author or filmmaker, a world perhaps quite different from your own. A sermon invites its listeners into the world it proposes so that we can see our everyday lives as the arena of divine action.

A sermon "scene" can draw on the biblical text of the day, theology in a broader sense, or human experience. By sketching slices of experience realistically, preachers help their listeners gain insight into the dynamics and relationships of their own lives. Each scene aims to function in a particular way. It might convict us of things done and left undone, confront us with a choice, or sketch the contours of the world as it could be and as it is meant to be, redeemed and renewed by the grace of God.

Putting Sermon Scenes in Order

The scenes of a sermon need to be arranged so that each connects with the one before it and prepares us for what comes next. Each "move" of the sermon flows from the last and leads to the next. Each asks us to consider a proposal or adopt a point of view. A sermon designed in moves or scenes doesn't necessarily need to enumerate its "points" any more than a good movie needs chapter headings. *Occasionally* a great film will signal that we're jumping to a different location and a different century, but this is rare; it just takes us there. Sermons, especially if the transitions between scenes are well crafted (a topic we touch on at the end of this chapter), listeners will move right along with us.

Webb encourages preachers to think less like lecturers and more like filmmakers as they design their sermons. A filmmaker creates a "storyboard"—a sequence of scene sketches that map out the action and dialogue of each shot in the sequence that creates the film experience. First, each scene should have a distinct function, or effect, for the listener. To clarify, what we mean by a scene's function is *the effect on the listener which that move aims to produce.* Maybe a move simply intends to impart information. Or maybe it seeks to draw a contemporary concern alongside a problem in the biblical text, as in the sermon beginning above. Closer to a sermon's end, a move might envision what faithful participation in God's redemptive activity would look like in the congregation's neighborhood.

A good way to become more adept at recognizing the function of sermon moves is to "map" the moves of some printed or audio sermons by an excellent preacher. Then reflect on the function of each one. We can ask, "What did the preacher mean to happen for us in this move? Did she mean for us to see something and draw a conclusion? Show us an accessible example of unexpected kindness to an outsider? Explain to us what it was like to be a tax collector in Jesus' time? Close the gap between the action in the biblical story and what can happen in our own setting?"

We can test the moves of a sermon we're developing in the same way. We could discover that when we think about what our moves are "doing"—what effect they're having—we're describing them all the same way. That is a problem; there either isn't enough variety in the sermon's ways of engaging the listener, or the sermon is stuck in neutral and isn't going anywhere.

Second, each of a sermon's moves or scenes should connect to what precedes and follows it so that listeners are not confused and left scrambling to figure out where the preacher means us to go.[7] The opening "scene" of the sermon, for example, has to connect not only with the next move, but with the concerns of the sermon as a whole. It positions listeners for the rest of the journey.

If we start with a typical human experience, it should meet two criteria: (1) it should be something most listeners—young and old,

---

7. Ibid., 106–7, 113–16.

women as well as men, native-born or immigrant—can identify with; and (2) it needs to orient us to the concerns of the sermon's core affirmation. For example, not long ago a student began her sermon by describing a simple scene in a supermarket. She found herself a helpless onlooker while a mother shamed her child mercilessly before a crowd of strangers. Her sermon explored how redemption means deliverance from shame-based lives.

Other good opening moves begin with the biblical text, but in a way that points us toward the sermon's concerns. It should be something any listener can easily recognize, not obscure or comprehensible only to students of ancient Greek or Hebrew. In a student sermon at a seminary located near a tough urban neighborhood, the preacher wanted to put us "on location" as quickly as possible, both in the biblical story and in present time. He began his sermon on Jesus' deliverance of the Gerasene demoniac (Mark 5:1-20) this way:

> Here in Mark's Gospel, Jesus gets out of the boat and immediately meets a man who is pacing, yelling, out of his mind—gripped by forces beyond his control. Walk from here just a few blocks, toward the highway [pointing], and you'll find yourself on a street corner. There you'll meet a man who is pacing, shouting, half out of his mind on drugs he can't live without—gripped by forces beyond his control.

With that, a sermon exploring our responsibility to take seriously the human toll of drug addiction was off and running.

No matter how the sermon begins, its first move has to capture listeners' interest, create anticipation for the next move, and relate to the sermon's central concern.

One of the most common errors in sermon writing is to do too much explaining. We explain and explain and then wonder why the people are not changed. If listeners are inattentive, maybe we aren't hearing what they're saying: "Don't spend twenty minutes *explaining* to me the love of God, the justice of God, why discipleship is costly, or why I should face trouble with hope. *Show me* the difference God's love, God's justice, following Jesus at a cost, or Christian hope makes in a situation I can understand and identify with."

A sermon that does nothing but explain is mentally exhausting. Our listeners live in a highly visual culture, not one that trades primarily in abstract concepts. Sermons need moves that make distinctions and clarify ideas from time to time; but they need more moves that evoke memory, help us see and feel the consequences of the wrongs we do, and imagine new possibilities. Preachers can take a page from the preaching of Jesus. Most of his preaching did not answer the question, "What does that *mean?*' but, "What does that *look like?*" Even in John's extended discourses, the language is evocative, metaphorical, and vivid.

No sermon design guarantees the transformation of lives; that is the work of God's Spirit. Nonetheless, preachers aim to make their sermons clear, vivid, relatable, and easily followed in service to the Spirit's work of transformation.

In thinking about the many options for sermon forms, one approach is to choose an image from the biblical text and use that image as a thread for the sermon. There are preachers who choose one image from culture and do the same thing but I think it is more effective to utilize a biblical image because if people remember the image that may bring them back to Scripture. For instance, if the biblical text highlights a "thorn in the flesh" one may choose to use thorn as a key image throughout, referring to it to represent human pain and suffering but then one might speak to how thorns can also be a part of roses, thus there is also the hope of a rose. Another example might be the image of bread we find throughout Scripture. Depending on the passage, one may preach on the lack of bread in the world, our need for bread to live, and then the bread of life we have in Jesus Christ. The point is that these images function as metaphors for our lives and the sermon can move using the images as the continuous picture. Handling a sermon in this way may be more effective than forcing a particular Scripture passage into a ready-made template. Sermon development is a fluid organic process and as one discerns the Word, how you might form your sermon becomes clearer. It can't be forced because sermon development is not a science; it is more like an art.- **LP**

One Text, Different Sermon Designs (Matthew 14:13-21)

To get a practical sense of the difference sermon design makes, as well as the kind of materials you might draw upon to build sermons, we focus in this section on a particular preaching context and text. Our preacher is Mikaylah, and she is the pastor of Springdale Methodist Church.

The Congregational Context

Mikaylah Thomson[8] arrived at Springdale Methodist Church three years ago. A midsized congregation in a city of about 75,000, Springdale Methodist is located in one of the city's older neighborhoods. Springdale Methodist is Mikaylah's second parish assignment.

The church is located within walking distance of a four-year liberal-arts college. The commercial district immediately around the church shows signs of decline. The small, privately owned businesses once located here could not compete with the big malls at the edge of town. Now small take-out restaurants, a thrift store, t-shirt shops, a used bookstore, a next-to-new clothing exchange, and a pawn shop have moved in. Within a one-mile radius of the church are several square blocks of modest-sized homes built in the mid-1900s.

The Sunday morning service attracts about eighty attendees. There are about a dozen aging couples who have belonged to the church for years, and another dozen widows and widowers. All of them have lived in town most of their lives and moved into the immediate neighborhood around Springdale Methodist when they were young parents with children.

8. Names and locations are fictitious, although the realities of this imaginary context reflect many of the realities affecting churches like this one around North America, especially in midsized Midwestern cities slow to recover from the economic downtown of the first decade of the twenty-first century.

Many of their neighbors of similar age have retired to other parts of the country. Some of those still at Springdale would like to do the same, but the closing of two manufacturing plants, a clothing maker and an auto-parts manufacturer, have resulted in a housing market flooded with real estate, much of it out in more desirable suburbs. Many homes around Springdale Methodist have been on the market for a year and more, their "For Sale" signs fading with the weather.

A few families with school-age children drive in from more upscale, distant suburbs. They prefer the close, family feel of Springdale and its anchorage in Methodist history to the big, independent churches out near the interstate. Some of Springdale's teenagers, though, prefer the youth programs at the bigger and newer churches. Springdale's membership is a third of what it was forty years ago, though the congregation can boast a growing Sunday school. Springdale Methodist struggles to meet its staffing needs as well as pay for repairs to the aging building.

A new cohort in Springdale's pews in the last decade is from abroad. Newcomers from India, Pakistan, parts of Africa, Thailand, and Vietnam have moved here, many of them taking jobs at the expanding medical center in town. Most are citizens now, and a few live within walking distance of Springdale Methodist. Others prefer downtown neighborhoods nearer the hospital where other residents from their home countries live as well. Their presence accounts for Springdale's growing Sunday school.

Neighbors in Crisis

Recently, Mikaylah and members of the church board have been meeting with pastors and lay leaders at other churches to meet a growing crisis in the city. Not far away from Springdale's neighborhood, closer to the center of the city, is a section everyone calls "the West Side." Twenty years ago it was a stable, working-class neighborhood, the compact but sturdy homes owned by hourly-wage workers at the two bustling manufacturing plants. But within the past two-and-a-half years, both of them closed, first the clothing factory, then, eighteen months later, the auto-parts plant. Two waves of unemployment have swept through the West Side, leaving hundreds of West Side residents jobless. In many households, two parents and perhaps a young adult child have all lost their sources of income.

Some in the first wave of job loss sold their homes and moved away to look for work elsewhere. Now, with a second wave of job loss, many families have lost their homes to foreclosure. Absentee landlords bought a good number of these and rent them to university students who are more willing to pay high rents and tolerate low maintenance standards. Families with no other options have moved in with relatives, so that, in many cases, a two- or three-bedroom home shelters three generations of adults and eight or nine children. Seventy-five percent of West Side families are on public assistance.

In light of the West Side crisis, the city's Council of Churches recently voted to begin a food-assistance program called "Healthy Weekends." Volunteers pack up ingredients to make two simple, nutritious meals in portions to feed four to six people. Families in need can pick up these "Healthy Weekend" kits at the Baptist Church on the West Side. Congregations who commit to the program will pledge volunteer hours, food donations, and funding to the program. Springdale Methodist has not yet decided whether to participate.

In consultation with the church board, Mikaylah has decided to preach a series of sermons around the theme "Faith in Action." The board hopes that such a series will help allay the fears of church members who worry that committing to this program will spread the congregation's funds and volunteers too thin. Her sermon on the feeding of the five thousand will be the first in this series. Mikaylah has decided that the core affirmation of her sermon will be: "As Jesus asked his disciples to turn over their limited resources for the feeding of a crowd, God asks us to let our limited resources be used to meet human need on the West Side, and beyond."

I. Preaching Matthew 14:13-21 Using Deductive Sermon Designs

Several factors might lead Mikaylah to choose a *deductive* framework of logic for her sermon on this text. First, she has learned from three years' experience at Springdale Methodist that the newer folks for whom English is a second language find it easier to follow a sermon that works deductively. They're accustomed to this style and can grasp what the sermon is about from the beginning. Mikaylah has learned the value of reviewing and summarizing along the way, using key refrain lines and simple stories that paint pictures to reinforce ideas.

Mikaylah might also decide on a deductive approach in light of the overarching purpose of the sermon series—to help Springdale members consider carefully whether and how they are being called upon to help their West Side neighbors. She might begin by bringing the congregation into Matthew's story, quickly moving to make the identification between the disciples who feel overwhelmed by the hungry crowd (Matt. 14:15) and the Springdale congregation, likewise daunted by the need on the West Side. Setting up a deductive sermon, Mikaylah would introduce the core affirmation early: "Yet, we know this story: Matthew wants us to know that our resources, no matter how inadequate they may seem to us, can be multiplied in the hands of God to meet human need." From there, Mikaylah could explore the story from three character perspectives:

1. *Who is the crowd?* In the crowd we see the faces of our West Side neighbors. We can't turn away from their very real need.

2. *Who is God?* Our God is the one we meet in Jesus, a God of compassion for whom no crowd is neither faceless, nor too large or too needy.

3. *Who are we?* We are today's disciples. We're asked to make our resources, however limited they may seem to us, available to the God who seeks to meet human need.

II. Preaching Matthew 14:13-21 Using Inductive Sermon Designs

We noted earlier that there is more than one way to design a sermon that basically develops inductively, leading us through a series of stories and observations that lead us *toward* its central claim. Using Mikaylah's setting, text, and sermon purpose, we'll test two inductive sermon plans. One is the story-shaped sermon. Considerable credit for the widespread embrace of this approach to sermon design in North America and beyond is due to Methodist homiletician Eugene Lowry. Lowry has devoted much of his career to describing and then theoretically refining the sermon that unfolds like a narrative plot.[9] Second, we'll test the "four-page" design proposed by Paul Scott Wilson. Although functionally similar to a narrative sermon, the four-page design is more driven by Wilson's theological commitment to a "law/grace" motif in the redemptive action of God.[10]

A. The Story-Shaped Sermon

In the last third of the twentieth century, theologians and Bible scholars began talking among themselves about a phenomenon everyone knew but no one had thought about all that much: stories comprise a large portion of our Scriptures. They began to explore

9. See Eugene Lowry, *The Homiletical Plot: The Sermon as Narrative Art Form*, exp. ed. (Louisville: Westminster John Knox, 2001).
10. See Paul Wilson, *The Four Pages of the Sermon* (Nashville: Abingdon Press, 1999).

what this means for theology, namely, that the nature of God is, in many ways, disclosed through story.

Also of interest was the unique way that narratives move us to new insight. They are not deductive arguments; that is, they don't make a statement and demonstrate its meaning. They are made up of ingredients like setting, character, action, and plot. They give us a world, with its possibilities and limits, and characters acting within that world—characters whose actions are interconnected so as to create suspense and progression—what we call plot. What we gain from stories is not primarily ideas, but insight.

Lowry was among those fascinated both by these elements, and by the remarkably stable patterns of action that seem to characterize almost every engaging story, however short or extended. We're introduced to a situation ("Arriving home in the dark, Lorna savored the enveloping quiet of her kitchen . . ."), but then trouble or tension develops (". . . until the click of a door closing upstairs signaled to her that she was not, in fact, alone."). The trouble doesn't go away; in fact, things become more complicated ("The intruder, whoever he was, seemed to be in the corner bedroom, talking low into a cell phone . . ."). But just when it seems there will never be a way out of the trouble, a new element is introduced—a clue that makes a difference, working against the trouble ("Her grown son's face appeared at the top of the stairs: 'Sorry if I scared you, Mom; I came home for the weekend to surprise you!'"). The situation shifts, the tension is released, and the story moves toward resolution and celebration. This is a familiar pattern; every TV sitcom or crime drama works basically according to this pattern.

We call sermons "narrative" when they progress according to this same story-shaped pattern. The four basic moves of a narrative sermon are: (1) *tension* or *trouble* develops in a situation ("the hour is late, send the crowds away so they may . . . buy food"; Matt. 14:15);

170

(2) instead of being resolved, the tension *complicates* or intensifies ("'You give them something to eat' . . . 'we have nothing but five loaves and two fish'"; 14:17); (3) a *clue* enters into the situation, either from within or beyond the story (Jesus says "bring them to me," and takes, blesses, and breaks the loaves; 14:19); and (4) the situation shifts, revealing a *new reality* ("all ate and were filled"; 14:20).

It's important to notice that the stories that stick with us don't move instantly from trouble to resolution. True to life itself, the tension intensifies. One of the arts of story-shaped preaching is to *trust* this tension, not giving in to the temptation to resolve it too soon. The preacher has to deepen the tension she or he has introduced—perhaps by showing how a troubling feature in the biblical text is echoed in human experience, or by widening the viewfinder of the sermon to show that a local problem the congregation faces is merely representative of trouble on a much-larger scale—before introducing the clue that releases the tension, casts the situation in a new light, and opens up new possibilities.

In Christian narrative preaching, the clue that reframes human experience is traceable in some way to the redemptive activity of God—past, present, or future. God's promise of newness reaches back across our present from the not-yet-realized future, seeding the graveyard of our failures, losses, and defeats with hope.

A classic story-shaped sermon of the African American tradition, one that many preachers have developed in their own way, just as jazz musicians make classic tunes their own through unique improvisation, has the core affirmation, "It's Friday, but Sunday's comin'!" Friday stands in such sermons as a metaphor for all that is life-denying, all that stifles dignity and personhood, and all that is deathly and deadly. It is the Friday of justice denied and truth smothered by falsehood. It is the endlessly dark Friday of tranquility shattered by violence and lives cut short. Death seems to triumph over hope itself. But then comes the clue, not shouted, but whispered: "But . . . Sunday's comin'!" Sunday. The Sunday of women hastening to dress a dead body with spices. The Sunday of absent body and present angels and a "gardener" who knows your name. The Sunday of angels who send us back to Galilee. The Sunday of testifying women and doubting male disciples. Sunday when the God of life delivers death its fatal wound. The Sunday that changes everything. Shout, people of God! God's Sunday reframes all the "Fridays" of our lives!

The most obvious reason for Mikaylah to preach the story of the feeding of the five thousand using story-shaped logic is simply that it *is* a story. However, her sermon will need to do more than simply repeat the story; she will need to "stitch" together the biblical story and the challenge that the West Side crisis presents. The moves of her sermon could be:

Move 1: *Present the trouble in the text.* Jesus' band of disciples is faced with a hungry crowd, with no resources in sight to meet the need.

Move 2: *Complication of the trouble.* The troubling situation intensifies in three ways. First, Jesus doesn't respond to the disciples' anxiety by spelling out precisely how God is about to act to meet the obvious need. There is no preview, no blueprint rolled out to show them how God plans to get the job done. Second, Jesus insists that they have a part to play ("You give them something to eat"; v. 16). This doesn't solve the crisis of the moment, but actually intensifies it. Third, when the disciples reluctantly reveal that they in fact have resources—ridiculously inadequate to the crisis, but resources nonetheless—Jesus asks them to hand them over. Is Jesus taking from them to let them starve and feed someone else? Jesus is asking them to let go, not only of some bread and fish, but their plans for their own survival!

Move 3: *The turn.* Thanking, blessing, breaking, giving: in a series of hauntingly eucharistic actions, five ordinary loaves and two ordinary salted fish are taken up into the redemptive work of God.

Move 4: *God's new reality disclosed.* The disciples' emergency rations, relinquished to God, become a feast of abundance for the hunger of many (meeting the disciples' own needs, as well).

Mikaylah will have to decide, on the basis of her congregation's listening habits and skills, whether to leave it to the congregation to make all the key connections between the needs of their West Side neighbors and this story, or trace those connections herself in brief but vivid ways.

Either way, her core affirmation will occur about two-thirds of the way through the sermon, and might sound like this: "Our resources, no matter how limited they may seem to us, can be multiplied in the hands of God to meet human need. If we're willing to take a risk, we can help our West Side neighbors." Moving from "reframing" the West Side crisis in the action of a God who multiples our resources to meet human need, Mikaylah might choose to move on to "imaginative rehearsal." The sermon might close with a vision of a West Side family breaking bread and passing it around the table, a vision that might point us to the table of the Lord's Supper, where everyone is welcome and no one goes away hungry.

Notice that Mikaylah can encourage a faithful response to the West Side situation *without* using imperatives like "must" and "should." She can rely on the indicative mood—inviting her listeners to imagine the West Side reframed by God's compassion as expressed by the caring faith communities.

B. The "Four Pages" Design

Homiletician Paul Scott Wilson constructs another inductive sermon design. Guided by the contrast between the sin that "law" reveals and the hope that "grace" reveals, Wilson contends that a sermon includes two vital proclamations: it exposes the trouble in the world and then introduces the unprecedented, unmerited grace that defeats the world's sin and trouble. In other words, sermons need to identify and name the life-denying, hurtful, toxic effects of sin and evil in the world, on one hand, and on the other, declare what God has done, is doing, and promises yet to do to overcome these realities.

Wilson's theological understanding of preaching produces a "four-page" map for the sermon that looks like this:

Page 1: Description of *trouble* present in the biblical text.

Page 2: Description of analogous *trouble* evident in the world of the sermon listener.

Page 3: Announcement of analogous *good news* in the world of the text, specifically in terms of redemptive action God has taken, is taking, or promises yet to undertake.

Page 4: Announcement of analogous *good news* in the world of the listener thanks to God's redemptive action.

It is helpful when building this kind of sermon to ask first, "Where is the action of God in this text, explicitly or implicitly?" (a step in the exegetical method discussed in the previous chapter). If we don't start there, we may identify the wrong fulcrum for change in the situation.

For example, what if Mikaylah were to start off by identifying "the crowds are famished" as the trouble and "the disciples hand out the bread" as the good news? While neither of these statements—either the "trouble" or the "good news"—is patently false, they miss the point. The disciples do not solve the problem; they participate in what *God* is doing. A gospel whose good news depends on human action alone is nothing to get excited about. Focusing on divine action prevents this model from devolving into little more than social analysis and moralistic scolding. Using Wilson's inductive design, Mikaylah could sketch her sermon this way:

Page 1: *Trouble in the text.* Faced with a hungry crowd of thousands, Jesus' disciples feel overwhelmed, especially when Jesus says, "*You* give them something to eat." Their meager emergency rations are no match for this hunger!

Page 2: *Analogous trouble in our world.* Human need on our town's West Side in the wake of the plant closings is overwhelming. Jesus asks us to care for such neighbors—but our resources are stretched here at Springdale already.

Page 3: *Good news in the text.* Jesus asks the disciples to place their own limited resources—resources they could justifiably keep—in his hands. Jesus gives thanks, blesses, breaks, and gives—and it is enough and more than enough.

Page 4: *Good news for our time and place.* "Placed in God's hands, our resources, no matter how limited they may seem to us, can be multiplied to meet human need." This claim can be imaginatively played out in the closing paragraphs of the sermon in ways immediately relevant to the listeners' time and place, including a description of the Healthy Weekends initiative.

Clearly, this is not a finished sermon. Both the biblical story and the West Side situation need to be fleshed out with vivid detail. At every point, the perspective on the story—that of the disciples—needs to be maintained. This sermon turns on that point of identification and point of view, and Mikaylah will want to maintain it so that it also becomes the fulcrum of response to God's action in the story and in the present situation.

A Word about Expository Preaching

Expository preaching is an approach to preaching that continues to be widely used in some Christian communities, particularly congregations within evangelical traditions. It is by no means as dominant as it once was. It is the modern-day version of what, in the ancient church, was known as the "homily," which consisted of commentary on the day's prescribed texts.

Since many good resources on expository preaching exist (one is included in the list of resources at the close of this chapter), we will not develop this technique here. Briefly, expository preaching usually consists of verse-by-verse, or section-by-section, explanation of the text's meaning, followed by an "application" of this meaning to believers' lives. The application may be an explanation of the benefits of divine action to believers or an explanation of the kind of obedient response for which the text is calling.

Today's best expository preachers know that a text is like a musical score: not every note in the score deserves the same emphasis. The same goes for the words and phrases of a biblical text. Phrases function differently, and a good expository preacher knows which phrases to unpack in order to let the text speak most eloquently to the situation of the listeners. Expert expository preachers interweave vignettes from ordinary experience and slices of history within and beyond the church into their preaching.

A pitfall of the expository approach, especially if it is used exclusively, is that it risks turning every sermon into a primarily cognitive experience. The gospel takes the form of a list of ideas. Stories, if used, function to amplify points. Seldom does an expository preacher trust the story form of the text to convey insight. Turning every genre through which the Spirit speaks in Scripture into a series of propositional declarations with moral consequences is to flatten the semantic landscape of Scripture—and unnecessarily. Perhaps meaning includes the *way* insight is conveyed. To strip the content of its form is to lose something of the content itself. The surprise of a story's gracious ending, flattened into a proposition (even said with feeling!) is no longer a gracious surprise.

Expository sermons need to move toward a concluding section that draws together a few main insights (for example, "First, relationships thrive with forgiveness and wither without it . . ."; "Second, we need forgiveness most when we deserve it least . . ."; and so on). It is no accident that sermons often work with sets of three: three observations, three perspectives, three consequences. Three is about the limit of what human memory, especially based strictly on listening, can absorb. Preachers need to remember that their listeners don't have the preaching notes in front of them; moreover, displaying the points on a big screen or putting them in the bulletin may not matter much on Wednesday, when a listener has access to neither of these things. What will matter on Wednesday is whether that listener has *seen* the world vividly enough reframed in the redemptive action, love, and justice of God on Sunday to reimagine the situation he or she faces on Wednesday similarly reframed.

Six Skills Every Preacher Needs

1. *Know how to craft a good beginning.*

- Begin, instead of talking about beginning.
- Throwaway entertainment is not a sermon beginning.
- The sermon's beginning should relate to its major issue and claims.
- Put your listeners in a location that evokes the issue with which your sermon deals. You could start, "In our world, it's always the same: human need outstrips our ability to meet it," but you might try: "Jesus' disciples had a situation on their hands: they were faced with upwards of five thousand hungry people, and not so much as a hot dog truck in sight." "Maybe, like me, you saw the news video of the first-aid workers arriving in [scene of disaster]. Staring back as they climbed out of their small panel truck were 3,500 gaunt faces."

2. *Write for the ear—the way ordinary people talk, not in essay-like sentences full of "however," "perhaps," abstract concepts, and lists*

full of commas. Use simple sentences (noun/verb/direct object) with active verbs. Don't hesitate to use contractions where appropriate ("isn't," "can't," "don't"). No need to be sloppy, but speak like an ordinary person.

3. *Know how to write a good transition sentence.* Transitions are like turn signals: they indicate where the sermon is going next. Connecting moves with a lame "also" or "but" creates little momentum. Ask yourself, "How does this next move relate to the one just before it?" Here are some possibilities:

- Contrast: "But on the other hand," or "It's not always that way, is it?," or just a pause, and "*—Really??*"

- Analogy: "That was true for Jesus' disciples, and in a way, it's true for us, too," or "That's true not only here but on the other side of the globe."

- Amplification of either trouble or possibility: "Not only that, but . . ."

- Shift of perspective: "Maybe there's another way to look at this"; or, shifting from contemporary experience to the text, "Our text today puts this in a new light . . ."

4. *Sketch the trouble the sermon confronts and the hope it points to by showing it instead of explaining it.* If you want us to feel in our hearts and stomachs what it is like to be lost in a strange city, don't say, "I felt lonely and disoriented." Take us with you, pushing through a crowd of strangers, past storefronts whose signs we can't read, on a day so cloudy you can't tell east from west. Or if you want us to know what freedom from captivity is, show us the father just released from prison, watching his children eat breakfast for the first time in seven years.

5. *Bring stories to life with spare detail.* Use only what listeners need in order to "get" the key dynamics on which you want to focus. Resist the temptation to over-explain ("We see, then, what Jesus

meant us to learn from this story . . .”). Human beings know how to make sense of stories. If you've cleared away possible cultural misunderstandings and established a definite point of view on the story's action, listeners will grasp the insight you're aiming for.

6. *Know how to write a good ending.* Keep the sentences short. Pick up concrete language that occurred earlier in the sermon. One sermon on the feeding of the five thousand ends this way: “It is up to you just to share what you have got, to feed whatever big or little hunger happens to be standing right in front of you. The rest will come. Because God is God, the rest will come. For now, for your part, how many loaves have you? Go and see.”[11]

Without question, salvation is not our work, but God's. Yet preaching serves that divine work, summoning us to the Spirit-enacted reality of God's new creation, begun in Jesus Christ. We preach not primarily to outfit our listeners with a flawless theology but to open their eyes to the ordinary scenes of their lives as the stage of God's redemptive judgment and hope. Playground and parking lot, mall and military base, campus and courtroom—even our own living rooms—become places of God's redemptive action. A compelling sermon turns us toward our Monday-to-Saturday world, eager to participate in what God is already doing in the present time, in these places, to renew all things.

Further Learning Strategies

1. Meet with three or four other students or working pastors to “workshop” possible designs for a sermon-in-progress. Bring your study notes and a draft of your core affirmation to this

---

11. Barbara Brown Taylor, “Local Miracles,” in *Mixed Blessings* (Boston: Cowley, 1998), 102.

session. Working together, see if you can sketch one deductive and one inductive sermon design based on each preacher's core affirmation. Then, with each preacher's anticipated preaching context in mind, discuss the factors that bear on making the best choice (genre and shape of the text itself, congregational listening habits, etc.). With the help of the group, sketch a couple of possible sermon designs.

2. For a period of time, make a practice of paying attention to the structure of every sermon you hear. Does it unfold deductively, announcing its central affirmation near the beginning? Is it inductive, starting with a question or problem, and probing Scripture and experience for answers? Does its structure hold together and lead you on a path you can follow? When this fails to happen, see if you can identify what threw you off the trail, or caused you to lose interest.

3. From time to time, access one of the websites listed below. Select three or four sermons, including those from both women and men, as well as some older preachers and others that are younger. Note how each preacher structures the sermon and connects moves. Use the questions above to test each sermon. *Note*: This exercise adapts well to group work. Agree with others on a list of sermons, then convene to share your impressions.

4. In a congregation where you serve as a pastor or seminary intern, gather a group of seven or eight volunteers from the congregation who are willing to (a) learn something about the way sermons are put together and (b) listen to two months' worth of sermons. At the end of each month, convene the group and discuss the sermons they've heard. See what you can learn about their preferred listening styles, as well as the strengths or weaknesses of each sermon. *Note*: This exercise works best when you provide a listening guide that directs attention to

sermon features such as main idea, major moves or sections, use of Scripture or experience, and so forth.

Further Reading

Allen, O. Wesley. *Determining the Form: Structures for Preaching.* Elements of Preaching. Minneapolis: Fortress Press, 2008. This brief, useful volume not only describes seven different sermon forms, but illustrates each one so that preachers can also visualize the ways each form makes its moves.

Allen, Ronald J., ed. *Patterns of Preaching: A Sermon Sampler.* St. Louis: Chalice, 1998. A collection of sermons grouped according to different patterns and occasions, each accompanied by the preacher's own interpretation of the sermon's structure and aims. Although not necessarily identified as "deductive" or "inductive," sermons of both types are included.

Allen, Ronald J., and Gilbert L. Bartholomew. *Preaching Verse by Verse.* Louisville: Westminster John Knox, 2000. An updated approach to expository preaching that demonstrates ways to keep an expository approach versatile and hearer-oriented.

Lowry, Eugene L. *The Sermon: Dancing the Edge of Mystery.* Nashville: Abingdon, 1997. A theoretical and practical summary of Lowry's narratively structured sermon design.

These websites, which require (free) membership sign-in for full navigation, post audio or video sermons by distinguished preachers from many worship traditions:

Chicago Sunday Evening Club (http://www.csec.org). This website describes its mission thus: "We tell stories that inspire people to put their faith into action to make Chicago better." Preachers will take special interest in the "30 Good Minutes"

181

tab, although there are excellent resources throughout the site to inform and inspire in an interfaith perspective.

Day 1 (http://www.day1.org). This website "offers an extensive library of lectionary-based sermons, audio, video, blogs, and other resources for lay persons and pastors."

8

Embodying the Sermon

Luke A. Powery

Harlem Renaissance writer James Weldon Johnson describes a sermonic scene in Kansas City that prompted his collection of poems and sermons known as *God's Trombones*. He says this riveting preaching moment was "a very rhythmic dance, and [the preacher] brought into the play the full gamut of his wonderful voice, a voice—what shall I say?—not of an organ or a trumpet, but rather of a trombone. . . . He intoned, he moaned, he pleaded—he blared, he crashed, he thundered. . . . I was, perhaps against my will, deeply moved; the emotional effect upon me was irresistible."[1] Johnson illuminates the embodied nature of African American preaching that is more than the voice but includes the entire body, even a dancing

1. James Weldon Johnson, *God's Trombones: Seven Negro Sermons in Verse* (New York: Viking Penguin, 1927), 6–7.

body. The somatic and sonic rendition of the word is what deeply moves Johnson. In his short account, he reveals implicitly how the human body is critical to preaching. It is more than words; it is an enfleshed word as the preached word takes on human form.

This should be obvious since being human includes having a body thus the body is always with us. However, there is a lingering "somatic dis-ease"[2] within homiletics despite its being insightfully defined as "theology processed through the body."[3] Sometimes, it may appear that no-body has to be present in order to preach but if there is no-body, there is no word. Preaching is an embodied practice, theology in flesh and bones. Ironically, however, sometimes in seminary, when students are in search for divinity, they lose their humanity; they suffer from somatic amnesia by forgetting they are embodied creatures. This chapter will help you reclaim and explore the significance of embodiment for preaching and offer some practical insights into the body's role in preaching, helping you to understand the ways in which preaching may be enhanced or inhibited by the (lack of) use of the body.

"Somatic Dis-ease" within Christianity

When dealing with the homiletical body it is important to remember that, historically, the human body has had a tenuous role within Christianity. In Western tradition and beyond, the body has been viewed as threatening and dangerous if not controlled. It was to be mistrusted, feared, and deemed unruly. There was a Christian ascetic attitude toward the body, which was viewed to be a part of the fallen creature; the term *flesh*, a metaphor of sinful humanity and irrational

2. Darnell L. Moore, "Theorizing the 'Black Body' as a Site of Trauma: Implications for Theologies of Embodiment," *Theology and Sexuality* 15, no. 2 (2009): 176.
3. Thomas H. Troeger, "Emerging New Standards in the Evaluation of Effective Preaching," *Worship* 64, no. 4 (1990): 294.

rejection of God, was equated wrongly with the body. In such an equation, the body was to be disciplined in order to control the fleshly passions.

The Protestant tradition, in particular, perpetuated these ideals. Certain scholars argue that

> The Protestant Reformation actually shifted the emphasis from sensual engagement with God to mental communion through the word of the gospels. Emphasis was placed on the mind's ability to grasp the revelation of God and the body was placed in a strait-jacket to keep it from the worst excesses of Catholic piety and superstition. The Reformation encouraged people to experience their minds as separate from and superior to their bodies which in turn led to an individualistic view of life. This was because salvation depended on mental, cognitive connection with God and a healthy distrust of things of the world, indeed the world itself.[4]

The Reformation emphasized intellectual comprehension of the word of God, which is important for preaching, but did so over against any usefulness of the "inferior" body, continuing a tendency even found in some of the early church fathers.

Christians devalued the body and prioritized the soul over the body, hypnotized by a neoplatonic Christianity in which one's distance from the earthly, physical, embodied realm determined the extent of one's spirituality; the farther away one was from the physical earth, the more spiritual a person was on the path toward immortality. The disconnection between Christian faith and the material body led to terroristic acts against bodies, and especially dark bodies (e.g., slavery). The body was viewed as worthless for Christian practice, though preachers always use their bodies to preach. This disembodied Christian legacy shapes historical homiletical emphases in divinity classrooms. Professors may be quick to discuss exegesis,

4. Lisa Isherwood and Elizabeth Stuart, *Introducing Body Theology* (Sheffield, UK: Sheffield Academic Press, 1998), 12.

theologies of preaching, and sermon form, but low on the teaching totem pole is anything about the body, because people are generally uncomfortable with their fleshly bodies.

Christians' difficulty fully embracing bodies—their own as well as Christ's—is indeed as old as Christianity itself. The phrase "God Incarnate" was so jarring to early believers that the heresy called docetism—the idea that Jesus didn't have a *real* body, but only appeared to—cropped up early and has been harder to discourage than crabgrass for two thousand years.

If we take seriously that God moved among us with a breathing, sweating, blood-and-bone body (one which may have been quite far from the first century physical ideal, in fact), shouldn't we rejoice in our bodies? Yet some of us come from worship or preaching traditions that, historically, have regarded the body as an unfortunate encumbrance—a distraction from the holy rather than the Spirit's habitation. Bodies are forced to be still and invisible.

Fortunately, North America is blessed with worship traditions, including but not limited to African American worship, that express the Spirit's redemptive claim upon the body—a claim that comes to expression in movement and sound. Exactly how any of us experience our bodies in preaching and worship will depend on the cultures that have shaped us. Claiming that certain ways of moving—or not moving—the body correlate absolutely with the presence (or absence) of the Spirit is neither charitable nor theologically defensible. Garrison Keillor's imaginary "frozen chosen," the reserved Lutherans of mythical Lake Woebegon, Minnesota, might find even liturgical toe-tapping quite a stretch. But amid the diversities of the preaching classroom or preachers' working group, we can learn from each other. We can breathe deeply, tell our critical selves to take a break, and let the Spirit move or settle us in new ways. **– SB**

A Theology of the Body

The irony of this legacy is that at the heart of Christian preaching is the incarnation of the divine in human form such that we read, "the Word became flesh and lived among us" (John 1:14). Through the incarnation, God embraces the human body by the divine Word becoming a body. God uses a body to spread divine love on earth. The incarnate Word is the embodied communication of the divine to humanity. When the *logos*, the Word, becomes flesh, then it comes to life in our world. The Word cannot touch the earth until it becomes enfleshed. Without movement in a body, the word event, preaching, is not alive, but dead. When God preached a Word, God chose to do it in and through a human body. When God wanted to demonstrate God's love, God performed an embodied Word in Jesus Christ, suggesting that even homiletical love is enfleshed.

There may be dis-ease with preaching bodies, but Jesus took on a body like ours and every time we stand in the pulpit we affirm the incarnation and the incarnational ministry of preaching. Homiletical bodies are means of grace, thus amazing grace baptizes every body as some-body. Every (dis)abled body can preach because human bodies are temples of the Spirit (1 Cor. 6:19). Bodies are homiletical sites of the Holy Spirit just as the incarnation of God in the flesh only happens through the Spirit.[5]

Spirit-animated preaching is embodied, as pneumatology implies materiality, not its negation. Through the Spirit, preachers discover their deeper physical selves. Sometimes a pre-sermon prayer voiced in the pulpit is, "Lord, move me out of the way." The irony of this prayer is that if a preacher is removed, and thus the body, there will be no word, no sermon. An alternative plea in the pulpit that affirms the body might be, "Lord, make me more fully present in the moment." This way the body can be accepted as an important aspect of the spiritual practice of preaching. In the Spirit, there is the convergence of the spiritual realm and material realm, suggesting the sacramentality of bodies such that the spiritual is made known through the corporeal. Homiletics can be an academic discipline that honors the body.

Of course, in certain traditions, and particularly in black religious settings, there has been a somatic sensibility throughout history that reveals the black body as a site of the Spirit's manifestation. There may be bodily ecstatic manifestations known as the "frenzy" or some form of the shout. In other cultural and religious traditions or denominations this is not the case because expressions of the Spirit

5. See Luke 1:26—2:21.

in and through the body are contextual, based on numerous factors. What is significant is that the body is a pneumatic vessel, which is vital for the embodied practice of preaching. The *how* of body performance will vary, but that should not change the body's importance.

Preaching with Your Mouth Shut

To go one step further, if the body is embraced as a temple of the Spirit, then in preaching, this suggests that the body is a "sacred text."[6] The body is to be honored and not underestimated because the homiletical body *is* a sermonic text. It preaches and performs the word in the Spirit as that word is set on fire, illuminating the grandness of the gospel. The Spirit breathes life through flesh-and-blood, real, human material bodies. Preaching is not just sonic; it is somatic. It can speak a word through a body. In the liturgy as a whole, including preaching, the body is less an object but more the subject of the event itself.[7] The body is that important.

A bad delivery can destroy a sermon and do injustice to hard preparatory work. Nonverbal body talk can assist or impede the preacher's message. For example, if you rock back and forth constantly without even knowing it during your sermon, this can become a distraction to the congregation and hinder what you are trying to accomplish. Thus, what you do with your body in the pulpit is critical and in preaching, as in any public discourse, the body is inescapable. Tom Long rightly reminds us, "There is a scandalous fleshiness to preaching, and while sermons may be 'pure' theology all the way through Saturday night, on Sunday morning they are

6. Dolan Hubbard, *The Sermon and the African American Literary Imagination* (Columbia: University of Missouri Press, 1994), 2.
7. James L. Empereur, "The Physicality of Worship," in *Bodies of Worship: Explorations in Theory and Practice*, ed. Bruce T. Morrill (Collegeville, MN: Liturgical, 1999), 145.

inescapably embodied and, thus, rhetorical."[8] The rhetoric of preaching includes the rhetoric of the body such that the ink of a sermon manuscript can become the flesh and blood of a real human person in motion.

Every year I meet a handful of students who dread preaching class. Some dread it because they suffer from stage fright. Maybe they have dealt, or still do, with a stutter, and nerves can bring it to the surface again. Another student can't shake a bad experience in a high school public speaking class. Each time he gets up to speak, that memory takes up a seat at the back of the room and grins.

But others dread preaching class simply because you can't leave the body out of it. Apart from occasion vocal participation in a discussion, you can get through classes in theology, history, and biblical studies without too much physical exposure. Preaching is different. Here, you have to put on display not only a theology and personal faith that may be under major reconstruction midway through seminary, but also your body. Short or tall, a little more round or hollow-chested than you could wish, there you are.

Some student preachers are ambivalent about occupying the *space* of the pulpit. Significant voices from the past tell them they do not have right to occupy that space. I remember a student who skittered to the edges of the space behind the lectern as if apologizing for being there. Instead of letting her hands and arms naturally evoke the space of the story unfolding in her sermon, her gestures were small and tight—a little like a squirrel fussing with an acorn! Wisely, this student shared her ambivalence about claiming the "space" of preaching with other students. She sought coaching from an experienced teacher of speech on our faculty and prayed for an open mind about her future. As graduation neared, she stopped insisting she only meant to "be some kind of assistant pastor" and claimed the Spirit's call to weekly preaching in a solo pastorate. She not only succeeded, but thrived. – SB

Without full embodiment of the sermon, sermons will fail. Homiletician Charles Rice remarks about his own experience, "I believe my sermon fell flat that Sunday morning at a Pennsylvania college because I was not sufficiently there as a *body*, responding in the flesh to the glory of a new morning . . ."[9] The Word must come alive in our flesh, therefore, how we prepare our bodies for

---

8. Thomas G. Long, "And How Shall They Hear? The Listener in Contemporary Preaching," in *Listening to the Word: Studies in Honor of Fred B. Craddock*, ed. Gail R. O'Day and Thomas G. Long (Nashville: Abingdon, 1993), 178.

9. Charles L. Rice, *The Embodied Word: Preaching as Art and Liturgy*, Fortress Resources for Preaching (Minneapolis: Fortress Press, 1991), 135.

preaching and use our bodies during preaching are important matters to consider. The performed word, not the read word, should be taken into consideration in our sermon preparation, especially in light of the insights of nonverbal communication theory.

How one preaches is just as vital as *what* one preaches. Issues of voice, body, gesture, movement, and sound should interact with typical preaching items such as biblical exegesis, theologies of preaching, and sermon form. The tendency is for the former issues of embodiment to be marginalized, either because of time or the view that they are less important. But the fact of the matter is that the body, as well as our mouths, speaks, leading to the notion that we also "preach with our mouths shut." In Toni Morrison's beautiful novel *Beloved*, one character, Baby Suggs, delivers an unforgettable sermon to the enslaved about loving themselves and their "flesh," their bodies. At the end of her message, Morrison writes, "Saying no more, she stood up then and danced with her twisted hip the rest of what her heart had to say while others opened their mouths and gave her the music. Long notes held until the four-part harmony was perfect enough for their deeply loved flesh."[10] This is a literary example of preaching with your mouth shut. Baby Suggs danced the rest of her sermon without using words.

This was a prophetic gesture then just as it is today, not only because of her race in the context of enslavement but because she was a woman preacher. The church has historically been uncomfortable with or at least ambivalent toward a woman's body in the pulpit, which has been dominated by male clergy. Any bodies other than male, heterosexual ones have been deemed unfit to preach. A woman's call to preach has traditionally been overlooked because

---

10. Toni Morrison, *Beloved* (New York: Vintage, 2004 [1987]), 102–4.

of her female body. In a rhetorical study of the gendered pulpit, Roxanne Mountford notes,

> Women's bodies are associated with natural inferiority and reproductive functions, and their confinement to the private spheres of community has been predicated in part of their sexual difference. Because preaching primarily occurs in the public sphere, women have long been banned from participation. Indeed, religion has been an important site for the disciplining of the women's bodies; every Catholic girl who was asked to kneel so that a nun could check her skirt length understands this point implicitly. World religions enforce chastity through restrictions on the bodies of women—where they can go, with whom they can associate, what they can say, and what they can wear in private and public. . . . When women preachers have challenged these same restrictions, they have risked banishment . . . or death.[11]

Because of their bodily differences, women were believed not to belong in the pulpit; thus what Baby Suggs does, similar to the bleeding woman in Luke 8 who reaches out to touch Jesus' garment, is a courageous act because it implicitly reveals that preaching is not solely a male act.

Homiletician Teresa Fry Brown testifies how the aesthetics of her voice and body were attacked unjustly:

> too much or too little makeup, too long or too short hair, too colorful or too dull dress, too low or too high shoes, too long or too shiny earrings, or too long or too red fingernails—was the source of criticism. My mannerisms were also evaluated—smiling too much, crying too much, speaking too loudly or too softly, being too happy or too sad, reading too properly or with too familiar language. There was a flood of criticism and a drought of affirmation.[12]

Despite opposition and critique, many women resist homiletical

---

11. Roxanne Mountford, *The Gendered Pulpit: Preaching in American Spaces* (Carbondale: Southern Illinois University Press, 2003), 9.
12. Teresa Fry Brown, *Weary Throats and New Songs: Black Women Proclaiming God's Word* (Nashville: Abingdon, 2003), 13–14.

patriarchy and press toward the mark of their calling to preach with their bodies. Women make up the majority of church membership yet function, in terms of the ordained preaching ministry, as second-class citizens. The gender prejudice is real and speaking about the body in preaching surfaces this conversation—one that is necessary to have in honor of Baby Suggs and other brave women proclaimers.

The homiletical dance of Baby Suggs reveals how a preacher's body movement can be the heart of the preaching event. It is not *all* of the preaching moment but a vital aspect of it. People hear and see sermons. Onlookers may see that the Lord is good based on how one uses one's body in preaching. Preaching then is not just word but also deed. It is active and action. The body speaks and may say some things that verbal speech cannot articulate. The body is the core of human communication. The word event, preaching, is an embodied event. There has to be some-body present to preach, and Christian bodies are temples of the Spirit, graced with the potential to sound and body forth human experience of the divine. Preachers are stewards of the holy in and through the body. Thus, great care should be given to our bodies in preaching.

Bodily Considerations

Our bodies matter and are vital to preaching thus it is important to explore what and how our bodies preach as they speak from a pulpit. There are many practical things to consider when thinking about the body in preaching; thus what is named in the following is not exhaustive but suggestive as a means to help you become more attentive to your body and other bodies in the pulpit. By reflecting on various aspects of the body, it is my hope that you will grow in somatic wisdom, knowing your body better as a means to understanding what role your body and other bodies play in preaching.

Breath

Practically (and theologically!), breath is important for the body to work and key as a starting point for bodily considerations. In fact, when thinking about the power source of the voice, breath is critical; all of my former voice teachers stressed this. Breathing properly gives the voice and body the support it needs to proclaim the word with strength, power, and fluidity. If there is no breath, the body will not move and it will only be a homiletical zombie (Ezek. 37:8). We may see flesh and bones but will not feel or hear any breath. Your preaching will not have life if there is no breath. Shortness of breath will lead to an unsustainable message and may in fact break up the meaning of what you are trying to say. A lack of deep breath can make your voice sound weak and will inhibit the amount of volume you can use. The more breath support you have, the more versatile you can be in terms of such things as pitch, pace, and volume. Solid breath support can make you feel grounded, stable, and secure. Without it, when you declare, "This is the word of the Lord," the people may not be sure you really mean it because it sounds sheepish or lacking confidence due to volume, pitch, or tone. In an extreme case, it could be so bad for the hearer (and preacher) that such a short phrase cannot be done with one solid breath. Breath is vital not only because it empowers the preaching body but because every breath is a prayer animated by the Spirit, and prayer is the source of deep connection with God and animation of the body, individual and collective.

Some teachers link a sense of presence and Presence with embodiment and (breathing) prayer. Through prayer, preachers become aware of the living God in their midst as they breathe in the good and breathe out the bad. This spiritual breath allows preachers to become centered within and connected to the community and the word. As homiletician Ron Allen teaches, "The preacher cannot put on presence, like an alb or a Geneva gown. It grows from prayer . . ."[13] It flows from breath. Embodiment is shaped by passion discovered through prayer that is breathing in the life of God. Holy breath is the life of preaching and partaking of this holy life-breath leads preachers to be more whole and holy.

The breath flowing through the body is the movement of the Spirit, and as such the body is an epistemological site of knowledge. Through bodily action, we come to know God and the word more intimately. Developing vocal and physical gestural fluidity is not of secondary importance; it is critical to condition one's whole self (including the mind through study) to acquire and reveal knowledge through the preaching event. Wherever breath is, there is life and movement, even music, for without breath it will be difficult to sing the gospel.

This became clear for one preacher at the wrong time. She was fired up about the word. Her volume was high and her rhythm was beating like a drum. Her pitch was at full praise throttle. She was rising to the heights of homiletical celebration, taking the excited congregation along with her for the spiritual ride. The congregation was celebrating with her as they talked back to her with the joy and hope of the gospel, when all of a sudden her pace and intensity got the best of her. Her spirit was high but her breath support was low—so low, in fact, that right at the point when she was about to sing or intone, she fainted! Because of this unforgettable moment, this preacher will never forget how important breath support is for homiletical body talk. Neither should you. Breath is vital for the music of preaching.

13. Ronald Allen, *Interpreting the Gospel: An Introduction to Preaching* (St. Louis: Chalice, 1998), 227–28.

Music

When it comes to preaching, it is important to remember that it is an oral/aural practice. The sermon is not the manuscript or notes on paper. The sermon is the music that happens off the page. Melody, pitch, volume, pace, rhythm, and phrasing are not peripheral to preaching. How language, voice, and gesture coalesce shapes the musical performance. A manuscript is basically musical notes to be played by the preacher, but not until the preacher preaches do we have music. The music of preaching varies. It can be rock-n-roll or hip-hop. It may be the blues or a classical symphony. The music heard depends on who the preacher is and is becoming. Every preacher has a song to sing, and the song is the gospel. I am not suggesting that every preacher has to be a professional musician or singer. What I am saying is that every preacher can make music and that preaching itself is musical. The questions thus are, "What kind of music do I make in preaching?" and "As I listen to others preach, what kind of music do I hear?" Every person does not appreciate or connect with every single musical genre for a variety of reasons. The same is true for preaching, even with the deep theological sense undergirding this book—not everyone will connect with or like our preaching all of the time. People are drawn to different types of music just as you are. Also, it could be that your volume or pace gets in the way of your message; it is not the musical genre itself that is the issue but how you are performing the music that is a hindrance in some way. As with music of any kind, listeners have to tune their ear to the style over time to come to fully understand the meanings that arise and how a musical piece works. The challenge and opportunity is to become as versatile as possible with your homiletical music depending on where and for whom you are preaching. Regardless of denominational tradition, preaching is music and music is a physical activity of body and voice, movement and sound.

Sound helps a sermon make sense to the listeners and provides a surplus of meaning to signify the presence of the Savior. A sermon manuscript or words on a page do not sound on their own. Paper is not a person or preacher and thus cannot proclaim. Words on a page must be spoken to be heard or it is not preaching, nor can it be music. In many African American churches, preaching has been music for centuries so it is easy to find someone who speaks of singing sermons and preaching songs. There is a long history of chanting or whooping sermons, revealing the synergistic relationship between music and the preaching ministry. When this convergence occurs, the preacher becomes the word performed, bringing the words on paper to life. It takes the human voice and body to give the Scriptures voice; without the human vehicle, Scripture does not sing.

The music of preaching is not confined to any one denomination or culture. Presbyterians, Lutherans, Episcopalians, and Seventh Day Adventists sing. It is not just Pentecostals or Baptists who can make music in the pulpit. All preachers can sing, and sermons can dance, too. Your sermon will not necessarily dance like Baby Suggs or Miriam (Exod. 15:20). You will dance like you. You will make music like you. Be yourself when you preach. Your music or dance is unlike any other and it is important to reflect on how you make music and dance in preaching. We sometimes have images of preaching that are dour and dirge-like and nothing that resembles music-making. However, consider that the body points us toward the possibilities of making music when we preach. As pulpit musicians, your aim is to dance to the rhythm of the Spirit as preachers dance with God, Scripture, and the congregation. It could be a waltz, the funky chicken, or jazz. Even as you tune your physical instrument to resonate with the wind of the Spirit blowing in the congregation, you should also be mindful that bodily considerations also include the body of the congregation because, as the saying goes, "It takes two to tango."

Community

It may be easy to overlook the congregation when thinking about embodiment in preaching but the emphasis on preaching as an oral/aural act necessarily includes the hearers in the congregation. What Evans Crawford calls "homiletical musicality" includes the congregation as part of the musical performance.[14] He has the "call-and-response" dynamic within many African American churches in mind, yet it would be a misnomer to suggest call and response only happens in these congregations. Call and response has a distinct form in African American congregations, but communal embodiment of the word happens in other settings. When people laugh or sigh in response to something said, call and response is happening. When a congregant shifts in his seat and leans forward to hear what you have to say, that is a response. Even if the response is not heard, that does not mean there is none. The response of a congregation is part of the sermon form the public body expresses. We do not normally think about the congregation when discussing embodiment in preaching, but we should. Listening to their body talk may inform how your body is talking or singing when you preach. Furthermore, their body talk may influence how your body talks while preaching. You may have to adapt what you are saying or doing based on the responses seen and heard. It also might mean that when you are tired (and

14. Evans Crawford, *The Hum: Call and Response in African American Preaching* (Nashville: Abingdon, 1995), 15–24; cf. William C. Turner Jr., "The Musicality of Black Preaching," in *Performance in Preaching: Bringing the Sermon to Life*, ed. Jana Childers and Clayton J. Schmit (Grand Rapids: Baker Academic, 2008), 191–209.

there will be times you will get tired!) the energy and strength of the congregation will buoy you and the word coming forth.

The example of Baby Suggs is a case in point. When she speaks with her twisted hip what was on her heart, Morrison writes that "others opened their mouths and gave her the music . . ." This is a literary example of communal embodiment. There has been much literature about the role of the listening congregation in preaching in the last twenty years or so, but the call-and-response dynamic is a distinct expression of the embodiment of the sermon in a community. It is the homiletical affirmation of what apostle Paul teaches: the individual body of a believer/preacher is not the only temple of the Spirit; the collective body of believers in a church is a temple of the Spirit, too (1 Cor. 3:16-17). The sermon is a collective symphony in which the entire body participates in the word event. Movement happens behind the pulpit through the preacher and in front of it through the congregation. Some may shout in agreement with the preacher by saying, "Amen!" or "Preach it!" or "Tell it like it is!" This "talk back" is part of the Spirit among God's people, as the sermon becomes a community's word and not sole possession of the preacher. It is a holy dance and spiritual song. It is verbal and nonverbal, vocal and nonvocal. What it looks like shifts across contexts but what remains the same is the community's involvement.

What I have named—breath, music, and community—are key overarching ideals to keep in mind when dealing with the body in preaching. These are not always discussed in relation to this topic, yet they are important matters to consider for the larger framework of homiletical embodiment. In the following, we will discuss some of the typical categories related to the body in preaching in order to help you reflect more deeply on your body habits in the pulpit and overall gestural repertoire.

Gestural Repertoire

I use the notion of "repertoire" because these aspects of your embodiment of the word in the Spirit comprise the range of possibilities for making music in preaching. These aspects of your gestural ecology provide you with options that coordinate with each other to make the most meaningful homiletical music possible in any given moment. At certain times during a sermon, different pieces may be more central depending on what you are emphasizing at the moment. Nonetheless, the hope is that you, as a preacher, will be able to utilize your full bodily arsenal for the glory of God. The truth is, you will never be able to escape your body so you might as well explore how best to utilize it in preaching, since it is always speaking anyhow.

Word and Movement

First, it is important to consider the interface of word and movement in preaching overall. As we see with Jesus, the enfleshed Word of God, he embodied the Word in word and deed. He spoke and acted. His words and actions comprised the totality of the word event of God in Christ in the power of the Spirit. His words did things and his actions spoke. There was a congruency between what he said and how he said it. His verbal expression reinforced his nonverbal expression and vice versa. There was a matching of sorts, which has been discussed in the field of the oral interpretation of Scripture that eventually became what we now call performance studies. Having what we say and how we say it "match" is vital because if they don't, we might send confusing signals to the hearers and beholders of preaching. Those in the congregation receive the word verbally and nonverbally through what Teresa Fry Brown refers to as "logosomatic language."[15]

In preaching, the word has a body and gestures according to what needs to be proclaimed. There is a fusion between word and movement in preaching; therefore, aiming to mean what you say and show, and to say and show what you mean, become critical to the effectiveness of the preaching event. Of course, just because we think our words and actions match in the moment does not guarantee the sermon will be God's word for the people in that time and place. We can dot every "i" and cross every "t" of theory and practice, but this does not assure us that divine power will grace us. Preaching is always a prayer to God to come, but this does not excuse us from putting forward our best word, voice, and body. We cannot assume that we are always aware of how our words and movement during preaching converge or diverge. Together they are to be one word animated by the Spirit. But it can be the case that they somehow speak different words so that people are unsure what is being proclaimed or if the preacher actually believes what is proclaimed. This is a serious consideration because "faith comes by hearing" (Rom. 10:17), yet it may also come by seeing and other senses, which is relevant in light of the Lord's Supper where we taste, feel, and see bread and wine. Thus, what we say and do affect what the congregation receives as the Word for them.

Voice and Verb

Second, and more specifically, you should reflect on your vocal and verbal gestures. Verbal gesture relates to the articulation and diction of actual words. It involves the physical articulators of the teeth, tongue, palate, and jaw. As one diction exercise says, "Diction is done with the tip of the tongue, the teeth, and lips." Verbal gesture, for example, involves if the words we declare are free and flowing

---

15. Teresa L. Fry Brown, *Delivering the Sermon: Voice, Body, and Animation in Proclamation*, Elements of Preaching (Minneapolis: Fortress Press, 2008), 77.

or like fire, legato or staccato, whether we elongate vowels and punch consonants. All of these verbal gestures make meaning and say a word about the Word. Vocal gesture, on the other hand, is more than words but includes the "how" of speech, that is, how we verbalize. The human voice is the vehicle for verbs. Aspects of voice are timber, volume, pitch, and overall issues of sound quality—for example, whether you sound as if you are under water or very nasal. Vocal gesture affects verbal gesture and vice versa because they work together in hope of conveying shared meaning.

One may speak words but not be "on voice" because the sound is a whisper rather than the sound made from the normative vibration of vocal cords. The voice affects the meaning of the verbs, the words. Once again it is a question of congruency. Did you say a word in the way it needed to be said to convey its meaning in the sermon? To declare "the joy of the Lord is your strength" (Neh. 8:10) is very different from the question of lamentation, "My God, my God, why have you forsaken me?" (Ps. 22:1). The content is different, thus the mood and tone of what you proclaim with your voice should also reflect a difference. If not, joy will sound like lament! When you speak of God's love and how nothing will separate us from the love of God in Christ Jesus (Romans 8), this should not sound like "Is there no balm in Gilead? Is there no physician there?" (Jer. 8:22). Different words or verbs require a different use of voice. A mindful preacher will be aware of this and the ways vocal gesture can reinforce verbal gesture, and how it is a challenge to separate the two.

In addition, to be "on voice" also means to be in alignment with one's vocation; thus we can speak of finding one's voice in preaching. Every voice is different, but every voice is essential. Your voice is your own. It cannot be duplicated nor should it be. It is the voice that helps shape the musicality of preaching. James Weldon Johnson's account at the beginning of this chapter centered on the voice of the preacher. Everyone may not be a trombone. Some may be a trumpet or flute or saxophone or violin. But every voice can sing the gospel. Every preacher can gesture successfully on behalf of the gospel so that it can get the widest hearing possible.

To speak of the voice and vocal gesture leads one back to the earlier discussion of the importance of breath for the body in preaching. To sing the gospel robustly requires hearty and full breathing. You may want to engage a vocal coach or acting coach to help develop these skills because it is vital for performing the sermon as best you can. Deep diaphragmatic breathing is crucial for the support of a powerful voice. Deep breathing that fills the diaphragm will move one away from thinking about breathing from the throat. We do not breathe from our throats. Doing so will lead to shortness of breath, a sign that the depth of one's breath is lacking. Breathing exercises can be done outside of the preaching moment with the goal that breathing deeply becomes a natural process; after all, you do not want to be working on your breathing *during* preaching. Rather, you want your breathing to be working your preaching. Just as it may not be natural to breathe deeply, it may not be natural for one to preach with one's own voice, making the music it was created to make. It takes time to learn your voice, to learn who you are as a person and preacher. Vocal gesturing can help you discover what you sound like, and over time you may eventually come to know yourself in a fuller way. In the meantime, the aim in preaching is for your voice to be free to express congruently what is being spoken in any given moment. Peace should sound like peace. Love should sound like love. Pain should sound like pain. You cannot depend on a church's sound system to do this for you. Your vocal and verbal gesture have to work together to do it. A sound system can enhance your preaching, but, believe it or not, it can also hurt it. This is why any aspiring preacher should know that he or she can make music on his or her own.

No piece of technology can do the preaching for you. You are the homiletical instrument through which the Spirit can play the word. You will rise high and you will stoop low. You will play fast and you will play slow. At times, staccato, and at other times, legato. But through your voice, you will make music; thus, how you use your voice is just as important as what you say with your voice.

Face, Hands, Eyes

Yet the voice is not the only part of our homiletical musical instrument or gestural repertoire. Thirdly, you should also consider your face, hands, and eyes. Does your face say what you want it to say? Does it match your words? If you want to express happiness, do you look angry or sad? If you want to convey a sense of confidence, do you look afraid, even without knowing it? Facial expressions speak and people watch you, therefore watching yourself in a mirror or on a video can be helpful in seeing the word you proclaim. It may not be what you think, for better or worse! Self-awareness is important, which is one of the most important things to take away from these bodily considerations.

The same is true of your hands. Do they aid or distract from your message? Do you flap your hands or fold your hands at times when it would make sense to do something else with your hands? Might those gestures be distracting at times? Once again, find opportunities where you can watch yourself and even get constructive feedback from trusted friends and colleagues. As a seminary friend once told me, "Check yourself before you wreck yourself"—or wreck the sermon. Eye contact and usage also need to be considered in how they fit with the portrayal of the Word for the day. Where do you look and why? Be careful where you look when you say John the Baptist's words, "You brood of vipers!" (Luke 3). You would not want to look directly at the congregation then (or maybe you would!). Are there particular moments in the sermon that you want to gaze in a specific spot? Are you seeing it before saying it? Do you see the still waters of Psalm 23 or the hills from Psalm 121 in your mind's eye? If so, at those moments you should not look at the people but gaze out with great focus as if you are looking at the waters or hills, which may help the congregation see those things as well.

Also, in other biblical and contemporary moments, it can be helpful to see what you are saying—the woman hemorrhaging blood for twelve years reaching out to touch Jesus (Mark 5); the paralytic man being brought down to Jesus through a roof (Mark 2); that little elementary-aged girl cheering and giggling as she sits on a swing and flies back and forth; the seven-year-old boy frustrated because he just struck out in a baseball game. "See it before you say it" is a mantra that may not only lead you deeper into a story or image but can lead others in the same direction; where and how you physically look will have an impact on this.

Whether it be the face, hands, or eyes, a key consideration is how meaningful your gestures are for the purposes of preaching. Have you given thought to these aspects of your physical instrument? Why do you do certain movements with your hands or look in certain directions or make certain facial gestures at certain moments? Does what you do make sense in order to convey the sense of the gospel?

Bodily considerations are significant for becoming the best preacher that you can become by God's grace. Attending to the body is not peripheral to preaching preparation and delivery; it is central because God became a body, you preach with your body, and preaching does not exist without a human body. But I must acknowledge that gestures can have different meanings in different contexts and cultures. A scream or shout in a sermon may lead one to think the preacher is angry in one church, but in another environment the people would believe that this sound indicates a heightened sense of the presence of God. There is variety and beauty in the possible diversity. Uniformity of expression is not the goal, at least when it comes to God. Unity, even the unity of a sermon, is enhanced by the body talk of the preacher. The gestural repertoire is to aid the music being made in the pulpit. Sermon unity can be achieved by different means but it is key that the "how" and "what" of the sermon converge and complement each other. It does not always happen nor does failure dictate God's presence and power. If God can raise Jesus from the dead, God can surely resurrect our sermons, even when we are in the way. Thus, even our body talk is a prayer for the Holy Spirit to breathe life into us, because it is only the Spirit who can make us the preachers we ought to be, mentally, spiritually, and physically.

Further Learning Strategies

1. Inhale as much air as possible in two seconds and attempt to fill your diaphragm like a tire. After you inhale, hold your breath for two seconds and then exhale all of your breath in two seconds. Increase your time by two seconds for every attempt as a way to work on breath control and stamina. Work your way up to ten seconds for the inhale, hold, and exhale. Has there ever been a time when you lost control of your breath or had shallow breathing? If so, what happened as a result? Why do you think this occurred?

2. Choose your favorite passage of Scripture. Try "body-talk biblical interpretation" by performing that text in some way so that someone observing you would understand the meaning you are trying to portray without using words. Sound it (without words), dance it, or try some other form of embodiment to enact the text.

3. Go to a church you have never visited before and "read" the

sermon text of the preacher's body. If you couldn't hear words and only watched the body talk, what would the sermon be about? Is there congruency between the preacher's words and movements? If you cannot attend a church service, answer the same questions by watching a sermon online on YouTube, making sure to mute the sound.

4. Gather in groups of three and discuss how your churches talk about the human body. Do they talk about it and its role in the life of Christian discipleship, or is there "somatic dis-ease"?

Further Reading

Bartow, Charles. *God's Human Speech: A Practical Theology as Proclamation*. Grand Rapids: Eerdmans, 1997. A theological and practical study of how the Bible read and sermon delivered are means of grace, stressing aspects of embodiment.

Childers, Jana. *Performing the Word: Preaching as Theatre*. Nashville: Abingdon, 1998. A study of the parallels between theatre and preaching and the ways in which the experiences and skills of actors and performance artists can be applied to preaching.

Childers, Jana, and Clayton J. Schmit, eds. *Performance in Preaching: Bringing the Sermon to Life*. Grand Rapids: Baker Academic, 2008. A collection of essays from homileticians who explore various aspects of performance in relation to preaching.

Crawford, Evans. *The Hum: Call and Response in African American Preaching*. Nashville: Abingdon, 1995. A study of the musicality of black preaching with particular attention to the historical communal dynamic known as call-and-response.

Fry Brown, Teresa L. *Delivering the Sermon: Voice, Body, and Animation in Proclamation*. Elements of Preaching.

Minneapolis: Fortress Press, 2008. An introduction to the rationale and methods for effective use of voice and body in the animation of the word in the preaching event. Numerous exercises are provided for conversation and actual practice.

Mountford, Roxanne. *The Gendered Pulpit: Preaching in American Protestant Spaces.* Carbondale: Southern Illinois University Press, 2005. Explores the relationship between bodies, space, race, and gender in rhetorical performance and American Protestant culture, particularly as it relates to women.

9

———

Preaching and Technology

Luke A. Powery

In the previous chapter, we learned how the Word became flesh in Jesus Christ and the ways in which this deepens our understanding of the role of the human body in preaching. While this is true, it is also obvious that in this digital age, some may assert that the Word has also now become digital. One cannot deny technology's pervasive presence in society, including the church and its preaching. The fact of technology and its use will not be disappearing anytime soon; thus, this chapter will explore what it means to engage technologies in preaching and some of the challenges and opportunities in doing so.

I serve in a university community where Sunday corporate worship is heard on the radio, viewed on hospital televisions, watched on YouTube, and listened to on iTunes. And guess what? God still speaks in all those mediums. During one late summer, I received a call from Duke University Hospital. A hospital chaplain asked if I would make a surprise visit to a man waiting for a heart transplant as a way to lift his spirits. I assured the chaplain that Coach K of the Duke men's basketball team might offer a better surprise visit; the chaplain disagreed. He said that this particular patient had become "enthralled" with Duke Chapel while in the hospital through the watching of our worship services on his hospital television. The chaplain told me that many heart-transplant patients require antidepressants when waiting for a new heart. But for this gentleman, Duke Chapel was his antidepressant.

God works in mysterious ways even through technology; thus, God is not limited by our limitations. In this specific case, it is not that technology was used to enhance a sermon per se (and I must confess that I do not use technology when preaching except microphones) but was used to make the sermon more public—locally, nationally, and internationally. Either way, it is important to reflect on what it means to have technology involved in the preaching moment. Despite problems with "Christian" television, it is not all bad. The extension of the gospel is global à la the day of Pentecost, and media, in whatever form, facilitates this. The media airwaves are not solely for televangelists. Big screens and sermons on iPads are not just for megachurches. God can speak through whatever means, even a dead dog, according to theologian Karl Barth.[1] This does not mean that there are not some theological and practical concerns with the use of technology in preaching. At the same time, we must recognize, in this digital age, that the enfleshed word can also be relayed digitally. Discerning the best path forward is the ongoing challenge and opportunity.

1. Karl Barth, *Church Dogmatics* Vol. I, Part 1 (New York: T&T Clark, 2009), 60.

Technology and Preaching: A Historical Tension

When it comes to a conversation about technology and preaching, one might easily think about the visual projection of images or the use of movie clips in sermons. Or one might ponder the use of an iPad for sermon notes or multisite churches that project the image and voice of their senior pastor on a screen at each site to assure that the same word is heard in each location every Sunday. Some may recall the liturgy of lament that arose online after the Virginia Tech massacre in 2007 or consider how technophiles have created apps for all kinds of spiritual purposes, including confession.[2] It would be easy to jump into this contemporary milieu, but it is important to recognize that the delicate dance of technology and its relationship to preaching is not really new.

The work of Walter Ong, along with others, has been critical to thinking about orality and literacy and how various technologies, including print media, have had an impact on preaching over time.[3] For instance, printing and writing have shaped preaching and the teaching of preaching in seminaries. Even though preaching is an oral/aural venture, many times it is still geared toward the printed page. Even at Duke Chapel, many expect printed copies of sermons to be available immediately following the Sunday-morning service. People want to read sermons, not only listen to them; this phenomenon has been shaped by a literate culture engulfed in written texts. This is just one example, but negotiating changes in technology while remaining faithful to the proclamation of the gospel has been an ongoing conversation. The technologies shift so quickly and

---

2. See Maureen Dowd, "Forgive Me, Father, for I Have Linked," *New York Times*, February 8, 2011, http://www.nytimes.com/2011/02/09/opinion/09dowd.html.
3. See Walter J. Ong, *Orality and Literacy: The Technologizing of the Word* (New York: Routledge, 1982); and idem, *The Presence of the Word: Some Prolegomena for Cultural and Religious History* (Binghamton, NY: Global Publications, 2000).

continue to "advance," influencing how people hear and see sermons and even shape what might be considered a "good sermon." All preachers have to deal with this reality using discerning wisdom and determine for themselves whether technological developments have or have not advanced the purposes of preaching.

The creative tension between technology and preaching has always been present. Even in 1964 when the Rev. Dr. Martin Luther King, Jr. gave his Nobel Prize acceptance speech, he noted how the "dazzling picture of modern man's scientific and technological progress" has not led to the sparkling of the human spirit. King says forthrightly:

> [I]n spite of these spectacular strides in science and technology, and still unlimited ones to come, something basic is missing. There is a sort of poverty of the spirit which stands in glaring contrast to our scientific and technological abundance. The richer we have become materially, the poorer we have become morally and spiritually. We have learned to fly the air like birds and swim the sea like fish, but we have not learned the simple art of living together as brothers.[4]

King, though not talking about preaching per se, speaks to the topic at hand through his realization that there is more to life—and thus more to preaching and more to ministry—than technological progress. There is the human spirit and the Holy Spirit, and if we forget this we will not be like a tree planted by the rivers of water that brings forth fruit in due season. We will be dry and ultimately die due to a spiritual famine as the inner life lags behind the outer life of technological progress, causing detrimental problems for the soul of preaching. There are those, including King, who urge us to remember the human and spiritual resources of preaching amidst the proliferation of innovate technological resources, though these

---

4. Martin Luther King, Jr., "The Quest for Peace and Justice," 1964 Nobel Peace Prize acceptance speech, http://www.nobelprize.org/nobel_prizes/peace/laureates/1964/king-lecture.html.

resources might be helpful to preachers and have been so throughout history.

Some of the tension at play here is that preachers might be rich in the latest, cool, and creative ideas for using technology, but poor, empty, and callous in heart and soul. This is highly problematic when the heart of preaching is a S/spiritual event. This is why some warn against allowing technology to override theology. Nonetheless, preachers may choose to use technology in a variety of forms and must be ready to negotiate why they do and how they do, especially in light of what I just mentioned. This is clearly a cautionary note (even from me!). The historical tensions have been present because more than the use of technology is at stake—it is about the what and why of technology and its consequences on our lives together, including preaching practices, as well. I am reminded of the popular phrase "the medium is the message,"[5] which implies that the medium of technology shapes and even controls how one preaches and how that preaching is received. This does not have to be solely about whether or not one uses projection screens but may include conversations about data speed, lighting, sound, photos/images, radio, TV, movies, laptops, iPads, iPhones, iPods, and more.

Why do you use the technology that you use when you preach and what is at stake by using it? Or, if you do not use technology, why not? There can be levels of technological usage, yet we should always keep in mind the ways the media of the sermon shape the sermon, preacher, and hearer. What are we saying about the Word when we put images on a projection screen as part of the preaching event? Are we implying that the Word is an image? Digital media such as PowerPoint or video and audio recordings challenge the medium of the traditional sermon but the question is, "What direction do

---

5. Marshall McLuhan, *Understanding Media: The Extensions of Man* (New York: McGraw-Hill, 1964), 8–9.

these media take sermons in terms of form and content?" Do they have a positive or negative impact on the congregation? No one can assume that all technology is bad or all technology is good. As you think about preaching animated by the Spirit, it is important to reflect on the impact of technology on and in preaching in order to make wise, thoughtful decisions about its interface with your proclamation. There are challenges and opportunities with technology. Some tensions will never disappear; thus, as preachers, we have to navigate this technological relationship, acknowledging both gains as well as losses when one uses technology in preaching. In the following two sections, I will probe what might be lost and gained with technology as it relates to preaching as an attempt to help you think further about your own perspectives on technology and preaching.

Losing with Technology

Technology is not going away; thus, we have to engage it in some way rather than hunker down in our traditional bunkers. What matters is how we engage it and for what reasons. Blindly adopting various media for preaching without some reflection on doing so can be harmful because, though we are in a digital age, we may not have considered what might be lost with the use of technology. We will explore what might be gained in a little bit but first take a moment to ponder a few negative possibilities as it relates to technology and preaching. This will reinforce the idea of the ongoing creative tension in the relationship between technology and preaching. Thus, the following is a skeptical and cautious perspective on this relationship. What do we lose with technology?

Loss of Incarnational Preaching

One of the first things we might discover is a loss of incarnational preaching, especially in light of the previous chapter on the body, our own and Christ's, and what that means for preaching the gospel. As we noted earlier, preaching is rhetorical but it is also deeply theological. It is more than *techne*. It requires a body, as evidenced in God's sermon in Jesus Christ called the Incarnation. The Word event is incarnational, thus preaching is as well. It is face-to-face, flesh-to-flesh communication in word and deed. Real human bodies, as opposed to virtual realities and bodies, are essential for the preaching ministry. Some congregations use holograms of their pastors because of their multisite campuses to convey a sense of in-person presence. You may have the image of the preacher but there is no body there, no flesh and blood present, except at the "main campus." This is not to say God cannot speak or use technology but rather to indicate the complexities of what is at stake when we use technology and what may be lost. One has to consider how the Word is received differently when a real body is present in the sanctuary compared to when one watches a sermon on a big screen. A preacher once referred to Jesus as God's selfie, but we know that Jesus, the Word of God, is more than a tweet or a Skype chat. He touched people and was physically present to them. He did not fax his love. Rather, he used his body on a cross to demonstrate it. Jesus was the Word incarnate, a person, an enfleshed sermon, not a text.

An incarnational sermon encompasses more than technology can offer, though there are trends in the church to utilize the Internet for various ecclesial practices such as communion. If we "do church" only online, the demise of pastoral visits to the sick and shut-in will surely follow. No one requests funeral sermons to be preached online rather than at a gravesite with a grieving family. At its heart, the Christian ministry is enfleshed, incarnational. Likewise, preachers want real people in the flesh in the listening congregation. Who wants to preach to high-definition images of a congregation weekly as opposed to people in the pews who you can see, smell, and touch? Of course, these are extreme examples, and technology does not necessarily have to head in the direction of extremes. But the use of technology in preaching raises questions about the incarnational nature of preaching.

More concretely, technology could be used as an easy way out of sermon development. For instance, a preacher might show an image on a projection screen rather than attempt to paint the image orally with human words. The word event includes incarnate words, and technology could limit one's effort at constructing one's own sermon language. We could show a picture of a deer by water trying to exemplify Psalm 42—"As the deer longs for flowing streams, so my soul longs for you, O God." But what this approach can do is dumb down the human imagination. Why show an image when you can describe a deer sipping from a cool, flowing stream? The reality is that what one person imagines will be different from what another person sees in her or his mind's eye. When you use a visual image it may not reach your ultimate goal because they are "finally literal. What you see is what you get."[6] This approach puts limits on the Spirit's work in the human imagination. When technology is used as a replacement for real incarnational relationships and interaction and real enfleshed preaching, we lose the core identity of preaching. Rather, technology should be a supplement to the incarnational dynamic of the word event, whether we are dealing with language or our bodies. Because preaching is so incarnational, it is very human. This points to another potential loss—the loss of our humanity.

Loss of Our Humanity

The loss of our humanity is closely linked to the incarnational nature

---

6. Thomas G. Long, *The Witness of Preaching*, 2nd ed. (Louisville: Westminster John Knox, 2005), 235.

of preaching and how the ministry of preaching, as all of ministry, is deeply human and requires human interactions to sustain the work and to illumine one's approach to preaching. If we lose our humanness, not only might our preaching become robotic, but it may lose its relevance to those who listen to our sermons. In reality, we may think we are "connected" with our congregants through LinkedIn or Facebook and still not really know them and be disconnected. You may see their faces but not know their hearts. The Spirit's work is critical in helping us to know people better, but we can get so consumed with using social media and other electronic platforms and think that those are the best way to get connected. It is always important to remember that technology cannot feel human feelings. Technology cannot love. Humans love and preaching is a rendezvous of love. Without the human element leading the way, preaching will lose its loving aims because it will have lost its humanity.

In the larger ecology of ministry, technology cannot serve food at a soup kitchen, visit a prisoner, or offer care at a birth or a death. All of these dimensions of ministry shape what preaching is; it is human, so we ought to be cautious of jumping on the latest techie-upgrade bandwagon. Just because we see someone's face on Facebook does not mean he or she is really our friend. We may think we know them but how is that possible if we never sit down with them face-to-face in a normal human encounter? To get to know someone, you have to listen and learn from them, laugh and cry with them. A problem with technology, at times, is that it may give us a false sense of a relationship without the commitment. Harvard minister and professor Jonathan Walton writes, "Intimacy without contact and familiarity without interpersonal exchange fosters false expectations of the other." He states further that faith leaders have "become little more than living avatars."[7] This is the danger of some media forms that provide connections without relationships; effective preaching is relational.

If preachers do not engage in relationships as a natural aspect of being human (and, of course, a key part of ministry) and primarily engage with others through technological outlets, this could lead to a lack of understanding of our mutual humanity. The preacher is human, and the means by which we proclaim the Word says something about this, but the people to whom we preach are also human. If we only see the congregation as those with whom we connect, we may forget their humanity and only view them as objects to be changed or preached at, rather than as brothers and sisters in Christ. Your approach to preaching will be informed by a sense of common humanity, and this is so much more than the latest technology fad. In an age in which people can engage online anonymously without accountability for what they say, even if it is racist, sexist, or just plain bullying, it is even more critical for Christian preachers to reflect their humanity in Christ through love and empathy. Some argue that the Internet is destroying empathy, as many become more detached even as they become increasingly attached to their gadgets and the computer screen. This digital age may nurture voyeurism without compassion, virtuality and not reality. Preachers have the responsibility to help others remain human in a media-saturated society, and the truth is that technology may not always help us reach this goal.

Loss of Sense of Community

Linked to the loss of humanity that is possible through technology is the potential breakdown of any sense of community. As noted in earlier chapters, preaching is a communal event of the Word. A

7. Jonathan L. Walton, "Staying Human in a Media Age," *Harvard Divinity School* 39, no. 3 & 4 (2011): 8–11.

community is vital to what preaching is and can be, but technology can get in the way of this community aspiration. Social scientist Sherry Turkle argues that "we expect more from technology and less from each other."[8] Through technological means we may have the illusion of companionship or friendship but it is just that—an illusion. People may be more intimate with gadgets than with other people but there is no emotional exchange, no real relational risk. But the gospel is risky and messy and even bloody. Technology can avoid all of that when one only interacts with a laptop screen or iPad. This way of being in the world makes an impact on what preaching is to preachers and congregations. It may lead people to be let down as they listen to sermons because they cannot control what is said or done in the pulpit, unlike their control of technology and personas developed through media. Also, as Turkle writes, "At the screen, you have the chance to write yourself into the person you want to be and to imagine others as you wish them to be, constructing them for your purposes."[9] Technology provides the illusion that we are sovereign, immutable gods in control of ourselves and others, which undercuts genuine dialogue in community. There should be no gods in community but, rather, a sincere relational antiphony.

A genuine homiletical community experiences mutual vulnerability in the presence of a God who became vulnerable for us. We *use* technology, meaning we control it to some degree, but in many ways creative community is formed when we lose control and offer ourselves to each other and God. Though we may believe we are in control, there are consequences. Many argue technology feeds a certain kind of loneliness, connected yet without communion. Preaching, however, aims ultimately for communion with God, our

---

8. Sherry Turkle, *Alone Together: Why We Expect More from Technology and Less from Each Other* (New York: Basic Books, 2011).
9. Ibid., 188.

eternal home. Jumping to technology may cause us to jump into depression without even knowing it. Technology may feel safer than having to interact with real people in the flesh because there is distance from potentially being harmed or having one's feelings hurt. This rationale for using technology can be a way of avoiding human community and avoiding having one's heart damaged. Of course, people get hurt over the Internet, but they can turn off the computer or switch homepages at any point. Preaching does not aim to hurt people, although it has at times. Its hope is the formation of community, Christ's community, the church in love.

These days there are digital churches, but consider what they may mean. People watch sermons or even a whole worship service online or on TV. Through this approach, however, the viewer has the power to change the channel or shut off the sermon if things do not go the way the viewer desires, if the Word is too demanding or challenging or convicting. Technology may make it too easy to stop anything we do not like. Congregation members do have the freedom to walk out of a service, but when a person is alone, watching a community at worship, there is perhaps more freedom to control the situation, even controlling when you want the sermon to end. The crux of the matter is, "How does technology help preaching form community, if it does at all?" God can use virtual choirs and virtual sermons to spread the gospel, but without the face-to-face time in a community, how would anyone really learn how to love like Christ? We learn how to be the body of Christ in person, and preaching in person can foster this. In person with persons we learn social skills that cannot be learned online. In fact, on one level, preaching is a social event.

Loss of Spiritual Growth and Depth

The incarnational and relational dimensions of preaching do not exclude it from being a spiritual practice. The hardwire of technology does not necessarily make preaching less holy, but the increase and even overuse of it may replace not only the incarnational heart of preaching, but its spiritual core also. Preaching as a theological act means there is relationship with God, and God is Spirit so we can talk about the spiritual realm and preaching's role in it. One with a skeptical eye toward technology may point out how the growth in technologies has not meant a growth in a person's spirituality. One might agree with Dr. King that "We have allowed the means by which we live to outdistance the ends for which we live."[10] People, including preachers and congregations, may get excited about the latest technology and how it can be used in ministry; but this excitement often appears to be more real than how they feel about Scripture and the story of God with God's people. In this way, technology does appear to override theology sometimes; thus, we should be careful not to equate technological use with spiritual growth.

> Is it possible that video-enhanced preaching can have the unintentional effect of making us somewhat *less* likely to take action in the world instead of motivating us? Imagine, for example, that the preacher decides to close her sermon with a couple of video clips in which someone takes a tremendous risk to rescue someone in danger. Viewers are moved to tears and the service ends in a moving song of personal devotion. Yet that moment of video "catharsis" *could* leave worshipers feeling as if they've *already* experience a compassionate response to human need when, in fact, the experience was strictly vicarious.
>
> The danger is that we can become cheerleaders for compassion and justice, not agents of these realities. What if imaginative visualization on our *own* mental "screen," prompted by a preacher's skillful words and featuring settings we recognize in our own daily experience, is a crucial link between worship and everyday Christian action? Technology can do much to enlarge our view of the world and activate emotion. It may present inspiring examples. But it's an open question: how can preaching best form listeners as active agents, not passive viewers? – **SB**

People do use technology to listen to sermons, read daily devotionals,

10. King, "Quest for Peace and Justice."

study Scripture, and listen to sacred music. By doing this, they aim to grow spiritually. But certain scholars also see technology as part of the problem that leads to spiritual dissolution. Homiletician David Lose writes, "The radical change in information technology—and particularly the rise of the Internet and the unparalleled access it grants to a dizzying array of comprehensive narratives—explains in large part why former patterns of communication and community building are increasingly ineffective."[11] Lose argues that technologies are a major reason for the destruction of a singular meaning-making narrative like the Bible while promoting multiple narratives that are easily accessible through digital means and searches like Google. We may get bits and pieces of a story from the Internet but it will not necessarily give us the whole story; therefore, it is difficult to grasp the totality of meaning. In addition, it is important to help people understand that we do not aim to commune with technology but God.

To grow in and toward God requires concentration and focus, but technology seems to work against this as companies market "the faster the better." Not only does technology break up a consistent story of faith (bits and pieces here and there), it does not necessarily allow for slow, deep reflection, for pausing to think and ponder about life and God. Tech-savvy preaching may feed into this and actually be working against itself because it is just as fast-paced as technology and has adapted a means that does not aid one reaching an end of eternal rest. Some churches promote texting and tweeting in service, but does that allow for a depth of theological and biblical reflection? Or has the church baptized a means for another end that is not the end of preaching? How can one grow over time if all we do is tweet 140 characters? Sermons can allow time and space for deeper

---

11. David J. Lose, *Preaching at the Crossroads: How the World—and Our Preaching—Is Changing* (Minneapolis: Fortress Press, 2013), 86.

reflection without rushing (though I am not advocating for longer sermons!). Sermons are not sound bites, though this is what is so prevalent in our day. Technology has rewired our brains to such an extent that people are less capable of reading and reflecting beyond a shallow level. People have become skillful at superficiality, and maybe this is true for preachers and the congregation as well because we have a case of "the shallows."[12] But shallow sermons will not prompt spiritual growth and depth; thus, preachers should be aware of how they adopt technology.

Gaining with Technology

For all of the losses associated with the use of technology in preaching, there are also potential gains. This is important to recognize, even when we do not wholeheartedly embrace its use in preaching. Technology by itself is not harmful; it is what you do with it and how it informs your life and ministry that makes it helpful or hurtful. I write this knowing that I do not utilize much technology in preaching but engage it more outside of the preaching event. Yet, how I use it or engage it outside of the ecclesial domain and in the everyday influences how I approach preaching, how I preach, and what I expect from it. The same is true for those who are on the listening end of a sermon. I have noted some losses, which are critical, but I acknowledge there are gains as well. We cannot write off technology point blank because, if we did, we might be writing off God and what God can do in and through it and its use in preaching. Nothing is impossible with God, including making some gains with technology. What do we gain with technology? I offer three suggestive possibilities as food for thought.

---

12. Nicholas Carr, *The Shallows: What the Internet Is Doing to Our Brains* (New York: Norton, 2011).

Gain of Cultural Knowledge

Throughout this book, we have emphasized the importance of contexts for preaching, that is, that preaching is not just about a text, a biblical text, but also relates to con-text, that it is with-text, suggesting that there are other variables that compose the task of preaching. Since preaching is more than Scripture and one needs more than a text to preach the gospel, preaching aims to relate to the world and the wider culture. This includes the wide tent of innovative technologies. By engaging technology in preaching, the church reveals itself as a part of the wider culture, indeed, that it is *in* it, though it may not be *of* it. To utilize technology or to be in conversation with it shows a willingness to learn from culture, to know what is happening in the world, which is where we live as preachers and congregations. Technology is so much a part of our lives, even as I type on a laptop right now (!), thus preachers should not ignore technology because that might send a signal that we are ignoring the people who are immersed in technological worlds. By relating to technology, we reveal how we, as ministers, are open to culture, not opposed to it. Of course, "Christian" preaching is rooted in Christ, but this does not have to translate into hunkering down in a holy, sanctified bunker away from the world. We must always be reminded that God so loved the world that the Word became flesh and entered the world because of love. Preachers can enter the world of technology as an act of love, not of technology per se, but of the people, many of whom are engulfed in technology.

By engaging technology, we can demonstrate that we care about culture, acknowledging all the while that we, too, are a part of the wider culture. We cannot escape it, even if we tried. By using it in some way, we reveal that we are willing to learn more about culture and attempt to relate to this digital age. This is a highly visual age, so thinking of opportunities to engage that sense might be helpful for a sermon at some point, especially if the visual image supports the spoken word and does not replace it. I am not suggesting an all-out endorsement or blessing of everything that occurs in technology; it can have a "dark side," and evil can be promoted through it, but the same could actually be said of preaching and preachers, too! However, what we do with the technology and for what end is key. Is the end the gospel (as it should be)? Preachers need to assess their motivations for using technology. If it is to just be "cool" without having timely reflection on the what and why of technology, you may run into homiletical problems, and definitely theological ones. But a careful embrace of technology might provide insight into the people to whom we are called to minister. We can learn about them via technology. We can learn about the world and preaching's larger contexts through technology and explore more fruitful ways of preaching the gospel, which inhabits the intersecting space of text and context.

Gain of Attending to Learning Styles

Preachers not only gain cultural knowledge by engaging technology but show their attentiveness to different learning styles by doing so. No one person learns the same way and this is true for members in any congregation. This is why it is important to think about ways to alter how you preach and how you put together your sermon. One does not want to organize his or her sermons in the same manner every Sunday. This is bad pedagogy and probably will eventually be boring for the hearers. Moreover, with a diverse congregational makeup, one should realize that everyone is different, including how they learn the gospel. Some may learn more from purely listening. Others are more visual learners and need to see. Some need to feel their bodies move in order to understand God in a deeper way. The point is to learn one's congregation's learning styles. There will be a wide array of listeners and in the age we live in, there are many who learn via technological means.

As ministers desire to serve the congregation in the best way possible, it behooves preachers to discern how best to preach. The use of technology, like movie clips, can connect to a pop-culture sensibility prevalent among one's hearers, and in this digital age with so-called digital natives, visual technologies may be a primary way that your congregants learn. Pastors need to know who is in their congregations because in a "graying congregation" the learning styles could be different. Seminary students are trained, for the most part, to view preaching as primarily hearing-oriented, but in a visual media environment, preachers should also be mindful of how people learn through sight. Seeing on TV, the Internet, iPhones, and iPads is so prevalent that we should consider what this means for how people learn and what they might expect from a sermon. This is not to say that all we do as preachers is to satisfy people's expectations, because this is not why we preach. What I am arguing for is attentiveness to different learning styles, which technology can help us do. Through technology, we can gain different ways of organizing a sermon, which may relate more effectively to certain learning styles. If your congregation includes generations accustomed to screens, pop music, and film, it is vital to assess how preaching may relate to these generations who learn in these kinds of ways.

Utilizing technologies that your people use in order to preach the gospel can be a revelation that the gospel travels across cultures, generations, time, and space. It could demonstrate that the gospel, Jesus, is for them, right where they are, though the gospel will not leave them where they are. Using technologies in preaching may be an implicit sign that they can bring their everyday experiences, their whole lives, into the community of faith to meet God. Nothing is out of the reach of God, including technology, thus preachers could be a resource for how one might integrate their whole lives, including technology, with their faith. Their faith includes their whole life, inside and outside the walls of a church. Digital use in the pulpit may obliterate the sacred and secular divides such that people come to see the gospel as relevant and real for every aspect of their life. Gadgets do not have to replace God but can be utilized to lead others to God and to reach out to those who learn differently and digitally.

Gain of Spreading Gospel Message

It may seem too obvious to mention, but another possible gain with technology is the wider spread of the gospel message. For those who cannot attend a service in person, Internet campuses, live streams of worship, YouTube channels, and radio feeds help share the Word. This should never be a replacement for one joining in a real church community, but the reality is that in this digital age, there are many opportunities for people to hear the word, even if they are not able to be present in a congregation at any given moment for funerals, weddings, or other services. People still yearn for a word from the Lord and these technological access points quench that desire. Plus—and I am a living witness of this—people are touched by God through sermons even if they are not present as they listen via the Internet or radio; God speaks through—and despite—technology. What preacher would not want people to hear the gospel wherever they might be? More people may hear the Word than would normally hear it, but the hope would be that they are already a part of a church or might eventually become a part of a church since nothing can substitute for face-to-face relationships in the church.

Multisite churches see this reality on a regular basis. They have the "home base" where the preacher is in the flesh but then at other locations, his or her image is placed on a big screen for the preaching moment. Their pastors affirm this approach because they can reach more people without having to build more buildings.[13] It could be that even at the home base, big screens are used because of the size of the building and in order to help congregants see the preacher better. Technology then is used as an extension of the body. There are many pastors who view the use of technology as a gain, despite some concerns. But one pastor put it this way to his congregation: "I know you're going to text, tweet and Facebook in church, so give them Jesus while you're at it! . . . It's a good way to share the Gospel with your friends and followers."[14] The idea that technology can help share the gospel should be viewed as a gain, even though we know there are tensions with technology in preaching. But just because there are tensions does not mean we cannot try different approaches. Technology can be viewed as making the church and the gospel more accessible to a wider audience.

Questioning Technology

Even with these noted potential losses and gains with technology, there are still questions that remain. Preaching's relationship to technology will be an ongoing conversation in the future. Just as technology is not going away, neither is preaching. The modern-day mantra says that "the church is dying," but I believe that preaching is not. Thus, to live in tension with technology is the way it must be because there are a variety of views on the role of technology in the church and for preaching in particular. There will never be universal or uniform agreement, but we can acknowledge that there are pluses

13. For an example of this, see John Blake, "'Virtual Preaching' Transforms Sunday Sermons," *CNN*, July 14, 2010, http://www.cnn.com/2010/TECH/innovation/07/14/virtual.preaching/.
14. See Trymaine Lee, "Churches Adopt Technology to Reach Out to Congregants," *Huffington Post*, December 11, 2011, http://www.huffingtonpost.com/2011/12/09/wired-church-technology_n_1139551.html.

and minuses to the use of technology in preaching. Our perspectives may have to do with tradition, experience, or our interpretation of Scripture. Regardless of one's take on technology—fan or full-blown opposition—there are some questions to ask as we continue to navigate the terrain of this techno-revolution. I raise three here.

Technology has extended the reach of Christian worship. Television and the Internet make worship accessible for persons who, for whatever reason (geographical isolation, mobility issues, and the like), cannot be bodily present with others in a worship space. The apostles did not hesitate to use the "technology" of their day—the hand-carried letter. In fact, a letter read to its addressees by someone trained for the task was considered a form of the sender's "presence." Yet, we pick up in many New Testament letters the apostles' eagerness to be bodily present to their congregations. There was finally no substitute for the human body and voice.

Maybe distinguishing between "preaching" and "proclamation" can help us to use technology wisely in worship. Christian "proclamation" includes preaching, but it is broader. Choral song, dance, visual arts, drama and video clips can contribute to "proclamation" of the gospel, yet not substitute for "preaching," per se. Skillful splicing of video, images, and song creates legitimate and powerful forms of Christian proclamation. Yet, historically, preaching refers to the stark simplicity of a human being standing up in all his or her (technologically unassisted) vulnerability and announcing the undefeated love of God in Jesus Christ, freeing us from sin and all that distorts and dehumanizes humanity. This unique wedding of body, voice, and message is portable. It can take place anywhere that human beings gather in longing, suffering, and hope, including places around the globe untouched by the "web world." – **SB**

How Much?

In affirming that there are losses and gains with technology, it is important not to operate within extreme modes of thought that draw a line in the sand and make this conversation black and white; it is not that simple. There are factors of your denominational affiliation, theology, experience, and much more that will guide you in how you engage technology or not. But any engagement with it for preaching has to consider the question, "How much technology is too much?" Is there a limit on what should be done in the preaching event? There is no limit on what *can* be done but how much of it is useful and purposeful is another story altogether. The adage, "less is more," could be helpful in thinking about an economy of use that nurtures technology's supplemental role in preaching. Included in this conversation is whether a certain type of technology is more helpful than others. How much of what technology? PowerPoint? Movie clips? Texting? There are choices to be made and perhaps they shift based on the sermon or the lectionary text of the day. Again, the consideration of how technology helps the end of the proclamation of the gospel is key. Maybe this shapes how much is too much. Nonetheless this is a question worth asking.

What about the Community?

Another important question to pose is, "What is the role of the community in discerning how to use technology?" We have argued that the community is significant for preaching, but how should a preacher involve the larger community when making decisions about technology? To discern what is constructive in a particular congregation will necessitate the communal voice being heard; otherwise, how does a pastor know what is most effective for a particular people? A preacher needs to exegete the congregation in order to learn how best to execute technology in preaching. Congregations should not feel pressured to duplicate Willow Creek, Saddleback, or Potter's House congregations in their uses of technology. Some churches may have electrical outlets for laptops or other devices at the seats in the main sanctuary. You do not have to duplicate that approach, but you should involve churchgoers in deciding the way forward in your churches. Their participation and opinions do matter on the path of discerning what to do, if anything.

When it comes to technology, preachers should want to have the support of their congregations because anything we do in preaching, or in the church as a whole, should have as its aim the growth of the congregation and an aim to live well together on the journey of faith. The influence of congregations should be felt in our decisions about technologies because technology in church shapes the church and not just the preacher. This is why communal discernment about these matters is important. Moreover, the identity of the congregation is shaped by having and using technology. Congregations, including the preacher, are who they are in relation to each other but also to technologies. What technology is used and how it is used has an impact on the whole congregation; thus, it is a communal matter, not the sole purview of the preacher. In an individualistic culture, it may be hard to swallow the fact that preaching is not just about the preacher. Furthermore, this topic of technology in preaching challenges us to remember that not everyone is having this conversation.

Is Everyone Doing It?

A third question that arises in this discussion is, "Are we assuming that everyone is using technology?" In this age of globalization, in a highly connected world, one might think the citizens of the world are drawing closer to one another. On one level this might be true, but on other levels, it is not. People might actually be more disconnected because of an assumption that everyone has access to technology, whatever it might be, and this is not the case. In some ways, one might argue that a discussion about technology in preaching is a privileged conversation because it assumes a certain level of resources that enable a community to purchase technology. Not every community or church has the means to buy state-of-the-art equipment because one has to have a certain amount of financial resources to do so.[15] Some rural and urban settings may not

15. For example, see Kim Severson, "Digital Age Is Slow to Arrive in Rural America," *New*

have access, or at least affordable access, which implies the role of economics and class disparities.

This conversation raises social-justice issues about power and privilege. Who is excluded when we start talking about technology and preaching? Even to talk about technology, the losses and gains, is a privilege when others may not be able to focus on this because the basic necessities of life are missing—food, water, jobs, and education. Technology is not a high priority for preachers when you or your people are lacking the basics to sustain life and life is a matter of survival. It is essential that we acknowledge this and affirm that not everyone is using technology. This conversation is not important for you when you are fighting for your life in a poor, violent community or your quality of life is low because every evening you have to return to your mold-infested, roach-infested apartment. A hard-knock life makes other things priority.

Going forward in this globalized, digitized world, as preachers of the gospel, it is important to remember not only "the haves" but also "the have-nots." Our congregations may include both. As technology grows, the question remains whether human beings are growing apart. This includes the church as well. Technology upgrades do not translate necessarily to a congregation growing in heart and mind, which creates tensions about its use in the church. Faster does not mean better, which is why we cannot depend on technology. It will constantly change even as it changes our communication patterns, probably changing us as well. However, the ministry of preaching depends on an unchangeable God, a firm foundation in Jesus Christ, the rock on which Christian preaching is built, and not the latest Twitter hashtag. When it comes to technology, we must continue to ask ourselves whether the means leads to the ends of preaching.

York Times, February 17, 2011, http://www.nytimes.com/2011/02/18/us/18broadband.html?pagewanted=all.

In many ways, this exploration of technology and preaching brings us back to the basics, with the realization that a high-tech sermon may not be for everyone. It brings us back to people, people who use technology and those who do not or cannot. People are the flesh and blood of preaching in the power of the Spirit. This reminds us that preaching is a Spirit-animated event, using human bodies to proclaim the gospel regardless of denomination, race, ethnicity, class, gender, or use of technology. The Spirit is poured out on all flesh (Acts 2) and not all technology.

Further Learning Strategies

1. Have you seen preachers utilize technology when preaching? If so, was it effective? If not, why not? What technologies were used and how did they help or hinder the sermon performance?
2. Beyond the potential losses and gains named above, what else do you see as the losses and/or gains of technological use for preaching?
3. Find any preacher who routinely puts his or her sermons online. Listen to one sermon from this preacher, in person, and then watch or listen to the same sermon online, in whatever format it might be. Compare your reception of the online sermon to what you heard offline. How are they different and similar?
4. What do you think is the future of technology in the church? Discuss with a friend or small group.

Further Reading

Detweiler, Craig. *iGods: How Technology Shapes Our Spiritual and Social Lives.* Grand Rapids: Brazos, 2013. A study of how various technologies, such as Google, Facebook, and Instagram, affect our lives in positive and perilous ways.

Kim, Eunjoo Mary. *Preaching in an Age of Globalization.* Louisville: Westminster John Knox, 2010. Kim takes globalization and its traits seriously and explores how one preaches in this setting. She posits "trans-contextual" preaching as a possibility and offers practical advice toward that end.

Lose, David J. *Preaching at the Crossroads: How the World—and Our Preaching—Is Changing.* Minneapolis: Fortress Press, 2013. An exploration of how the major cultural influences of postmodernism, secularism, and pluralism present challenges and opportunities for preachers today.

Schultz, Quentin J. *High-Tech Worship? Using Presentational Technologies Wisely.* Grand Rapids: Baker, 2004. A wise guide in helping the church use the gift of technology to convey meaning and foster connection with God and others.

Wilson, Len, and Jason Moore. *The Wired Church 2.0.* Nashville: Abingdon, 2008. A "how-to" guidebook for those in multimedia ministry in churches. Covers topics such as blogs, podcasts, streaming video, and more.

Wiseman, Karyn. *I Refuse to Preach a Boring Sermon! Engaging the Twenty-First-Century Listener.* Cleveland: Pilgrim, 2013. Explores issues from imagery to technology and offers techniques to help preachers be more creative and to take risks.

10

Preaching and Christian Formation

Sally A. Brown

A few minutes before five o'clock on a Sunday afternoon cars are pulling into the parking garage beside a multilevel, steel-and-glass structure in the redeveloped downtown of a Midwestern city. The building complex is inviting. With covered walkways and shaded benches, open courtyards and play areas, it invites the passersby to explore. Windows of all sizes and shapes reflect the late-afternoon sun.

Signs point to businesses and human-service enterprises throughout the four levels of the complex. There is a daycare center here for children, a community center with programs for grade-school age kids and senior adults, a couple of cafés, three restaurants, a fitness center, and a walk-in healthcare facility. A life- and corporation-coaching firm is housed here, as well as the offices of a counseling center. On the side of the complex nearest the bus stop and subway station is a community food bank, a thrift store, and a job training and placement agency. Everything here is accessible.

On Sunday afternoons, an auditorium and integrated multiuse rooms on the third level of this complex become the rented home of the Open Door Community. Signs directing visitors to the Open Door on Sundays bear a caption: "A welcoming Christian church for seekers and pilgrims." Among those making their way to the auditorium are Alex and Norah, Jordan and Carey.

Alex is new to Open Door. Eight weeks ago, he would have been hanging out in one of his friends' apartments at this hour, probably watching football or basketball, depending on the season. He wouldn't have dreamed of coming to a church on a Sunday afternoon. But that was before he met Norah. They met at the thrift store, both checking out the "gently used" coats. Alex, whose single mother had no religious affiliation, has always thought of himself as spiritual but not religious. He would categorize himself as an inquiring skeptic. But so far, he's intrigued—as much by the commitment of Open Door members to bring love and justice to their downtown neighborhood as anything. In worship, he feels a sense of holy presence. The community's three preachers have passion, vision, and a way of communicating that makes him feel they "get" him.

Norah has been a committed Open Door member for a couple of years; but two-and-a-half years ago, she was in the same position as Alex—inquiring. Thanks to the sermons she has heard here, as well as discussion classes held at a restaurant on the complex's ground level right after the services, Norah asked to be baptized. She considers herself on a spiritual journey these days, learning what it means in her time and place to be a follower of Jesus. She wants to devote more time and energy to participating in God's mission of redemption in the world.

Jordan and Carey, married for nine years, are parents of two active children, a boy, Max, and a girl, Luci, who are both adopted. The family has walked to church this afternoon from the nearby remodeled brownstone they bought a few years ago. Jordan and Carey are committed Open Door members and among Open Door's leaders. They head up a mission group committed to just and safe living for senior adults in the neighborhood around Open Door. Members of this group volunteer their time to provide transportation to the senior center in this same complex, deliver meals to those who need them, drive folks to doctor visits, and help them with taxes and medical-insurance issues.

Preaching to Support Faith Formation

Alex and Norah, Jordan and Carey represent not simply different individuals we might find in today's churches, but different stages of formation in Christian faith. In this chapter, we are widening the camera angle, so to speak, on the work of preaching. One of the pressing tasks of every preaching ministry today is to help our listeners develop a more aware and more active Christian faith, both as individuals and as a community.

According to the Franconia Conference of the Mennonite Church, U.S.A., Christian formation refers to "those efforts of the church to help one another grow as disciples of Jesus and to be formed more and more into the likeness of Christ, including all dimensions of human and interpersonal experience."[1] These definitions emphasize that Christian formation is holistic; that is, growth in a living relationship with God, through Jesus Christ and in the power of

---

1. See http://franconiaconference.org/vision/definitions-of-missional-terms/.

the Spirit, involves more than private spirituality. Christian faith is irreducibly a communal experience; we grow in relationship not only to God, but to ourselves, to others, and to the wider created order. A vital Christian faith translates into concrete choices to devote careful thought, compassion, time, and resources to God's mission of redemption in the world.

We focus in this chapter on ways preachers can inspire, support, and equip individuals and communities for holistic Christian faith and practice. Ultimately, preachers cannot create faithful Christian lives any more than they can create faith; both are the work of God's life-giving Spirit. But here again, preachers can conscientiously plan their preaching in service to this divine work.

For purposes of this discussion, we will think of the faith journey as unfolding roughly in three phases. Phase 1 is the stage in which a person *discovers or rediscovers Christian faith*. Phase 2 begins when a seeker *becomes a disciple*. God's redemptive work in Christ is embraced; Christian faith is owned. Phase 3, which we call here *living out of faith*, may emerge only after years of active faith. At this stage, believers embrace leadership in and beyond the faith community and make major, intentional commitments motivated by determination to participate in God's redemptive work in the world.

Faith formation is not always a steady process. It can languish or be disrupted. Young adults who have been raised in a faith-practicing household often move into a period of skepticism, brief or lasting. Others suffer profoundly disruptive experiences that derail the beliefs of childhood and youth: someone close is claimed by fatal illness; military deployment takes them to the battlefield where they witness horrifying violence and loss of life; failure in marriage or vocation shatters self-confidence and, with it, faith; addiction to drugs or alcohol takes over. Yet, years later, an individual can find (or be found *by*) a community of Christians who take the suffering seriously and listen deeply. This can become a doorway into faith rediscovered, although this will be a faith cautiously rebuilt in light of difficult life experiences.

In this chapter, we describe ten preaching strategies that function to support Christian faith formation. By speaking of preaching *strategies* rather than *topics*, we mean to direct attention toward the cumulative effect of a steady preaching ministry.

In addition to evaluating our individual sermons, every preacher needs to reflect on the cumulative effect of his or her preaching. Over time, what overarching vision would our listeners receive about God's redemptive work in the world? What would they understand about the practices of worship and social witness? What help would our sermons have offered as they assemble a working understanding of the way different Christian doctrines relate? Most preachers discover they tend to stress some things but underemphasize others.

The first three preaching strategies we describe here support *every* phase of faith formation. These three are: Strategy #1, laying down key storylines found in the Scriptures; Strategy #2, casting an overarching vision of the way God has worked, and continues to work, for the redemption of humanity and all creation; and Strategy #3, relating Christian faith to the issues that confront us as citizens of a community, a nation, and the world. Strategies #4 through #10 are grouped under the three phases of faith formation described above, and support the tasks of each phase in specific ways.

Preaching Strategies That Support All Phases of Christian Formation

Strategy #1. *Allow the narrative "backbone" of Scripture to show through in every sermon you preach. Tell the stories of the Bible. Include stories of particular individuals and events, but from time to time trace overarching storylines from both the Old and New Testaments.*

In the mid-twentieth century, when church attendance was more the norm than the exception in North America and many faith communities emphasized religious education, many Christians were modestly familiar with their Scriptures. Today, fewer North Americans in general identify with a faith tradition, and steady religious education is rare. As a result, Christian preachers cannot assume their listeners know the major storylines that run through the Old and New Testaments or the characters that feature in those stories. These need to be introduced and connected, so that listeners gradually pick up their chronological connections and their significance for faith today.

A sermon series, either rooted in the Revised Common Lectionary or independent of it, can trace one of the longer narratives of the Bible. Stories basic to Christianity's "narrative backbone" include: the stories of humanity's beginnings in Genesis; stories of the patriarchs (Abraham, Isaac, Jacob, and the sons of Jacob, including the fairly long story of Joseph); the saga of the Hebrew slaves' exodus from Egypt and into the land of promise; stories of the kings and prophets of Israel and Judah; the exile to Babylon and subsequent return of a remnant of Israel; the life of Jesus; and the beginnings of the Christian church. Often a single figure stands at the center of a book (Ruth, Daniel, Esther, and prophetic books) or is the chief figure in a running story (Elijah, Samuel, David, and so on). Building biblical literacy doesn't require that every sermon be devoted to storytelling, but you need to plan time for this and not leave it to chance.

Congregations should hear these stories read from Scripture itself or even performed by a trained storyteller. Necessarily, these same stories need to be told more briefly in sermons using basic skills of excellent storytelling. These skills are so critical it is worth devoting space to them here.

1. *Sketch the setting, action, and characters using selective detail.* For example, when you tell the story of the angel Gabriel's announcement to Mary that she will bear a son, don't say, "Suddenly there was a beautiful angel standing there!" (No need to rhapsodize about shining wings, particularly since there is no hint of wings in the text. For all we know, Gabriel looked like the fish vendor at the market.) Instead, try: "One moment Mary was alone with her thoughts and the onions she was peeling. The next, she was face to face with a stranger." Simply report Gabriel's message, verbatim. Then, instead of using the voice of third-person narration ("Mary found this confusing"), try it from Mary's own perspective, focusing on revealing detail: "'*Favored* one?' The hairs on Mary's arms bristled." A journalistic, documentary-style report laced with details that signal emotion instead of describing it in abstract terms invites listeners to *experience* the action instead of analyzing it from afar.

2. *Create and release tension.* Homiletician Eugene Lowry has argued that creating and releasing tension is fundamental to all preaching. It is particularly important in managing a story's dramatic progress.[2] Imagine you're telling the story of Abraham's servant who's been sent to the family homeland to find a wife for Abraham's son Isaac among Abraham's relatives. Draw out the tension the servant must have felt, sent on this errand. How is he supposed to find the right woman? How will he know? To convey his concern, don't report: "He wondered how he'd find the right woman." Imagine his internal dialogue, maybe even contemporized a bit: "How do you find the right girl anyway? Pretend to drop something and read the label on her sandals?" Let listeners hear Rebekah's offer of water for

---

2. Eugene L. Lowry, *The Homiletical Beat: Why All Sermons Are Narrative* (Nashville: Abingdon, 2012).

the servant and his camels ("Can I draw water for you, sir . . . ?"). Is she suspicious of the lavish gifts? Could be. Don't skip past the dramatic pause of Gen. 24:21: "The man gazed at her in silence, to learn whether or not the Lord had made his journey successful." Waiting, watching: discernment in our lives can be like that.

3. *Refrain from dictating how listeners should react to stories, or the sense they should make of them.* It weakens a preacher's storytelling if he or she always feels compelled to direct listeners to make the "right" sense of the story. Telling the story of Gabriel's announcement to Mary and then adding the pushy query "Isn't that a wonderful story?" empties the story of mystery and interest. Truth be told, for many this is *not* a wonderful story, but a very troubling one. This is a mind-bending tale of a divinely caused pregnancy.

Honoring this trouble instead of trying to usher it quickly out the kitchen door respects both story and listener. One might transition out of the story this way: "We don't know how Mary interpreted her situation. We *do* learn that, some time later, a pregnant Mary visited her cousin Elizabeth, who confirmed the visitor's strange message about Mary's baby."

One reason that Scripture's stories function helpfully for worshipers at different stages of faith formation is that they are, by nature, multivalent. They yield meaning of different levels depending on the listeners. Wide-eyed children hearing the story of the annunciation will probably have questions on the ride home from church, but their questions may be about the dress code of angels, not virgin birth.

Gary, the brilliant, tough-minded high school kid whose parents still make him come to worship, has slid as far down in the pew as is humanly possible. He's staring at the toes of the laced-up boots he favors lately and has adopted a look of fierce boredom. Gary is skeptical about many traditional Christian claims, but he respects you.

Now and then on Saturdays, he stops by your office on his way home from his morning job at the bakery down the street, brings you a bagel, and quips that he's there to "talk about the holes in Christianity." Watching Gary, you make a mental note that Peter, Andrew, James and John didn't have to check a box, "I believe in the virgin birth of Jesus," when they were called away from their boats.

An artist in the congregation may be struck by the realization that Gabriel might have looked perfectly ordinary. She imagines painting this scene, the figures modeled on neighbors of hers—two ordinary people—with light and color to hint at something of the mystery of the scene. Maybe there are more divinely appointed conversations in all of our lives than we would ever guess.

We need to give up the idea that our job is to "control" what people make of biblical stories. Flattening stories into take-home propositions hinders the multivalence that allows them to be avenues of insight for widely diverse listeners. Preachers can trust these stories—and trust the Spirit.

It is faith speech to say that ultimately the formation, which happens through preaching, is an act of the Spirit. Preachers are co-laborers with God, which means we have a role to play as well, however, this doesn't mean that we can control the outcomes of our sermons. We preach as a "letting go" of our work in order for God to do God's work. This means we give up trying to "control" what people make of biblical stories or our sermons. We can't control how our sermons will be received or what people will hear or imagine. The truth is that people will hear things you never said in a sermon, good or bad. Someone else is at play in minds and hearts. We offer the Word and leave the future of the Word in God's hands and by doing so, we imply that forming people is something God really does by using us. At the same time, we should offer some caution that there are situations when preachers may be engaged in malformation and not transformation. This is why every sermon is always a prayer to God for a blessing. – LP

Strategy #2: *From time to time, and with an eye to the world your congregants live in week to week, take up public issues in the pulpit. Model in sermons what it means to think critically about difficult questions in light of faith. Acknowledge that faithful Christians can, and will, arrive at different conclusions on public issues.*

Some preachers studiously avoid public issues in their preaching. They worry that such topics distract from the core issues of faith. But such avoidance can unwittingly signal that—as skeptics suspect—Christian faith is irrelevant to ordinary life.

The authors and compilers of the canonical books were not in a position to anticipate many conundrums of modern life. At the same time, there is plenty of material in the Bible about the use and abuse of power, the power of lust and wealth to distort our judgment, appropriate treatment of society's most vulnerable members, relating across lines of cultural difference, and care of the environment and earth's nonhuman creatures. Sermons and informed discussion about these and other matters can contribute to clearer thinking about the issues we face every day.

Preaching is a public discourse, and the gospel is all encompassing. It is personal, communal, social, and political. The latter doesn't mean political parties or partisanship. We can confuse a political gospel for governmental politics. But engaging in the world, taking up public issues, dealing with the *polis*, the city, is critical if we believe the gospel of Jesus Christ impacts every domain of life. In the power of the Spirit, this is the case. The gospel is not just about Jesus in one's heart, but Jesus in every aspect of one's life. For instance, the gospel speaks to economic structures, racial issues, and gender equality. It does so because the ministry of Jesus dealt with all of this. Jesus did not run for president and Jesus would never run for president because his ministry was an indictment of the political and religious powers of his day. His was another way and the gospel is subversive many times, which has nothing to do with endorsing this or that candidate for political office. Preachers are not called to be politicians of the pulpit. We are called to be proclaimers of the gospel and this gospel shapes how we engage in public. A level of discernment is always required when it comes to this topic of politics and preaching. – **LP**

A handful of especially difficult issues have proven very divisive within and beyond the church in the last several decades. People have strong views on matters such as abortion; how persons of diverse sexual orientations do, or do not, fit into the church; euthanasia; and immigration policy, to name but a few. These issues are viewed differently in different sociocultural contexts in North America today, to say nothing of different faith communities.

Congregations are rarely of one mind even on the question of where Christians should turn for guidance on issues like these. In the Methodist tradition, four sources are typically brought into play to inform deliberation: Scripture, reason, Christian tradition in a broad sense (including theology), and human experience. Yet, having this "four-legged stool" in place still leaves open the question about the relative weight that should be given to insights from each of these sources.

An added layer of tension within Christian communities is that Christians do not agree about how Scripture is meant to shape our thinking. While most Christians believe that we depend on the Holy Spirit to illumine our understanding of Scripture, they disagree about how clearly or directly Scripture speaks to current issues. Some are persuaded that no matter what the issue, Scripture speaks timelessly and clearly. Others believe that Scripture sheds light on our thinking, but in a less direct way. If the import of Scripture were transparently obvious on every matter, we would not need biblical interpretation, preaching, or the illuminating activity of the Holy Spirit.

Before preaching a sermon on a highly polarizing issue, a preacher needs to be clear what the sermon is meant to accomplish. Is it meant to clarify the issue itself? Foster a particular way of bringing Scripture to bear on issues in general? Or is it meant to help construct an open, respectful environment for ongoing discussion? Is the hope to move listeners to a decision, or would that be premature? Some issues are so many-sided and sensitive that the place to start is not with a sermon, but well-planned forums for education and discussion. If we can help seekers and committed Christians alike get a stereoscopic view of difficult issues, drawing on multiple resources, they are likely to do better critical thinking about them. Face-to-face conversation, with basic "rules of engagement" in place, encourages participants to differ with honesty and mutual forbearance. Sermons on difficult issues function best when they are part of an open, two-way communication environment. As in all preaching, preachers need to be mindful that, whether they realize it or not, the issues they touch upon from the pulpit are not abstractions for some in the pews, but matters at the heart of personal identity and family life.

Strategy #3: Preach sermons that cast an overarching vision of God's redemptive purposes in the world.

There are preachers who deliver a well-crafted, helpful sermon every week, yet, over time, fail to offer their congregation anything like a guiding vision of God's redemptive work in the world or the congregation's place in that redemptive mission. Vision, or what we might call "an arc of coherence," is crucial for Christian formation at every stage, from inquiry into faith all the way to leadership in worship and public witness.

Crafting an overarching vision of mission and ministry is the shared responsibility of a community's leaders and not up to the preacher alone. Consultation and accountability can only strengthen the vision shared from the pulpit. The resulting vision is best expressed in language that is simple, concrete, and consistent over time.

During a ministry that lasted over three decades, one preacher offered a sermon every year or two that envisioned Christian faithfulness as the practice of "four loves"—love of God; love of the God-given, God-intended self; love of the significant others of one's life; and love for neighbor, near and far.[3] Other sermons—his own and those of staff members—picked up this language from time to time, reinforcing this flexible but coherent framework for interpreting Christian life. It anchored newcomers and seasoned members alike in a common framework.

* * *

The three preaching strategies we've discussed so far support persons in every phase of faith formation. In the rest of this chapter we focus on strategies that specifically support the tasks of the three phases of faith formation.

Preaching That Supports Those Discovering or Rediscovering Christian Faith (Phase 1)

Strategy #4: *Use language that is invitational rather than authoritarian. Handle your Scripture text in a spirit of shared discovery. Invite listeners to be fellow explorers with you of all that God has done, is doing, and promises to do to renew all things.*

One of the definitions of preaching listed in an online dictionary reads: "to give moral advice to someone in an annoying or pompously self-righteous way."[4] Some who stay away from churches do so because one or more bad experiences in which the preaching they heard fits this definition all too well. This is sad because it is so unnecessary. Preachers can prompt people to examine their lives and motivate them to act otherwise *without* being self-righteous, pompous, or scolding.

As we have stressed throughout this book, the core of Christian preaching is news about God's promises kept and being kept in Jesus

---

3. This sermon, with slight variations, was preached frequently between 1972 and 2001 by the Rev. Keith A. Brown at the First Presbyterian Church of Bethlehem, PA.

4. See https://www.google.com/?gws_rd=ssl#newwindow=1&q=preaching definition.

Christ. Preaching at its heart is news in the indicative mood about what God has done, is presently doing, and will continue to do to defeat sin and evil and draw all things to completeness in Christ, firstborn of God's new creation. God's action creates the opportunity, basis, and sustaining context for faithful Christian lives.

Strategy #5: *Speak about human sinfulness and the saving significance of Jesus' life, death, and resurrection, working with the broad palette of images and metaphors of redemption that the biblical witness offers.*

God's redemptive mission toward humanity and all creation is motivated by God's unending love. God seeks our freedom from patterns of behavior—greed, vengefulness, and duplicity—that the Christian tradition calls "sin." There will be times in every Christian's pilgrimage to feel regret, remorse, and shame. But shame is not the motivating basis of right action. God's love is.

Speaking about sin is challenging today, when words like sin and repentance have largely disappeared from the cultural lexicon. Nonetheless, preachers can demonstrate what sin looks like by showing how acts of greed, abuses of power, lack of self-control, and duplicity destroy the fabric of our lives, personally and socially. One only needs to spend some time at the local library scanning a week's worth of local, national, and international news to find material. Human beings continue to live up to their biblical reputation for taking what isn't theirs, dealing in half-truths or outright deception, behaving in ways ranging from ugly to murderous toward ethnic or religious groups different from their own, as well as toward family members. Sin is the abuse of power and opportunity on many levels; and we preachers need to name it for what it is.

Preachers also need to speak as vividly about God's redemptive work in our lives, individually and socially as about sin and the damage it does. This requires a language as rich and broad as the salvation/redemption vocabulary of the New Testament.[5] By the end of the twentieth century, the language of redemption heard in many North American churches held to a single, dominant account of the saving effects of Jesus' death called "penal substitutionary atonement theory." So widely assumed is this metaphor of sin as shameful crime and the cross as punishment that many think the New Testament speaks of nothing else in relation to the cross.

In fact, the Scriptures offer us many salvation metaphors (images that reveal crucial aspects of the saving impact of Jesus' death) to interpret Jesus' life, death, and resurrection. For example, the early church fathers spoke of redemption primarily as God's ransom of humanity from Satan's clutches. Such an image may have spoken particularly well to a culture well familiar with political conquest and subsequent captivity. The New Testament itself speaks of Jesus Christ as the One who "made captivity itself a captive" (Eph. 4:8, quoting Ps. 68:18). We can reclaim this redemptive image today in helpful ways. It interprets the saving power of Jesus' death and resurrection especially well for anyone recovering from addiction to alcohol, drugs, gambling, or a preoccupation with pornography, as well as for women or men who suffer from eating disorders.

Preaching That Supports Those Living *into* Christian Faith (Phase 2)

Strategy #6: *From time to time, focus on a particular Christian doctrine.*

Many in the pews need our help to see how basic Christian beliefs

---

5. For further discussion of New Testament images and metaphors in relation to Jesus' death, see Joel B. Green and Mark D. Baker, *Recovering the Scandal of the Cross: Atonement in New Testament and Contemporary Contexts* (Downers Grove, IL: InterVarsity, 2000); and Sally A. Brown, *Cross Talk: Preaching Redemption Here and Now* (Louisville: Westminster John Knox, 2008).

fit together and how they connect to acts of worship and to public witness. A preacher might do a series of sermons, each taking up one question: What is the church? What is the role of the Holy Spirit? Why do Christians worship God as a "Trinity" of persons? How is Jesus like a priest for us? A prophet? A gracious ruler or leader? What images does Scripture use to speak of the destiny of humanity and creation?

Good sermons on doctrine do not have to be boring. Spending a half-hour explaining and defining is *not* a particularly good approach to preaching about doctrine. We can speak in simple language, telling lively stories from church history where they are relevant. We can show through snapshots of human experience the difference a doctrine has made at some point in Christian history—for example, during the Reformation and subsequent reform in the Catholic church. This helps put flesh on the bones of doctrine.

Strategy #7: *Preach from time to time on core Christian practices and how practicing them has a positive impact on our whole lives.*

According to philosopher Alasdair MacIntyre, a practice is a sustained, coherent, goal-directed pattern of communal action. It is guided by specific standards of excellence peculiar to that practice. Its goals relate to the values of a specific, historic, and living tradition, values that are exhibited in classic guiding narratives.[6] Judged according to MacIntyre's definition, playing baseball is a practice. Conducting a choir is another. Playing in a jazz band counts as a practice. High-altitude hiking is a specialized social practice.

Christians engage in an array of distinctive practices. Worship as a whole might be considered a practice, although it is probably more

---

6. Alasdair McIntyre, *After Virtue: A Study in Moral Theory*, 2nd ed. (Notre Dame, IN: Notre Dame University Press, 1984), 187–92.

helpful to think of worship as a web of interconnected practices. Some Christian practices are common to all faith communities. Others, such as the form of ecstatic prayer known as speaking in tongues, are common to some but not to all. Some churches baptize infants or include children in Holy Communion, while others wait on offering these sacraments until they have publicly professed their faith. Practices can vary from one congregation to the next in the same denomination. Episcopalians use a common prayer book, yet the details of their services vary in texture, sound, and formality around the world. Worshipers appreciate learning from their preachers about the history of the church's worship practices, why worshiping communities' practices differ, and the theology that articulates those differences.

What we do together inside the sanctuary shapes what we do outside the sanctuary. The fact that we all come to the table of the Lord as equals—brothers and sisters equally hungry and thirsty for communion with God, equally in need of God's outpoured grace—relates to Christians' long history of hospitality to stranger and society's most vulnerable. Those are the sorts of Christian practices beyond worship that sermons can reinforce.

Strategy #8: *Preach about giving, a central and many-sided practice of Christian faith.*

Generosity within and beyond the church is a core Christian practice that deserves attention—and not only in so-called "stewardship" or "pledging" seasons. The God we have come to know through Jesus Christ is a God of mercy and self-giving love. A sure sign of growing Christian faith is a growing instinct toward generous giving.

Preachers need to be unafraid to speak about money. Money is a powerful force in virtually every culture around the globe. It provokes anxiety, confers power and status, and fuels violence. We live in a world obsessed with buying and selling. Money talks, opens doors, and wins friends. Having too little money to meet our needs and the needs of those who depend on us can create such anxiety that it compromises our health. Money inspires desire so powerful that people will kill for more of it. Money has a dark side. No wonder Jesus described money as a master that can be god-like in its influence (Matt. 6:24).

On the other hand, some preachers give the unfortunate impression that giving is an unpleasant obligation. Wealth turned loose for human good is a concrete sign of love for the neighbor and stranger. Holding wealth lightly reminds Christians that our ultimate security does not depend on our retirement fund.

With two-career households the new norm in much of North America—and necessarily so with the skyrocketing costs of education, healthcare, and retirement—volunteering is more difficult for many today. Time given for the sake of others is a precious gift. Devoting time to face-to-face, human contact is a witness to the world that we do not belong to ourselves but to God.

Preaching That Supports Those Living *Out of* Faith (Phase 3)

At this stage, a believer's faith commitment has become the pivot around which other life choices revolve. She or he has begun to see things almost instinctively through a lens of love for God, neighbor, and the radically "other." Their faith motivates and informs their leadership within and beyond the church.

Strategy #9: *Preach about leadership.*

Preachers can choose texts, narrative and otherwise, that foreground best leadership practices. The advice that Moses' father-in-law,

Jethro, offers him near the beginning of the Hebrews' journey toward the promised land (Exodus 18) promotes the wisdom of delegation. It suggests there is a difference between leadership and the desire to control situations through micromanagement or by making ourselves indispensable.

Themes of trust, risk, conflict, compromise, success, and failure all arise in the stories of Israel's first three kings, Saul, David, and Solomon. Esther and Ruth are models of risk-taking courage. Paul's references to colleagues in the early mission of the church (the book of Acts and many references in Paul's letters) highlight the importance of fellowship and accountability. Jesus' own habit of stepping away from the thick of activity to pray and meditate (as in Luke 5:16) may say something important about the practices that feed discerning leadership.

Strategy #10: *Instead of pushing from behind with guilt, motivate by making the horizon of hope vivid. Use local, accessible figures and realistic settings.*

The more seasoned worshipers are in the life of faith, the more sermons they have heard. The more sermons they have heard, the less likely they are to be pushed into action by guilt-producing rhetorical strategies.

Motivate by painting pictures of the world as it could be and should be, thanks to the redemptive love and justice of God. Keep the vision local and realistic. While we can point to the inspiring lives of figures like St. Francis, Mother Teresa, Martin Luther King, Jr., or Bishop Desmond Tutu, preachers need to identify and celebrate risk-taking, generous, creative Christian lives nearer at hand. Our listeners need concrete examples of changed lives, situations, and institutions that are part of the world they deal with every day. Through us, and in our time and place, the Spirit is working redemption and hope.

A Final Word

Preachers are always on a formational journey themselves. We cannot hand down spiritual advice from the pulpit as if our listeners are weaker or lesser than we are. We are fellow pilgrims. This makes us fully accountable to the word that we speak. Time and again, preachers find that the Spirit confronts them through the words they hear themselves saying. This, too, is the life-restoring work of the Spirit.

Further Learning Strategies

1. As we've pointed out, the vision shared from the pulpit needs to be developed in consultation and accountability with a Christian community's leadership, broadly speaking. One contributing factor will be the preacher's own sense of what counts as "the gospel." Open a blank page in a journal or computer screen. Then free-write (keep going without editing) in response to this question: "What is the heart of the 'good news' (gospel) that I hope my listeners will grasp over time?" You may choose to work with a group and then share and discuss your responses.

2. As you prepare sermons, either as a student or pastor, test them against what you've written in exercise #1. After six months or a year, reflect on your original statement. Would you revise it?

3. Share with fellow students or pastors three or four life practices, spiritual and otherwise, that seem most essential to sustain your preaching life. These might include prayer, keeping a journal, reading current theology, reading particular journals, and meeting with fellow preachers, but also consider practices that

support emotional and physical well-being (hiking, running, yoga, seeing films, reading novels or poetry, cooking, woodworking, etc.).

Further Reading

Baker, Mark D., ed. *Proclaiming the Scandal of the Cross: Contemporary Images of Atonement*. Grand Rapids: Baker Academic, 2006. This collection of sermons and educational plans demonstrates how using multiple images of the significance of Jesus' death and resurrection can enlarge a congregation's vision of redemption.

Honeycutt, Frank G. *Preaching to Skeptics and Seekers*. Nashville: Abingdon, 2001. The author explores the impact of select sermons (included in the text) on seekers and skeptics who agreed to attend church, listen, and provide feedback.

Hull, William E. *Strategic Preaching: The Role of the Pulpit in Pastoral Leadership*. St. Louis: Chalice, 2006. A comprehensive study of the role preaching plays in several strategic leadership tasks. Detailed case studies are included.

Johnson, Susanne. *Christian Spiritual Formation in the Church and Classroom*. Nashville: Abingdon, 1989. Working against the backdrop of an individualistic popular culture of "self-help," Johnson develops an "ecclesial" formational vision that sees the congregation as an "ecology" of formation.

Tisdale, Leonora Tubbs. *Prophetic Preaching: A Pastoral Approach*. Westminster John Knox, 2010. Specific strategies for developing well-structured sermons that speak a prophetic word amid contemporary issues, doing so in ways suited to their congregational contexts.

Index